R Blackwell .

STRIKING A BALANCE?
Employment Law after the 1980 Act

STRIKING A BALANCE?

Employment Law after the 1980 Act

Roy Lewis

Senior Research Fellow
SSRC Industrial Relations Research Unit
University of Warwick

and Bob Simpson

Lecturer in Law
London School of Economics and Political Science

Martin Robertson · Oxford

First published in 1981 by Martin Robertson & Company Ltd.,
108 Cowley Road, Oxford OX4 1JF.

British Library Cataloguing in Publication Data

Lewis, Roy
    Striking a balance?
    1. Great Britain. Employment Act 1980
    2. Labour laws and legislation — Great
    Britain
    I. Title   II. Simpson, Robert
    344.104'1125   KS3004.5

ISBN 0-85520-442-7
ISBN 0-85529-443-5 Pbk

Typeset by Freeman Graphic, Tonbridge
Printed and bound in Great Britain by Book Plan, Worcester

Contents

Preface   vi

Abbreviations   viii

 1 Law and Power: The Employment Act in Context   1

 2 Employment Protection   23

 3 The Right to Organise   60

 4 The Closed Shop   75

 5 Trade Union Membership   99

 6 Trade Union Ballots   123

 7 Collective Bargaining   136

 8 Picketing   153

 9 The Right to Strike   183

10 Conflict and Controversy: The Employment
      Act and Beyond   223

Notes   232

Table of Statutes   251

Table of Cases   257

Index   264

Preface

Industrial relations law has developed rapidly over the last twenty years. As it has grown it has become more controversial. After the Donovan Report and *In Place of Strife* in the late 1960s came the Industrial Relations Act 1971, and then the Trade Union and Labour Relations Acts 1974–76 and the Employment Protection Act 1975. Over the same period the industrial tribunals developed into a system of 'labour courts' for determining the ever more extensive range of statutory rights for individual employees. Now the Employment Act of 1980 holds sway. The Act is claimed by the government to strike a 'fair balance' between the different policies adopted by previous administrations, one that will work and be acceptable to employers, workers and trade unions. Though Parliament may enact further legislation, a mastery of the principles of this Act is likely to remain an essential prerequisite for understanding both day-to-day legal problems at the workplace and the possible future development of labour law.

This book attempts to explain as clearly as possible, but without over-simplification, the 1980 Act, its accompanying codes and regulations, related labour laws such as the 'July Orders' on dismissals and redundancy consultation, and also the government's Green Paper *Trade Union Immunities*. What changes are made in maternity rights or the law of unfair dismissal? What legal rules now apply in closed shops? Who has a legal right to be a member of a union? When is picketing lawful? When is it illegal for workers to go on strike or take other industrial action? Our aim is to provide comprehensible answers to such questions.

Employment law cannot be understood as a set of technicalities in isolation from a wider legal and social context. The Employment Act operates by way of amendment to other statutes and to the doctrines of judge-made common law. A useful account of the ways in which the Act may affect the lives of everyone at work must include some explanation of the general framework of labour law and its interaction with the actual behaviour of management and trade unions. Our analysis therefore reaches beyond the legal technicalities into the realms of industrial relations and public policy.

Authors of books about Acts of Parliament only rarely acknowledge their debt to the authors of the legislation. Our account of the Employment Act however makes extensive use of the official reports of the legislative proceedings, especially the marathon thirty-two sittings of the House of Commons Standing Committee 'A', and of the various debates in the House of Lords. As it happened, the opposition's front-bench spokesmen in the Lords were Lord McCarthy, a fellow of Nuffield College, Oxford and one of the country's leading experts on industrial relations, and Lord Wedderburn of Charlton, Cassel Professor of Commercial Law at London University and the foremost authority on industrial relations law in Britain today. In response to the innumerable legal and practical objections raised by this formidable pair, government spokesmen had to justify with some rigour the Act's overall approach and its detailed 'small print'. For this we are duly grateful. We have also made use of the very informative reports of the House of Commons Select Committee on Employment, which is conducting its own investigation into trade union immunities.

We owe a very special debt to Professor Wedderburn, our friend and teacher over many years. His thinking has strongly influenced the structure and content of this book, not least its treatment of the law of industrial conflict. We would also like to thank Linda Dickens, Mark Freedland, David Winchester and Penny Wood for their advice and assistance. In so far as we have succeeded in making the law comprehensible to the layman and in placing it in a realistic context, we are indebted to our long-term guinea pigs at the LSE, the personnel management and trade union students who attend 'The Elements of Labour Law' lecture course for which we were until recently jointly responsible. Although we have been immersed in the subject matter since the publication of the government's first consultative documents in July 1979, this book was written and rewritten, typed and re-typed, within a period of four months, a feat only possible with the help of our exceptionally able and tolerant secretaries — Norma Griffiths of the Industrial Relations Research Unit at Warwick University and Catherine Swarbrick of the LSE's Law Department. Finally, the opinions and any errors contained herein are of course entirely our own.

Roy Lewis and Bob Simpson
1 May 1981

Abbreviations

ACAS	Advisory, Conciliation and Arbitration Service
ACTT	Association of Cinematograph, Television and Allied Technicians
APEX	Association of Professional, Executive, Clerical and Computer Staff
ASLEF	Associated Society of Locomotive Engineers and Firemen
ASTMS	Association of Scientific, Technical and Managerial Staffs
AEF	Amalgamated Engineers and Foundry Workers
AUEW	Amalgamated Union of Engineering Workers
CAC	Central Arbitration Committee
CBI	Confederation of British Industry
CEGB	Central Electricity Generating Board
CIR	Commission on Industrial Relations
CO	Certification Officer
CPSA	Civil and Public Services Association
CSEU	Confederation of Shipbuilding and Engineering Unions
DE	Department of Employment
DHSS	Department of Health and Social Security
EA	Employment Act 1980
EAT	Employment Appeal Tribunal
EEC	European Economic Community
EEF	Engineering Employers' Federation
EETPU	Electrical, Electronic, Telecommunications and Plumbing Union
EMA	Engineers' and Managers' Association
EOC	Equal Opportunities Commission
EPCA	Employment Protection Consolidation Act 1978
EPA	Employment Protection Act 1975
ETU	Electrical Trades Union
GMWU	General and Municipal Workers' Union

ILO	International Labour Organisation
IPCS	Institute of Professional Civil Servants
IPM	Institute of Personnel Management
IRA	Industrial Relations Act 1971
IRC	Independent Review Committee (of TUC)
ISTC	Iron and Steel Trades Confederation
ITF	International Transport Workers Federation
NALGO	National and Local Government Officers' Association
NASD	National Amalgamated Stevedores' and Dockers' Society
NGA	National Graphical Association
NIRC	National Industrial Relations Court
NUBE	National Union of Bank Employees
NUJ	National Union of Journalists
NUR	National Union of Railwaymen
NUS	National Union of Seamen
POEU	Post Office Engineering Union
PSI	Policy Studies Institute
SI	Statutory Instrument
SLADE	Society of Lithographic Artists, Designers and Engineers
SOGAT	Society of Graphical and Allied Trades
TASS	Technical, Administrative, Supervisory Section (of AUEW)
TGWU	Transport and General Workers' Union
TSSA	Transport Salaried Staffs Association
TUC	Trades Union Congress
TULRA	Trade Union and Labour Relations Acts 1974 and 1976
UCATT	Union of Construction Allied Trades and Technicians
UMA	Union Membership Agreement
UKAPE	United Kingdom Association of Professional Engineers
USDAW	Union of Shop, Distributive and Allied Workers
UPW	Union of Post Office Workers

1

Law and Power:
The Employment Act in Context

One of the aims outlined in the Conservative Party election manifesto of 1979 was the restoration of 'the health of our economic and social life, by controlling inflation and striking a fair balance between the rights and duties of the trade union movement'. The manifesto added that

> by heaping privilege without responsibility on the trade unions, Labour have given a minority of extremists the power to abuse individual liberties and to thwart Britain's chances of success;

and further that

> between 1974 and 1976, Labour enacted a 'militants' charter' of trade union legislation. It tilted the balance of power in bargaining throughout industry away from responsible management and towards unions, and sometimes towards unofficial groups acting in defiance of their official union leadership.[1]

Since the 1979 election the government's labour law programme has been repeatedly justified in terms of 'redressing the balance' between employers and trade unions and between individual liberty and collective power.

The passing of the Employment Act was the sequel to a decade of rapid inflation and of the intensification of industrial conflict, culminating in the notorious 'winter of discontent' of 1978–79. Major developments in labour law have usually occurred at times of economic and social crisis. The increasing incidence of strikes in the late 1960s led first to *In Place of Strife* and then to the Industrial Relations Act 1971. In an earlier era the General Strike of 1926 paved the way for the Trade Disputes and Trade Unions Act 1927. The resurrection of the Triple Alliance of miners, railwaymen and transport workers in 1919 was the pretext for the Emergency Powers Act 1920. The rise of a militant shop stewards' movement prompted the Munitions of War Act 1915. And we can only speculate on where the spate of massive strikes and the spirit of revolutionary syndicalism in the years before the First World War would have led. It sometimes happens that the judges are presented with opportunities to develop new legal principles in advance of Parliament. A line of cases in the 1960s, for example, anticipated many of the liabilities in the Industrial Relations Act, and a series of judgments on secondary action and picketing decisively influenced the provisions of the Employment Act. In other words, 'the nature and extent of legal regulation have been determined not by some abstract rule-making force but by the interplay of judicial innovations, public policy controversy, the relative power of management and labour interests, and party politics with a view to electoral advantage'.[2] The Employment Act is no exception. It is symptomatic of a widespread belief that trade unions have too much power. To quote a former permanent secretary at the Department of Employment: 'In the last ten years three successive Prime Ministers have been prevented by the industrial and political power of the unions from pursuing policies they declared essential in the national interest.'[3]

In the modern mass consumption and interdependent economy, it is argued, official and unofficial strikes cause inconvenience and disruption to the public, economic losses to the strikers themselves and to their employers, and, in view of the severity of international trade competition, to the national economy. If trade unions or informal but union organised work groups engage in collective bargaining without strikes the consequences may sometimes be even more damaging: inflationary wage settlements which the employer is unable or unwilling to resist. If they impose their own unilateral rules without collective bargaining the result is inefficiency and restrictive labour practices. If they attempt to maintain internal solidarity and discipline through the closed shop, they are charged with the imposition of unreasonable restrictions on the liberty of the individual. And if the trade union movement engages in political activity (as it always has done), then the constitution and the sovereignty of Parliament are threatened. These sentiments have become the dominant climate of opinion among not only Conservative politicians but also boards of directors, financiers, top civil servants, judges, some leading academics, newspaper proprietors ·and, on the evidence of public opinion polls, a segment of the electorate including many trade unionists.

There is of course a counter-viewpoint that making scapegoats of the unions is a diversion from the real problems. Restrictive labour practices and many strikes are arguably a rational response to job insecurity, fluctuations in earnings, managerial inefficiency, and the pervasive 'dog eat dog' atmosphere of an economy in steep decline. Can industrial peace and efficiency be achieved or even aimed for in a society marred by the persistence of an antiquated class system, enormous inequalities of wealth and power and now mass unemployment? This is not the place to debate these arguments and counter-arguments except with regard to one aspect which is central to the approach of the Employment Act. The Act tries to 'redress the balance' in a variety of ways. It repeals certain statutory procedures which were enacted for the benefit of trade unions and their members, it erodes the legal position of employers and trade unions who may wish to uphold the closed shop and it restricts the so-called trade union 'immunities'. All these matters will be analysed in some detail but a preliminary word about the nature of the immunities may be helpful. It is widely asserted that unions enjoy exceptional legal privileges which swing the balance of industrial power in their favour. Professor Friedrich Hayek, who (together with Professor Milton Friedman) provides much of the intellectual inspiration for the present government, goes so far as to depict union 'legal privileges' as the 'chief cause' of inefficiency, poverty and unemployment.[4] What then are these alleged legal privileges?

DO TRADE UNIONS ENJOY LEGAL PRIVILEGES?

The legal freedom to organise industrial action in Britain rests on a structure of statutory immunities from judge-made liabilities. This unique characteristic is a legacy of the dramatic conflicts between Parliament and the courts which have been a recurrent theme in the historical development of strike law. During the nineteenth century the legal suppression of the emerging trade unions was effected mainly through the criminal law, until the great emancipatory statutes of 1871—75 removed some of the most restrictive consequences of criminal liabilities. It was significant for the future development of the law that the Conspiracy and Protection of Property Act 1875 provided that a combination of persons to do any act should not be a criminal conspiracy unless that act itself would be punishable as a crime, so long as they acted 'in contemplation or furtherance of a trade dispute' (the modern equivalent is to be found in the Criminal Law Act 1977). The blocking of *criminal* liability, apart from the regulation of picketing where the criminal law was and still is of critical importance, prompted the judges to develop new *civil* liabilities for torts (civil wrongs which may be restrained by injunction and compensated by damages). Tortious liability is an area of maximum judicial discretion because torts are the creation of the judges and not of Parliament.

By the turn of the century judicial creativity was reaching a climax. The House of Lords (in its judicial capacity composed of Law Lords who form the highest appellate court) built the civil liability for the tort of 'simple' conspiracy on their disapproval of basic trade union aims (*Quinn* v. *Leathem*, 1901). The tort of inducing breach of contract was a further hazard for trade unionists, as was 'interference' with another person's freedom to use his capital or his labour, though the latter liability was rejected by the House of Lords in 1897 (*Allen* v. *Flood*). But the biggest legal blow was struck in the famous *Taff Vale* v. *ASRS* case in 1901, in which the Law Lords held that a union itself as distinct from its officials could be liable in tort for damages. The defendant, the Amalgamated Society of Railway Servants, paid damages and legal costs totalling £42,000 and it seemed that the threat of bankruptcy loomed over any union which dared to threaten industrial action. As Professor Wedderburn has explained, *Taff Vale* 'became part of working-class culture, part of the way "they" treat trade unions if they can. Such feelings have not died.'[5] Indeed the memory of previous conflicts is itself a salient feature of recent political and industrial struggles over labour legislation.

The Trade Disputes Act of 1906, which reversed *Taff Vale*, entrenched the legal structure of immunities. The Act gave trade unions a blanket immunity by prohibiting legal actions in tort against them, and, for persons acting 'in contemplation or furtherance of a trade dispute', it gave immunities from liability for the torts of simple conspiracy, inducing breach of employment contracts and interference with a person's freedom to use his capital or labour, as well as providing them with some legal protection for peaceful picketing. The alternative approach would have been the enactment of a more comprehensive labour law code with positive legal rights and obligations. This had in fact been advocated in embryonic form by some of the passages in the Report of a Royal Commission of 1903—06. But by 1906 the unions were already too suspicious of the law and lawyers to accept any tight system of legal regulation. As will be apparent from our later discussion, restoration of the principle of *Taff Vale* and the idea of positive rights are central to the contemporary controversy about the future of labour law.

The tension between Parliament and the courts did not end in 1906. Inherent in the structure of the law was the possibility that the judges might expand the common law liabilities, or give narrow interpretations of the statutory immunities or of 'in contemplation or furtherance of a trade dispute', the 'golden formula' (to use Professor Wedderburn's celebrated phrase) on which the immunities depend. British labour law is characterised by this pendulum that has swung between judge-made law and Parliament's enactments. In fact the last two decades have been the most prolific period of judicial creativity since the final quarter of the nineteenth century. The harbinger of a new wave of restrictive judgments was *Rookes* v. *Barnard* (1964), where the law Lords held that the threat of industrial action in breach of employment contracts could provide the ingredients of liability for the obscure tort of 'intimidation'. A Labour administration responded with the Trade Disputes Act 1965 providing an immunity against the narrow ground of liability in *Rookes*. The immunities however were to be outflanked yet again by the development of liabilities for inducing breach of commercial contract (*Stratford* v. *Lindley*, 1964) and for interference with commercial relations short of breach (*Torquay Hotel Co. Ltd.* v. *Cousins*, 1969). Such liabilities had not been envisaged by the architects of the 1906 Act, and it seemed that the 'labour' injunction was about to become an accepted weapon of industrial conflict even before the enactment of the Industrial Relations Act 1971. That Act was repealed in 1974 by the Trade Union and Labour Relations Act which restored the immunities in much the same terms as the Act of 1906, leaving untouched the expanded liabilities in respect of commercial, that is, non-employment contracts. Eventually the Trade Union and Labour Relations (Amendment) Act of 1976 legislated immunities to protect against these most recently developed liabilities. The policy of TULRA 1974–76 has been summed up by Lord Scarman: 'Briefly put, the law now is back to what Parliament had intended when it enacted the Act of 1906 – but stronger and clearer than it was then.'[6]

Soon however even TULRA 1974–76 seemed ineffective as a new line of authority emanating mainly from the Court of Appeal drastically reduced the ambit of the golden formula 'in contemplation or furtherance of a trade dispute'. This particular phase was brought to an end not by Parliament but by the Law Lords. In the leading cases of *NWL Ltd.* v. *Woods* (1979), *Express Newspapers Ltd.* v. *MacShane* (1979) and *Duport Steels Ltd.* v. *Sirs* (1980) they recognised that the judicial restrictions on the plain, ordinary and unambiguous meaning of

the golden formula had reached the borderline of idiosyncratic per-
versity. As Lord Scarman said in what must be taken as a thinly veiled
reference to Lord Denning, the Master of the Rolls and head of the
Court of Appeal: in our kind of society 'justice is not left to the un-
guided, even if experienced, sage sitting under the spreading oak tree'.[7]
Aware that judges are not necessarily the best arbiters of the rights and
wrongs of industrial conflicts, he added that he was not unhappy that
the courts were not called upon to be 'some sort of backseat driver in
trade disputes'.[8]

But most of the other Law Lords went out of their way to condemn
the very statute which they felt they must under protest apply. Lord
Diplock described his conclusion on the plain meaning of the golden
formula, in the context of what he regarded as the 'much extended'
immunities in TULRA 1974–76, as

> intrinsically repugnant to anyone who has spent his life in the
> practice of the law or the administration of justice. Sharing these
> instincts it was a conclusion that I myself reached with consider-
> able reluctance, for given the existence of a trade dispute it in-
> volves granting to trade unions a power, which has no other limits
> than their own self-restraint, to inflict by means which are con-
> trary to the general law untold harm. . . . Recent experience has
> shown that almost any major strike in one of the larger manu-
> facturing or service industries, if it is sufficiently prolonged, may
> have the effect (figuratively) of bringing the nation to its knees. It
> is the ability in the last resort to carry out a threat to do this
> without involving any breach of the civil or criminal law as it now
> stands that gives to trade unions, individually and collectively,
> their 'industrial muscle'.[9]

Similarly, Lord Keith saw trade unionists as 'privileged persons' able to
'bring about disastrous consequences with legal impunity'.[10] This was
the invitation to legislate against secondary action which the government accepted with alacrity in section 17 of the 1980 Act.

It is correct to regard the immunities as 'privileges'? It should be
clear from our cursory historical survey of strike law that the immunities do not put trade unions above the law or make them privileged
persons. Without the immunities, left to the full rigour of the common
law, trade unions could not exist or function lawfully. The immunities
are in essence the British legal form of basic democratic liberties, the
equivalent of what in other countries takes the form of a positive right
to strike guaranteed by legislation or by the constitution. Nor does it
follow that the immunities endow unions with what Lord Diplock

called 'industrial muscle'. The inter-action between legal norms and behaviour is too complex to be reduced to a simplistic assertion that the law can somehow directly generate (or directly restrict) the ability, motivation and needs of trade unions to take industrial action. It was the late Professor Sir Otto Kahn-Freund who described law as a 'secondary force in human affairs, and especially in labour relations',[11] and who coined the phrase 'what the state has not given, the state cannot take away'.[12] It must be remembered, as the government's Green Paper *Trade Union Immunities* acknowledged, 'that the way in which the law on industrial action has developed so far in this country has been characteristic of our industrial relations as a whole. Compared with most other countries there has traditionally been a minimum of legal interference and regulation. The conduct of our industrial relations is basically voluntary'.[13] There is indeed a delicate inter-connection between legal intervention, voluntary industrial relations and the wider society, an organic relationship which is crucial to any practical impact of the Employment Act.

THE VOLUNTARIST SYSTEM

The attempt to limit judicial intervention by means of the negatively expressed statutory immunities was of great importance in determining the basic pattern of the relationship between legal and industrial institutions. Generally the law played only a minor role in the shaping of British industrial relations. The historic emphasis was not on legal regulation but on voluntary self-regulation by employers' and workers' organisations. This characteristic was reflected not only in the immunities but in the overall framework of labour law.[14]

The industrial revolution encouraged the spread of laissez-faire ideology in nineteenth-century Britain and as part of this trend freedom of contract became the dominant legal doctrine. The contract in question so far as workers were concerned was the contract of employment, a legally enforceable relationship between each individual employee and his or her employer. Judges insisted that the parties to the contract were free and equal in coming together to form the contract and in the negotiation of its terms. The supposed equality was a legal fiction to legitimise the superior strategic strength of the employer who could dictate the terms to the individual employee. This situation was however modified by the gradual enactment of statutory protections from a few of the grossest forms of exploitation. The state intervened to control the notorious practice of 'truck' by stipulating the payment of wages in cash rather than kind for manual workers. It also attempted to regulate industrial safety and, mainly in respect of women and young persons, health and welfare at work. What is remarkable is that until the 1960s, with the exceptions of truck and industrial safety, protective legislation was largely conspicuous by its absence. This bare minimum of state intervention in the individual employment relation gave all the more scope to the development of voluntary institutions and collective bargaining.

The key voluntary institution was of course the trade union. The Trade Union Act of 1871 gave unions immunity from the restrictive legal consequences of the common law doctrine of 'restraint of trade'; this protection is today embodied in s.2(5) of TULRA. The status of unions as voluntary unincorporated associations was retained by the 1871 Act, which provided for the voluntary registration of unions with the Registrar of Friendly Societies. The Registrar's functions have now been taken over under the Employment Protection Act by the Certification Officer. The overall principle (with some exceptions, for example, in respect of amalgamations and party political expenditure) was historically one of minimal state interference in the internal affairs of unions.

Collective bargaining developed in Britain without state regulation and with very little state support. The lack of a positive right to strike was complemented by the absence of an enforceable right to organise in unions or a legal obligation on employers to recognise them. Such collective bargaining law as existed was supported by indirect sanctions or by none at all. The state machinery for conciliation and arbitration of collective conflicts was not (apart from a few exceptional wartime measures) underpinned by legal sanctions. The statutory wages councils for particular trades and industries, which date back to the Trade Boards Act of 1909, were seen as exceptional stop-gap arrangements to be dismantled on the development of voluntary collective bargaining. The collective agreement itself came to be regarded as a 'gentleman's agreement' which, unless the negotiating parties specified otherwise, was not intended to be a legally enforceable contract. On the contrary collective agreements in Britain were enforced not by legal but by social sanctions. The theory of the non-contractual status of collective agreements, which had been first advanced by Professor Kahn-Freund, was eventually confirmed by the Donovan Royal Commission, then by the

High Court (*Ford Motor Co.* v. *AEF*, 1969) and is now embodied in s.18 of TULRA. The legal impact of collective bargaining tends to operate instead at the level of the contract of employment where suitable collectively agreed provisions may be and often are incorporated as part of the individual contract.

This unobtrusive legal framework was conducive to the development of a distinctive style of voluntary collective bargaining. Such bargaining was informal and infinitely varied, with each factory or workshop evolving its own 'custom and practice'. Agreed procedures were considered to be more important than formal written agreements with detailed substantive terms. The emphasis was on the practical resolution of disputes as opposed to contractual interpretations turning on the lawyer's distinction between conflicts of rights (the meaning and application of the existing terms) and conflicts of interests (matters outside the existing terms).

A legal framework which thus abstained from regulating the core of the collective relationship was not historically inevitable but there were powerful factors which fostered its evolution. British trade unions did not campaign to secure laws guaranteeing basic organisation rights. Why not? In the oldest industrialised country in the world collective bargaining had spread in advance of the growth of union political influence and of the extension of the franchise to manual workers. The unions had learnt from experience to rely on their own industrial strength, and also that contact with the law tended to be difficult, expensive and usually to their disadvantage. In addition, a structure of immunities and overall non-intervention was more consistent with the spirit of laissez-faire which pervaded even trade unionism for much of the last century. Although the collective organisation of unskilled workers in the late 1880s was associated with a more militant socialist ideology, which expressed itself in what proved to be unsuccessful demands for a legal minimum wage and legal maximum hours, the voluntary principle was steadily entrenched as an article of faith. Eventually this attitude came to be shared by employers, the government and even by the judges. During the Second World War, when the unions reached the zenith of their acceptability and prestige, the House of Lords decided that industrial action to promote the closed shop or other genuine trade union objectives did not after all constitute the tort of simple conspiracy to injure (*Crofter Harris Tweed* v. *Veitch*, 1941). In the period after the war industrial self-government was elevated to an ideological belief common to both sides of industry. Abstention of the law was a central plank of the prevailing 'voluntarist' ethos in industry. The nineteenth century doctrine of individual laissez-faire gave way to what Kahn-Freund brilliantly described as 'collective laissez-faire'.

The ethos of voluntarism grew out of the relatively harmonious social and prosperous economic climate of the mid twentieth century. Compared with the smouldering class conflict of the past, there was a notable degree of consensus over the legitimacy of the labour movement and a whole range of fundamental socio-economic issues: the mix of the mixed economy, the welfare state and full employment. A mature system of industrial relations resting on a rough equilibrium of power apparently delivered industrial peace and a measure of social and economic justice. The state seemed to be a neutral force in collective labour relations: it might intervene where there was a serious disequilibrium of social power but for the most part it abstained from intervention and merely, to use Kahn-Freund's terminology once more, 'held the ring' or set the 'Queensberry rules' for the conflicts between the autonomous social forces.

This intricate pattern of legal norms, ideology and social reality was challenged and transformed under the pressure of Britain's persistent economic decline of the last twenty years. The worsening economic problems appeared to be not unrelated to the failures of the industrial relations system. These included restrictive labour practices, inflationary wage drift, and the rising incidence of industrial conflict, which in the 1960s tended to take the form of action that was both unofficial (not sanctioned by the union) and unconstitutional (in breach of agreed procedures). Broadly speaking governments have pursued two different remedial strategies both of which have had a dramatic impact on labour law: reform and restriction.[15]

THE STRATEGY OF REFORM

This strategy was advocated by the Donovan Royal Commission.[16] Donovan's definition of the problem was how to preserve and protect the voluntary institutions of industrial relations and yet to restore order, peace and efficiency. The solution was a voluntary reform of the institutions whereby management and trade union officials would regain control over workplace activity through factory-wide and comprehensive collective agreements. A system of extensive joint regulation (or 'management by agreement' as it is sometimes called) would supplant the disruptive spontaneity of the shop floor and some traditional areas of managerial prerogative. On this analysis it must be emphasised unions were still legitimate bodies and a reformed system of collective bargaining was still a viable means to order.

The reform strategy did not however confine itself to the practices of collective bargaining. It always involved an incomes policy, preferably on a voluntary basis, in order to restrain and rationalise the growth of money incomes. It involved too a more interventionist framework of labour law. The underlying assumption of traditional non-interventionist legal policy — that what was not regulated by law would be regulated by collective bargaining — was found in many instances to be fallacious. New labour laws might help to remedy the omissions of collective bargaining and to hasten its reform. Another coincidental but important pressure for new employment legislation was the need to harmonise British law with international and, from 1973 onwards, Common Market standards. On the other hand, the aim to reform and not to destroy collective autonomy logically demanded that the new laws ought not to subject the collective labour relationship to detailed legal regulation. Reform, according to the Donovan Report (para. 190), was 'to be accomplished, if possible, without destroying the British tradition of keeping industrial relations out of the courts'. This general line of reasoning was adopted by Labour administrations in 1964–70 and 1974–79, and a not totally dissimilar strand of reform, though with greater emphasis on the law, was implicit in some of the policies of the Conservative government of 1970–74.

Individual labour law

The trend towards legislation promoting the reform strategy has been clearly and consistently indicated by the growth of 'individual' labour law, that is, the law regulating the relationship between the individual employee and his or her employer. This development has involved a massive expansion of the work of the industrial tribunals, composed of a legal chairman and two lay persons, one employer and one trade unionist. The tribunals started in 1965 with the single jurisdiction of hearing appeals against training levies. Subsequently they have developed into a system of 'labour courts' for dealing with complaints arising from the individual employee's statutory floor of rights — unfair dismissal, redundancy pay and consultation, guarantee pay, equal pay, trade union membership and activities, time off work for union duties, safety representation and other specified purposes, maternity pay and leave, and protection from discrimination on grounds of sex, marital status or race. (Certain of these provisions are the subject of detailed consideration in chapter two.) By the late 1970s about 40,000 cases were registered annually with the tribunals, the large majority being complaints of unfair dismissal.

Much of the statutory framework could until the Act of 1980 be regarded as bipartisan. Both Conservative and Labour governments had made important contributions. The Conservatives initiated the process with the Contracts of Employment Act 1963, providing for 'written particulars' of employment and minimum notice periods. Labour followed with the Redundancy Payments Act 1965 to ensure that employers made a minimum payment to workers who were sacked through redundancy. The right not to be unfairly dismissed, which had been first recommended by Donovan in 1968 and then included in a Bill which fell in 1970 with the Labour government, was finally introduced by the Conservatives in their Industrial Relations Act 1971. It was the only part of the Act to be re-enacted in 1974. Labour went on to strengthen and extend the statutory rights of individual employees with the Employment Protection Act 1975 (EPA) which together with TULRA constituted the main labour law component of the 'Social Contract'. Later the individual rights in this and various other statutes were consolidated in the Employment Protection (Consolidation) Act 1978 (EPCA). During this period Labour also passed the Health and Safety at Work Act (though the Conservatives had planned something similar), the Sex Discrimination Act 1975, which supplemented and amended the earlier Equal Pay Act 1970, and finally an extended Race Relations Act 1976 replacing earlier legislation.

The largely bipartisan nature of this unprecedented development of individual labour law provides a key to understanding the underlying public policy. Social justice for the individual worker was of course a fundamental consideration but other objectives were equally important. Statutory redundancy pay, for example, was intended to facilitate the acceptance of technological change of in fact the 'need' for redundancy whatever the cause. Unfair dismissal laws were designed to encourage an improvement in personnel management and to eliminate industrial discipline as a cause of strikes. The maternity provisions had as much to do with the efficient operation of the labour market as with the rights of women. The whole thrust of employment protection was really to encourage the efficiency of and to modernise British industry, and it is no coincidence that comparable measures exist in most other European countries.

These strongly interventionist aims took the law far beyond the earlier precedents of the regulation of 'truck' and industrial safety. It is now generally acknowledged that the overall tradition of non-intervention has been abandoned in the field of individual labour law. But what were the implications of this development for collective labour law and relations? The Donovan Royal Commission was adamant that the tribunals which it originally envisaged should have jurisdiction over neither collective disputes nor over issues between trade unions and members or applicants for membership (para. 576). Nevertheless the enactment of an individual right not to be unfairly dismissed, for example, raised an immediate question concerning the closed shop — what was to be the position of an employee who was sacked for belonging to no union or to the wrong union? The legal answer to this question has been radically altered (for the fourth time within the space of nine years) by the Employment Act, and we shall return to it in detail in chapter four. Or what of the rights of strikers who are sacked? If a tribunal was allowed to determine the merits of such individual dismissals would it not also be determining the rights and wrongs of the collective industrial action? This possibility was foreseen and the law has attempted to avert it by a curious compromise, the current form of which is as follows: where an employer dismisses all the strikers the tribunal cannot decide on the fairness of the dismissals, but if he victimises some strikers but not others, those who are dismissed are eligible to make a claim for unfair dismissal (EPCA s.62). Whether the Employment Act has thrown the tribunals into the centre of collective conflict is another question we shall raise later on.

It is indeed arguable that even in advance of the 1980 Act the growth of individual labour law had a profound impact on the organic relationship between law and industrial relations. The statutory floor of individual rights is the starting point (and in times of mass unemployment doubtless often the finishing point) of collective negotiations on all the issues covered by the legislation, whether redundancy pay or discipline or equal pay or maternity rights. Some of the individual legal rights are also specifically designed to have their primary impact at the collective level, for example, the right of union officials to paid time off for industrial relations duties (EPCA s.27); or the right not to be dismissed because of trade union membership or activity (EPCA s.58); or the right not to be compelled by action short of dismissal to join a union (EPCA s.23(1)(c) amended by EA s.15(1)). Notwithstanding the ingenious solution concerning unfair dismissal and strikers, the tribunals have to deal more and more with essentially collective issues including the interpretation of collective agreements on the entire range of subjects from hours of work to union membership. In the EPA's redundancy consultation procedure moreover it is the trade union (not the individual employee) who makes the initial complaint, which by definition relates to collective issues. Paradoxically the tribunals are in theory also given jurisdiction over collective agreements by some of the 'contracting-out' provisions, which are supposed to ensure the primacy of collective bargaining by allowing the collective negotiators to vary the application of statutory rights.[17] To make matters worse, the tribunals themselves are said to be exhibiting a discernible trend towards unnecessary legalism (see chapter two). In short the idea that individual labour law can somehow be isolated from collective labour law and relations is beginning to look untenable. We shall in fact argue that the Employment Act's restrictions on individual legal rights may have an important impact on the collective relationship.

Collective labour law

Collective labour law, that is, the legal rules applicable to the collective relationship between management and trade unions has also developed at a formidable rate. However many of the statutory initiatives in this area, which is far more controversial than the floor of rights for individual employees, have proved to be short-lived. The story begins with the Labour administrations of the 1960s. Although Labour welcomed the general approach of the Donovan Report and as we have seen disapproved of judicial efforts at increasing the legal resources of employers via civil liabilities, it was itself prepared to back up direct state intervention with criminal sanctions. A statutory incomes policy was introduced by the Prices and Incomes Act 1966, which stipulated criminal sanctions against those who used industrial action to contravene government legal orders designed to delay the implementation of pay awards.[18] In terms of the tradition of non-intervention this statutory policy was revolutionary as it interfered directly with free collective bargaining. The statutory process eventually lapsed but similar criminal sanctions were revived by the Conservatives' counter-inflation legislation of 1972–73.

The Labour White Paper *In Place of Strife* (1969) envisaged a range of criminal restraints on management, unions and individual employees.[19] The major proposals included a compulsory conciliation pause, under which workers on strike in breach of collectively agreed procedures might have been legally ordered to return to work; a compulsory strike ballot; and a statutory union recognition procedure covering inter-union disputes whereby fines could be imposed on defaulters. These 'penalty' clauses ignited a fierce conflict within the labour and trade union movement and were eventually withdrawn. *In Place of Strife* proved to be the prelude to the Conservatives' Industrial Relations Act, which we discuss later in this chapter.

In the mid 1970s the framework of collective labour law was reconstructed. TULRA, which repealed the Industrial Relations Act, restored some of the basic principles of non-intervention, notably the statutory immunities and the presumption that collective agreements are not intended to give rise to legally enforceable contracts. The voluntary approach to state-sponsored conciliation and arbitration was also re-affirmed and these vital functions were removed from the control of a government department and placed under the aegis of the Advisory, Conciliation and Arbitration Service (ACAS), whose tripartite governing council is composed of employers, trade unionists and independent experts. Then came the EPA, which put ACAS on a statutory footing and introduced a series of legal rights for trade unions: a union recognition procedure (ss.11—16, now repealed); a legal duty on employers to disclose information to recognised trade unions for collective bargaining purposes (ss.17—21); arbitration for the 'recognised' or alternatively the 'general level' of terms and conditions — a procedure at the option of management as well as unions (Schedule 11, now repealed); and compulsory consultation rights for recognised trade unions over questions of redundancy (Part IV). Further consultation rights were enacted to cover industrial safety (Health and Safety at Work Act 1974 s.2) and occupational pensions (Social Security Pensions Act s.31(5)). In this context it is also worth noting the procedure to ensure that collective agreements conform with the principles of equal pay (Equal Pay Act 1970 s.3).

What were the implications of these new laws for the voluntarist character of industrial relations? Although the statutory consultation rights on safety and to a lesser extent on redundancy appeared to have generated more efficient personnel management practices and more formal bargaining,[20] the overall impact has been less than one might have expected. In a few instances the recognition procedure encouraged the development of collective bargaining, but its effect overall was almost bound to be limited as collective bargaining was already wide-spread by the time the EPA's procedure was introduced. Of critical importance moreover was the fact that the legal sanction was indirect. It was neither an injunction nor a fine but an arbitration award on terms and conditions of employment by the Central Arbitration Com-mittee (CAC – the permanent tri-partite body with the function of voluntary and statutory arbitration). The CAC's award was incorpora-ted into the individual contracts of employment of those covered by the claim, and ultimately a recalcitrant employer might have been sued by the individual employee in the County Court for breach of contract. Schedule 11 operated in a similar way and the final sanction in the dis-closure of information procedure still does. Breach of the duty to con-sult over redundancies also leads to an indirect sanction. A trade union may complain to an industrial tribunal, which may make a modest 'protective award' for the benefit of individual employees, who then have to make their own claim in the tribunal if the employer fails to pay up. In legal theory the duty to consult over industrial safety could be enforced by the Health and Safety Executive by means of 'improve-ment' notices and criminal prosecutions in the magistrates' courts. In practice the Executive will not as a matter of policy use its legal powers to enforce industrial relations procedures and consequently there is no legal enforcement at all.[21] Generally the most serious risk of legalism arose from the attempt by the judges to subject ACAS and, to a lesser extent, the CAC to meticulous scrutiny and direction in the exercise of their powers under the recognition procedure and Schedule 11, a danger which has in fact been averted by the Employment Act's repeal of the recognition procedure and Schedule 11 (see chapter seven).

Trade union power and collective labour law

Can it be claimed that these legal rights (as well as the restoration of the immunities) tipped the balance of power in favour of the unions? Is an argument of that kind sustainable despite the indirect sanctions? It is true that the EPA was part of the Social Contract and, according to the Labour Party Manifesto of October 1974, the objective was to bring about 'a fundamental and irreversible shift in the balance of wealth and power in favour of working people and their families'. Beyond the EPA moreover there was the Bullock Report's suggestion of a law to secure a radical extension of industrial democracy through union representation in company boardrooms.[22] Clearly trade union aspirations were reflected in the EPA and the Bullock Report, though the latter evinced only a tepid White Paper from the Labour government.[23] We suggest however that the dominant policy was not to transfer power but rather to continue the reform strategy as mapped out by the Donovan Report.

In this strategy ACAS was to have the pivotal role. It was apparent from the express provisions of the EPA that ACAS was (and is) intended to be much more than the custodian of the official peace-keeping machinery. Its functions as defined in law are influenced by the original concept of the now defunct Commission on Industrial Relations, which had been set up by Labour in 1969 in order to encourage the reform of industrial relations on Donovan lines. ACAS is 'charged with the general duty of promoting the improvement of industrial relations and in particular of encouraging the extension of collective bargaining and the development and, where necessary, reform of collective bargaining machinery' (EPA s.1(2)). The responsibilities of ACAS for inquiries and the issuing of codes of practice are expressly defined in terms of promoting the 'improvement' of industrial relations (EPA ss.5 and 6). ACAS is also to provide industry with a free advisory service covering (according to s.4 of the EPA) the whole field of industrial relations and personnel management including pay structures, job evaluation, manpower planning, discipline, employee communications, and, in so far as it affects collective bargaining, the internal organisation of management and trade unions. As Professor Kahn-Freund noted with some enthusiasm, this activity would be conducive to the 'so urgently necessary modernisation' of British industrial relations.[24] It is from this perspective too that we must view at least some of the new collective labour laws of the Social Contract era.

A union recognition procedure was seen by the Donovan Report as an alternative to the industrial power struggles which had determined management recognition policies in the past. The idea was to avoid damaging conflicts in the future and to ensure a more orderly extension of collective bargaining to white-collar employees in particular. The conciliation, investigation and report by ACAS were therefore the critical stages of the EPA's recognition provisions. These applied not only to situations of fresh recognition but also, though this was largely ignored in practice, to 'further' recognition (s.11(3)). The 'further' recognition option was intended to provide a remedy to the severely limited scope of much collective bargaining. The reformist intent was underlined by the principle, carried over directly from the 'bargaining unit' provisions of the Industrial Relations Act, that the procedure applied only to single or 'associated' employers but not to employers' associations. The exclusion of multi-employer bargaining units related to the need, as diagnosed by Donovan, to secure orderly and comprehensive arrangements in the middle levels of bargaining below the decaying industry-wide structures. This same principle, again carried over from the analogous provisions of the Industrial Relations Act, applies to the EPA's disclosure of information duty. Finally, as in the case of the new individual labour laws, the pressure for measures of reform was reinforced by international obligations. The law on redundancy consultation and notification was based not on trade union demands but on the Common Market Directive on Collective Redundancies.[25]

The idea that the new collective labour laws were a great extension of trade union power is even less tenable when one considers the wider context of the period 1974—79. Against a background of mounting unemployment, persistent inflation, public expenditure cuts (though not on the subsequent scale), fluctuating living standards and the basic failure of Labour in office to implement the Social Contract's overall economic and industrial strategy, the new labour laws were certainly not to be regarded as a reflection of trade union strength. They were moreover with all their imperfections, omissions and weak enforcement, offered to the unions as a major part of the consideration for their active involvement in a restrictive incomes policy. In this situation the new laws were indicative not of a transfer of power but rather of the encouragement which the government offered to trade union leaders to assist in the maintenance of social and economic stability. Given the decentralisation and democratic traditions of British trade unions, attempts to integrate them are likely to be of only limited success and the Social Contract duly perished in the 'winter of discontent' of 1978—79, a reaction to an over-rigid 5 per cent pay policy. In February 1979 a belated effort to salvage some understanding between the unions and the Labour government was made in the form of the 'Social Concordat', which included the TUC's own Guides on *Negotiating and Disputes Procedures, Conduct of Industrial Disputes* and *Trade Union Organisation and the Closed Shop*.[26]

The argument for the policy of reform always contained a note of warning. If the unions did not co-operate and exercise self-restraint then more coercive measures might have to be imposed. Although the Donovan Report, for example, proposed that collective agreements should retain their non-contractual status in the immediately foreseeable future, eventual legal enforceability of procedure agreements was envisaged on a selective basis where the reform of collective bargaining failed to curtail unconstitutional strikes 'due to irresponsibility or to agitation by eccentrics or by subversives' (para. 508). The explicit note of warning reappeared in the writings of those academic analysts most closely identified with the reform strategy. According to Allan Flanders writing in the late 1960s 'the longer the process of reconstruction is delayed the more punitive they [public and private sanctions] may have to be'.[27] A decade later Otto Kahn-Freund wrote that unless the unions shoulder the task of reform 'the freedom to strike without which they cannot exist may one day be in mortal danger'.[28] The prophesised legal nemesis has arrived in two major instalments: the Industrial Relations Act 1971 and the Employment Act 1980.

EXPERIENCE OF THE INDUSTRIAL RELATIONS ACT

The 1980 Act inevitably invites comparison with the Industrial Relations Act 1971, the last attempt by a Conservative government at recasting labour law. The earlier statute pursued two objectives: the reform of industrial relations and the restriction of trade unions. The reform strategy implicit in the IRA and explicitly set out in the accompanying Industrial Relations Code of Practice (1972) bore many resemblances to that of the Donovan Report but, in great contrast to Donovan, the law was envisaged as the government's main instrument in achieving reform. This strategy nevertheless assumed the legitimacy of the unions and indeed reflected a collectivist ethic. The restriction strategy on the other hand reflected an individualist ethic, according to which unions distorted the market relations between the employer and the individual employee. The solution was to use the law to reduce the organisational strength of trade unions and their capacity to take collective industrial action. There was a further strand to the individualist ethic, namely, that the union aspiration to control jobs and labour markets posed a threat to the personal liberty of the individual employee. Individuals were therefore to be given new legal rights vis a vis unions and the closed shop was to be outlawed. The Act's duality of aims led Professor Wedderburn to suggest that it appeared to be the work of two draftsmen: 'The first may be thought of as a civil servant or "organisation man" concerned mainly to bring "order" and a tidy structure into collective British industrial relations. The second is quite different, a Conservative lawyer involved above all else with doctrines of *individual* rights, often without regard to the shop-floor problems of collective bargaining.'[29]

In the forefront of the Act's reforming measures was the provision that, unless there was an express clause to the contrary, collective agreements made in writing would be presumed to be intended to create legal relations. *Fair Deal at Work,* a Conservative Party policy document published in 1968 before the Report of the Donovan Commission, had forcefully argued that lack of legal enforceability was the precondition for the informal style, vague content and pervasive disorder of collective negotiations. But the Act's encouragement of contractual collective bargaining was totally ineffective because the optional clause disclaiming any intention to create legal relations became virtually a universal feature of agreements. A legal procedure for determining 'bargaining units' and 'sole bargaining agents' was another major plank of the Act's reform strategy. The main justification was that the lack of such a North-American-style procedure had encouraged the overlapping and illogical pattern of union recognition and membership. In the event the sheer complexity of this measure meant that few people in industry were able to comprehend what it was supposed to achieve. Moreover the unions affiliated to the TUC boycotted this and other procedures, refusing to register with a new Registrar of Trade Unions so as to bring themselves within the Act's definition of a 'trade union'. The other measures relevant to reform (apart from unfair dismissals) included the registration of procedure agreements, which was in practice unimportant; a duty on employers to disclose information for collective bargaining, which was not brought into effect; and a mechanism to impose legally enforceable procedure agreements, which was never used.

The strategy of restriction was promoted by a series of provisions to curtail the legal freedom of unions to take industrial action. The Act restored the principle of *Taff Vale,* whereby organisations as distinct from individuals could be made legally liable. Also plaintiffs were given the opportunity to press claims in a specially-created National Industrial Relations Court (NIRC) for a new range of civil liabilities called 'unfair industrial practices'. Unofficial groups and also unregistered unions were vulnerable particularly after *Heaton's Transport* v. *TGWU* (1972), where the House of Lords held that the unregistered TGWU was vicariously liable for the apparently unofficial acts of its shop stewards in the docks. Meanwhile a group of dockers' shop stewards in

London, the 'Pentonville Five', had been imprisoned for contempt of court after deliberately flouting injunctions. The courts, with the aid of the Official Solicitor (the fairy godmother of trade union folklore), were constrained to resort to some very unorthodox devices in order to release the dockers and so avert an industrial and constitutional crisis. Further legal embarrassments arose from the policy of the AUEW, the second largest union, not to observe legal orders or voluntarily pay fines for contempt of court. At one point the AUEW called off a national strike only after the NIRC had accepted an offer from a group of anonymous donors to pay the fines and compensation owed by the union (*Con-Mech. Ltd.* v. *AUEW,* 1973). Fortunately relatively few employers chose to avail themselves of the dubious benefits of litigation. The government was no less reluctant as regards its own right to apply to the NIRC for restraining orders under 'national emergency' cooling off period and ballot procedures. It only did this once in the railway dispute of 1972 (*Secretary of State* v. *ASLEF*), with the consequences of strengthening the unions and exposing the NIRC to the accusation that it was an instrument of class justice.

The Act's legal rights for individual employees included: the right to belong to and participate in the activities of a registered trade union and, what was far more important, the right not to belong to any organisation of workers, as qualified for registered unions only by the possibility of an 'agency' or 'approved closed shop'; the right to be admitted to a trade union if appropriately qualified; and the right to challenge through a legal procedure the continuance of most collective bargaining arrangements. These measures potentially threatened not only trade unionism but the very principle of joint regulation through collective bargaining. The right not to belong, together with a specific prohibition on 'pre-entry' arrangements, directly clashed with the practice of the closed shop, though widespread management connivance allowed the vast majority of existing closed shops to continue and even a few new ones to develop. In addition a further complication was injected into some difficult situations by virtue of the ability of registered but unrecognised staff and professional associations and breakaway unions and their individual members to use legal tactics at the expense of TUC-affiliated bodies and established procedures.

The 1971 Act was a spectacular failure. It foundered on the rocks of union opposition and management indifference. Its strategies of reform and restriction were contradictory. How could the law encourage trade unions to control workplace activity while at the same time undermining their security? Above all the Act failed because it attempted to change at one dramatic stroke the historically organic relationship between law and collective labour relations in Britain.

Have the architects of the Employment Act (and of the eight consultative Working Papers[30] on which it was based) learnt the lessons of the Industrial Relations Act? Certainly the structure of the 1980 Act is quite different from that of the 1971 Act.[31] It operates mainly by way of amendment to other statutes and the judicial interpretations of them. It does not try to establish any comprehensive framework of rights and obligations administered by a new set of institutions. There is no NIRC, no Registrar and no grandiose procedure to restructure collective bargaining. With the possible exception of funds for union ballots, the strategy of reform is almost entirely absent. Indeed the Act repeals the EPA's union recognition procedure and Schedule 11 and it erodes the statutory floor of individual rights. The Employment Act is in essence based on the single strategy of the restriction or coercion of trade unions. This strategy accords with the same individualist ethic which underpinned the Industrial Relations Act. The reduction by the 1980 Act of the immunities in TULRA for those engaged in picketing and secondary industrial action may be markedly different in legal form from the unfair industrial practices of the 1971 Act but in substance the intention to restrict the ability of unions to engage in industrial action is not dissimilar. Again the new legal rights for individuals against employers and unions in and sometimes outside closed shops take a different form from the IRA's right not to belong. But the potential implications for union solidarity, the stability of collective bargaining and the problems of multi-unionism are analogous. And the Green Paper *Trade Union Immunities* once more raises issues such as the vicarious liability of unions, the legal enforceability of collective agreements, and special legal restriction in disputes which give rise to national emergencies. The trade unions have made it clear that they consider that their vital interests are under threat. Although the 'step-by-step' tactics of the 1980 Act contrast with the 'at a stroke' approach of the IRA, it would seem that the latter statute is of more than historical interest. The relevance of the Industrial Relations Act to the analysis of the Employment Act is one of the recurrent themes of the following chapters.

2

Employment Protection

Half of the sections of the Employment Act operate by way of amendment to the EPCA which provides the modern framework of most of the statutory floor of rights enacted in the 1960s and 1970s for the protection of individual employees.[1] The Act concentrates on two aspects of that protection: unfair dismissal and maternity rights. In neither of these areas however is the EA the only source of changes made by the present Conservative government. The right to complain of unfair dismissal was severely restricted by one of the 'July Orders', which extended the basic qualifying period of employment from six months to one year. Other amendments to the law on guarantee pay, redundancy consultation and social security benefits can also legitimately be considered as part of a policy to halt and reverse what had previously been a progressive expansion of individual employment protection rights. This chapter analyses these developments and their practical consequences and also examines the important modifications in industrial tribunal procedure which took effect at the same time. (The new provisions in EA s.7 which are concerned with closed shop employment, together with the allied provisions concerning organisational rights in EA ss.10 and 15, are considered separately in chapters three and four.)

The government's general argument in support of its measures was that certain of the employment protection laws bore overharshly on employers, discouraging recruitment especially in small businesses. Small firms lacked specialised personnel departments to handle grievances and procedures and, it was asserted, found the whole paraphernalia of employment protection a practical and psychological disincentive to the employment of more labour. Freed from these bureaucratic and legal constraints they could expand, become more prosperous, create more jobs and help to regenerate an ailing economy. The creation of legal rights had outstripped and was impeding the creation of wealth

and the time had come to redress the balance. The erosion of employment protection was therefore a response to economic decline. The Earl
of Gowrie, one of the ministers in the Department of Employment,
revealed a great deal when he declared:

> In the words of the old song, 'something's got to give', and in our
> case it is the ability of our economy to sustain, without the raging
> inflation which has the same job destroying effects in the end, the
> levels of employment to which we are accustomed . . . as all noble
> Lords are aware, we in this country have accustomed the elec-
> torate to a greater degree of mental and physical comfort than
> our national situation allows. . . . The message is that this legisla-
> tion in its present form diverts management attention from the
> central task of running a business. . . .[2]

In evaluating these arguments we have the advantage, as did the
government, of two comprehensive and objective investigations into the
effects of the legislation on key sectors of private industry. The first,
commissioned by the DE and the Manpower Services Commission, was
carried out by W. Daniel and E. Stilgoe of the Policy Studies Institute
(PSI).[3] It consisted mainly of a survey of 301 manufacturing firms
employing from 50 to 5,000 workers. The second was undertaken by
R. Clifton and C. Tatton-Brown, two members of the DE's own staff,
with interviewing assistance from the specialist Opinion Research
Centre.[4] This was a survey of 301 small firms employing fewer than
fifty people in manufacturing and service industry.

Daniel and Stilgoe identified unfair dismissals as the aspect of employment protection having most effect. But they found that the idea
that employers were refraining from taking on extra staff because of
fear that the law might make it difficult to get rid of them later on was
simply a myth. The impact of the law was not to stop dismissals but
rather to encourage employers to take more care over selection and disciplinary procedures. It had thus encouraged more effective and better
personnel management and industrial relations, an exercise in en-
lightened self-interest which most employers understood and appreciated. The Clifton and Tatton-Brown survey of small firms also exploded
the myth of the disincentive effect of employment protection. Of the
firms who had a greater volume of work but who had failed to recruit
more staff, only 4 per cent cited employment protection as a reason.
When all the firms in the sample were asked to list the main difficulties
in running their businesses only 6 per cent mentioned employment
protection, which ranked thirteenth in the scale of difficulties. Issues of
much greater concern were lack of finance (44 per cent), staff shortages

(35 per cent) and VAT (16 per cent). Such difficulties one may surmise must have intensified under the present administration, which increased VAT and regarded high interest rates as a central component of its 'monetarist' solution to inflation.

Against this the government placed some reliance on submissions and surveys of various interest groups such as the EEF, the National Federation of Self-Employed and Small Businesses, the Small Business Bureau (a Conservative Party pressure group), the Association of Independent Businesses, the London and Birmingham Chambers of Commerce, the Forum of Private Business and the Alliance of Small Firms (motto: 'Mind your own business is the only moral law'). But serious doubt as to the validity of the findings of the PSI and DE studies could not be raised on the basis of these views. An exhaustive survey of this evidence carried out at the Small Business Research Unit, a genuinely independent research body based at the Central London Polytechnic, concluded that it was (with the partial exception of the EEF questionnaire) based on surveys which were politically biased and statistically unreliable.[5] Rather than dispute this the government preferred to rely on more intangible criteria. To quote Mr. James Prior, the Secretary of State for Employment: 'In so many cases with small employers it is the psychological aspect that is important. It is the anecdotal evidence more than the practical evidence.'[6]

Rising unemployment however makes the need for employment protection greater than ever before, particularly in small firms where the counter-balance of trade union organisation is frequently absent and where the incidence of both labour turnover and unfair dismissal is higher than average. Research indicated, for example, that in 1978 a quarter of all unfair dismissal claims involved firms employing fewer than twenty people and such firms lost a proportionately higher number of cases in the tribunals than larger firms.[7] The Employment Act's special qualifications and exclusions for small firms only serve to create a second or inferior class of employee. They were strongly opposed by the IPM which argued that 'small, far from being beautiful, would become synonomous with disadvantaged'.

UNFAIR DISMISSAL

Doubling the service qualification

As from 1 October 1979, in advance of the main Employment Act, a large proportion of potential applicants were excluded from the industrial tribunals. This was because the service qualification for unfair dismissal claims was as a general rule extended from twenty six to fifty two weeks by one of the two July Orders.[8] No qualifying period is required only if the reason for a dismissal is 'inadmissible', that is, if it relates to union membership or activities, or non-membership in a closed shop, see chapters three and four. Also where the reason for dismissal is to avoid the impact of the medical suspension provisions in EPCA ss.19–22 the qualifying period is only four weeks. The general rule however is that the employee who wishes to complain of unfair dismissal must have a minimum period of one year of continuous service with his employer.

This was the first of several measures which the government put forward as a way of helping small businesses but which in fact limits the rights of all employees whatever the size of their employer. As a variant of the recruitment disincentive theory, it was also argued that employers should be free without worrying about unfair dismissal to treat their new employees as probationers until they have proved themselves capable of doing the job. However the EAT has clearly laid down that the tribunals must give due regard to the notion of probation in considering the employer's reason for dismissal and whether he acted reasonably. In such cases it is usual for the tribunals to say that the employee has some sort of duty to establish himself (*Post Office* v. *Mughal*, 1977). Probation, in other words, relates to the fairness of a dismissal and not to the quite separate question of the service qualification.

If the service qualification is not supposed to be a probationary period, what is its rationale? It is all about the work load of the industrial tribunals. When the unfair dismissal law was first introduced in 1971 the service qualification was set at two years in order to avoid the possibility of the tribunals being flooded with claims. When it became clear that they could carry the case load, the qualifying period was reduced by TULRA to a year and then to six months. By 1979 the tribunals were coping quite well with the vastly increased volume of work and the question might well have been asked as to whether the period should be reduced to three months (as was actually envisaged by the previous government) or even abolished altogether as in some European countries. The irony was that the power for amending the EPCA by ministerial regulation was enacted on the assumption that future changes would enhance rather than weaken the rights of individual employees.

In high turnover industries (catering for example) the July Order marked the effective end of employment protection for many of those most in need. Those with good employers or with strong unions do not feel the full impact. For them the internal grievance procedure is more important than the industrial tribunal. The number of tribunal applications from a particular service or industry has always been inversely proportional to union membership density. But if a bad employer of a well organised workforce is tempted to revive arbitrary dismissals for shorter service employees, we may expect more strikes on the hoary old issue of management prerogative. For the most part however it is the ill-organised, predominantly low-paid, predominantly female, often seasonal employees who bear the brunt.

Service qualification in small businesses

While the general service qualification is one year, the Employment Act requires a minimum period of continuous service of two years if 'at no time during that period did the number of employees employed by the employer for the time being of the dismissed employee, added to the number employed by any associated employer, exceed twenty' (EPCA s.64A, inserted by EA s.8(1)). There are only two exceptions: when the reason for the dismissal is 'inadmissible' in which case there is no qualifying period, and when the dismissal is made to avoid the EPCA's provisions giving a right to paid suspension from work on certain specific medical grounds where the qualifying period is four weeks. Generally however the employer now has a complete 'defence' against an unfair dismissal complaint by an employee with less than two years' service if his business employs a workforce not exceeding twenty.

In counting the number of employees those working for the employer of the dismissed employee are added to those of any 'associated' employer. The concept of the associated employer is of critical importance in employment protection and many other areas of labour law. An ever growing proportion of people work for employers who are part of a wider group of companies with complex and interlocking structures often stretching across national frontiers. So far as the law is concerned two employers are associated 'if one is a company of which the other (directly or indirectly) has control, or if both are companies of which a third person (directly or indirectly) has control' (EPCA s.153(4)). This definition seems quite broad but, in view of the complexities of corporate groupings, the question whether particular employers are associated is often unclear. However the Court of Appeal has ruled that employers in the public sector cannot be associated because they are not limited companies (*Gardiner* v. *Merton Borough Council,* 1980).

Another big complication is that only 'employees' in the strict legal sense may be counted. Indeed on the evidence of the reported unfair dismissal cases the question of whether the complainant is an employee is increasingly contested by employers. Consequently the employer's defence of 'I employ no more than twenty employees' is likely to be a further encouragement to the spread of the notorious 'lump' (nominal self-employment). The lump has already wreaked havoc in the building trades, and in many other industries lawyers are busily devising ever more elaborate schemes of self-employment in order to avoid legal responsibilities to do with unfair dismissal, redundancy, safety, social security and taxation. The consequence has been a continuous stream of expensive litigation to ascertain whether particular workers are or are not 'employees' for particular purposes. The test of an employment contract used to be whether the 'master' controlled the 'servant' in the way he did the work. Then came the 'organisation' test: was the worker integrated into the organisation or was he in business on his own account? To these criteria were added the 'mixed' test and finally, as the judges' last resort, the so-called 'common sense' test. In one recent case it took a hearing in the industrial tribunal, an appeal to the EAT, and then a lengthy judgment in the Court of Appeal to decide whether a sheet metal worker was an employee or a self-employed independent contractor. It was finally held that, though he had been treated as self-employed by the Inland Revenue, on a true legal construction he was an 'employee' and was therefore able to claim unfair dismissal (*Young and Woods Ltd.* v. *West,* 1980). This particular firm employed between twenty and twenty five people on the shop floor, and it is easy to imagine that some employers will classify new recruits as self-employed if the total of their employees would otherwise exceed the magic number of twenty.

What is the effect of this provision on the small firms themselves? They are not freed from the need to maintain records and develop procedures, if only because they will usually employ some employees with more than two years' service. But will it help to dispel the recruitment disincentive (assuming that this exists)? It is worth noting for the record that the government's original proposal in the Employment Protection Working Paper and in the Employment Bill as first published was much more clearly aimed at eliminating disincentives. Undertakings employing not more than nineteen employees were to be exempt from unfair dismissals during their first two years' of trading as a specific encouragement for new enterprises to develop. As the Bill proceeded through Parliament this proposal was withdrawn and the two year service qualification for all small firms was substituted. Any disincentive which this removes would have to relate to employees with more than one year's service (the general rule) but less than two. But there is no evidence to suggest that small firms in particular perceive a problem about a one year as opposed to a two year service qualification. Clifton and Tatton-Brown found that only a tiny proportion of small firms without prompting mentioned employment protection as a factor inhibiting recruitment and specifically that the large majority of firms did not even know the length of the service qualification. In fact small firms are generally less worried about getting rid of staff than about attracting and retaining the right kind of employee. The extension of the service qualification in small firms may have harmful effects on recruitment if it (a) inhibits recruitment altogether as firms attempt to stay within the twenty employee limit, or (b) encourages the spread of nominal self-employment or (c) discourages labour mobility into and within the small firm sector as employees decide to stay where they are in order to preserve their accrued service rights.

If the effect of this measure on recruitment is dubious, it nevertheless deprives many individual employees of any protection against unfair dismissal. A surprisingly large proportion of the nation's labour force is affected: it is estimated that as many as four million workers are employed in firms with a staff of fewer than twenty people. Between a quarter and a third of men and up to a half of all women are employed in the same job for two years or less, and these proportions are much higher in certain high turnover industries such as construction and catering where the employers are often small. Moreover the small firm is statistically more likely to dismiss unfairly and yet this is where the Employment Act creates a new category of second class employee. It was significant that the Donovan Commission, which provided the blueprint for our unfair dismissal law, was specifically opposed both to a two year service qualification and to any exclusion of small firms (paras. 555–56). Their enactment not surprisingly provoked a barrage of criticism from many directions including the TUC, the Equal Opportunities Commission, the Royal College of Nursing and employers' organisations such as the IPM, the Association of County Councils and even the CBI (though its Smaller Firms Council took a different view).

The burden of proof

Claiming unfair dismissal involves four key issues: was the complainant
an employee with the requisite service qualifications, was he dismissed,
what was the reason for the dismissal and did the employer behave
reasonably? The onus is on the complainant to prove both that he was
qualified to claim and that he was dismissed. The employer however,
must show that his reason or principal reason for the dismissal falls
within the statutory list of acceptable reasons, that is, it relates to
capability, qualifications, redundancy, conduct, the statutory requirements of the job, or, alternatively, that there was some other substantial reason such as to justify dismissal. Given that the employer can
almost invariably point to one of these very broad heads of acceptable
reasons, the crux of a claim for unfair dismissal (unless one of the
provisions in EPCA ss.58–62 governing special situations applies) is
usually the fourth stage: did the employer act reasonably or unreasonably in the circumstances, having regard to equity and the substantial
merits of the case, in treating the reason shown as sufficient for dismissing the employee? The reasonableness of the employer's action is thus
decisive in determining the fairness of a dismissal and it is here that the
Employment Act shifts the onus of proof from the employer. The Act
removes the requirement that the employer should prove the reasonableness of a dismissal and merely leaves the words 'that question shall
be determined in accordance with equity and the substantial merits of
the case' (EPCA s.57(3) as amended by EA s.6).

This provision puts the clock back to the Industrial Relations Act of
1971. That Act was silent as to where the burden of proving reasonableness lay and left the issue to be determined by the tribunals in accordance with equity and the merits of the case. The tribunals proceeded to
apply the general legal principle that, in the absence of a contrary
provision, he who makes a claim must prove it. The onus of proving an
allegation of unreasonableness therefore rested on the employee, and it
was only subject to that principle that the tribunals could determine
reasonableness in accordance with equity and the merits.[9]

In 1974 the law was changed and the onus of proving reasonableness
was put on the employer. This helped to clarify and simplify tribunal
hearings and to minimise undue legalism. It also brought the law into
line with the social reality that the employer has the greater knowledge
of his own actions and state of mind. It is for the same reason that the
onus in redundancy claims has always been on the employer to show
that the dismissal was for a reason other than redundancy (EPCA

s.91(2)). In unfair dismissal cases moreover the tribunals determine the reasonableness of dismissal for the reason shown according to the standards of the 'reasonable employer' (*N.C. Watling Ltd.* v. *Richardson,* 1978). The logic of putting the onus on the employer has in fact become an integral part of the judicial formulations of the tests of fairness and reasonableness (*Weddel* v. *Tepper,* 1980). But under the Employment Act, the employee may be hard-pressed to discharge the burden of proof in respect of the employer's actions and subjective motivations.

The government's argument as set out in its Employment Protection Working Paper and reiterated in Parliament was that the principle of the employer having to prove reasonableness had resulted in a

> widespread feeling among employers that they are 'guilty until proved innocent' . . . it is believed that the provision has put employers at an unfair disadvantage in cases where the substance of the employee's complaint is not clear to the employer or where the employee's case is weak. The government therefore proposes that the onus of proof as to reasonableness should be made neutral as between employer and employee.

Was there really a widespread feeling of 'guilty until proved innocent'? According to a survey of employers who had been involved in unfair dismissal cases conducted by the Industrial Relations Research Unit at Warwick University only 5 per cent mentioned the onus of proof as an adverse feature.[10] Nor was it clear that an employer faced by a claim he considered obscure or weak was hampered by the burden of proof — he could always have requested further and better particulars and (since 1978) the originating application has specifically required more details on the substance of a claim. Finally there is the assertion that remaining silent on the burden of proof achieves 'neutrality' as between the parties. As experience under the Industrial Relations Act indicated, there is no such thing as a neutral legal burden of proof. It is now up to the employee to prove the unreasonableness of the employer's behaviour and even of his state of mind. Some lawyers argue that this will make little difference in practice because in many cases the evidence is very strong on one side or the other. But there are also cases where the evidence is evenly balanced and the winner is the party upon whom there is no legal burden of proof.

Size and administrative resources of the undertaking

The Employment Act stipulates that, in determining the reasonableness of a dismissal, the circumstances to be considered by the tribunal must specifically include 'the size and administrative resources of the employer's undertaking' (EPCA s.57(3) as amended by EA s.6).

The size of the employer's organisation is of course an important consideration but there are other considerations as well. In determining reasonableness the tribunals are guided by the Code on *Disciplinary Practice and Procedures in Employment* issued by ACAS. The Code sets out general standards of what is sometimes called 'procedural fairness'. The need for procedural fairness is part of the overall scheme of employment protection and links up with other legal requirements, for example, the employer's duty to give each employee 'written particulars' of employment specifying important terms and conditions such as the job title and also a note of the disciplinary rules and the first stages of individual grievance and disciplinary procedures with reference to the subsequent stages (EPCA s.1). A dismissed employee is also entitled not to have a request for a written statement of the reason for his dismissal unreasonably refused (EPCA s.53). Under the stimulus of this legal framework, particularly the tribunals' use of the Code, there has been a steady improvement and extension of disciplinary procedures in industry over the last decade. Not infrequently these follow the guidelines of the Code: the individual should know the case against him, he (or his union representative on his behalf) should be allowed to put his version of the events, he should not normally be sacked for a 'first offence' and there should be a system of warnings.

The standards of procedural fairness may vary according to circumstances including the size of the employer's organisation. Without any explicit statutory compulsion the tribunals have taken the employer's size into account. For example, a hierarchy of stages in an appeals procedure might be inappropriate in a small firm. The EAT has clearly laid down the principle that the size of an organisation — in the particular case it was a girls' public school with forty members of staff in all — could have the effect of scaling down the procedural requirements (*Royal Naval School* v. *Hughes*, 1979); size may also affect the appropriateness of the remedy and, according to the EAT, reinstatement should not normally be ordered against small firms (*Enessy Ltd*. v. *Minoprio*, 1978). Now however the tribunals are under specific instructions to take account of the 'size and administrative resources of the employer's undertaking'. Whereas other aspects of reasonableness are left to the common sense of the tribunals, size and administrative resources are to be subjects for compulsory consideration and doubtless for legal disputation.

Does one measure 'size' only by the number of employees? What do 'administrative resources' amount to? Are profitability, financial resources or capital assets relevant? The most excruciating technicalities could arise from the concept of the 'undertaking'. This is not defined in the Employment Act, though the Industrial Relations Act did have a definition: ' "undertaking" includes a business and, in relation to any body of persons (whether corporate or unincorporate) whose activities would not, apart from this provision, be regarded as constituting an undertaking, includes the aggregate of those activities' (s.167(1)). But what does that mean? Needless to say it gave rise to litigation particularly as, under the 1971 Act, 'undertakings' with fewer than four employees were exempted from unfair dismissal claims (s.27(1)(a); *Kapur* v. *Shields* (1975)). Whether 'undertaking' is wider or narrower than the notion of 'associated' employer is difficult to say for certain but it might be much more restrictive; for example, an 'undertaking' might be a single plant or shop or garage without regard to the corporate structure which owns or controls it. Moreover 'administrative resources' as distinct from 'size' is a separate consideration. What if a medium or even large firm argues that it lacks the administrative resources to run a proper personnel function at a particular undertaking? Such a possibility goes much further than the ostensible objective of assisting small firms to overcome the supposed disincentive effects of unfair dismissal.

The one certain effect is an erosion of the rights of the individual employee. Though workers in small firms are often more in need of protection than others, the tribunals could begin to treat the 'size and administrative resources of the employer's undertaking' as an almost overriding consideration. This would lower the standards of procedural fairness and encourage a purely economic or 'accounting' interpretation of the substantive merits of a dismissal with the consequences of injustice to the individual and more industrial strife.

Waiver of unfair dismissal rights

The right not to be unfairly dismissed is by definition dependent on the occurrence of a 'dismissal'. The law recognises three varieties of dismissal for this purpose: (a) the termination of the contract of employment by the employer whether or not he gives notice, (b) the expiry of a fixed-term contract of employment without renewal, and (c) 'constructive' dismissal, that is, the employee leaves of his own accord but he is entitled to do so because of the employer's conduct (EPCA s.55). There is a similar three-fold definition of dismissal under the statutory scheme of redundancy payments (EPCA s.83). We are here concerned exclusively with dismissal by the expiry of a fixed-term contract. Such a dismissal it must be emphasised is not to be mechanically equated with the question of fairness, which turns on whether the employer acted reasonably in not renewing the contract (*Terry* v. *Sussex County Council*, 1977).

An employee may agree in writing during the currency of a fixed term contract to waive his rights on the expiry of the contract to claim unfair dismissal and/or a statutory redundancy payment (EPCA s.142). The waiver is however effective only if the fixed term contract is of a certain minimum duration. In the case of the unfair dismissal waiver, EA s.8(2) reduces this minimum duration from two years to one year. This amendment is apparently a 'tidying up' operation to ensure consistency with the new one year qualifying period for unfair dismissal claims introduced by the July Orders. (There is to be no change to the minimum duration of two years in fixed term contracts under which an employee may agree to waive his right to a statutory redundancy payment since this period corresponds with the minimum of two years' service required for a redundancy pay claim.) In addition, the government made the more general argument that its new provision would encourage employers to create jobs where there is scope for genuine fixed term contracts rather than deter them with the prospect of a complaint of unfair dismissal.

The assumption of the waiver principle is that, in the words of the government's Employment Protection Working Paper, 'employers and employees should be able freely to enter into fixed term contracts which provide that at their conclusion the employee will not have the right to bring a complaint of unfair dismissal'. The key word is 'freely'. In reality the employee is not in a free and equal position vis à vis his actual or prospective employer, particularly when jobs are scarce. Fixed term contracts with waiver clauses drafted by the employer's legal advisers are now becoming fairly common. They are frequently encountered, for example, in the contracts of research and teaching staff in higher and further education. Non-unionised workers are the most vulnerable perhaps, though many a union member has signed away his rights especially when, as is usually the case, the waiver clause is included in his general terms and conditions.

Indeed the lawyers have now devised an ingenious method of automatically excluding employees' rights even without the formality of a waiver agreement. Under the so-called 'task' contract the contract ends on the performance of the task. There is no dismissal and therefore no right to claim unfair dismissal or a redundancy payment. Whether or not there is such a thing as a 'bona fide' task contract, there is undoubtedly a growing problem of the sham task contract. In one case a ship repair worker was taken on over many years for successive tasks. It was held that his job ended on the completion of each task and, on this reasoning, he was not dismissed and his claim for redundancy pay was denied (*Ryan* v. *Shipboard Maintenance*, 1979). The implications of the task contract were considered recently by the Court of Appeal in *Wiltshire County Council* v. *Guy*, 1980. A technical college teacher was employed under a 'hybrid' contract of employment, which included elements of both a fixed term and a task contract. During the course of each academic year she was to teach only those courses specified by the employer. When the courses finished she was not required any more that year. Did she work under a fixed term contract, the expiry of which was a dismissal, or under a task contract, the performance of which was not a dismissal? The Court of Appeal held that she had a fixed term contract but it also confirmed that, despite her many years' of service, she would have forfeited her rights if she had had a task contract.

The reasoning behind this judgment would deprive certain categories of employees of their unfair dismissal and redundancy pay rights, for example, construction workers taken on until a power station is built or research officers engaged specifically to produce a report on a particular topic. Did those who drafted the statutory definition of 'dismissal' intend to exclude such employees from statutory employment protection? Of course they did not, but until recently task contracts were rare whereas now they are spreading. The legislation ought to be amended, on the analogy of the expiry of a fixed term contract, to define the performance of a task contract as a dismissal for the purposes of unfair dismissal and redundancy. Instead the government is content to do absolutely nothing about task contracts whilst taking steps which can only encourage the more frequent exclusion of rights under fixed term contracts.

Reduction of the basic award

Assuming the unfair dismissal claimant wins his case in the tribunal (in 1979 only 27 per cent of applicants were successful), the primary legal remedies are in theory reinstatement and re-engagement. In practice no more than 3 per cent of successful applicants get re-instated or re-engaged. Compensation is the normal remedy. In 1979 the median tribunal compensation award was £402, and the median figure for compensation agreed in conciliation was £193.[11] These figures are less than princely but the Employment Act aims to reduce the basis of compensation awards.

Compensation is awarded under two heads: a 'compensatory' award and a 'basic' award. A compensatory award is to compensate for the financial loss resulting from an unfair dismissal, mainly for loss of earnings and pension entitlement. It is currently subject to a £6,250 ceiling, which is reviewed annually but was not increased for 1981. It is reduced by up to 100 per cent to the extent that the employee contributes to his own dismissal.[12] It is also reduced if the employee fails to mitigate his loss, for example, by not seeking another job. Deductions are made too for ex gratia payments from the employer and for redundancy payments in excess of the amount of the basic award.

The basic award is to compensate for loss of job security, that is, for the loss of all the worker's 'property' of accumulated rights in his employment. It is calculated by a computation of age, length of service and pay in the same way as is a statutory redundancy payment. It is currently subject to a ceiling of £3,900 for an employee who earns at least £130 per week (reviewed annually) and who has at least twenty years of service since his 41st birthday with the same employer. Redundancy pay is deducted from the basic award, which is further reduced to the extent that the employee has contributed to his own dismissal. However there was, until the Employment Act of 1980, an irreducible minimum award of two weeks' pay except where a redundancy payment was received.

The Employment Act aims three heavy blows at the very concept of the basic award. Firstly, where a tribunal finds that an employee has unreasonably refused an offer of reinstatement it must now reduce the basic award by an amount it considers just and equitable (EPCA s.73(7A), inserted by EA s.9). What social behaviour or problem is this supposed to regulate? The answer was given by the Under-Secretary of State for Employment: 'somebody may have been unfairly dismissed, and, that finding having been made, he may immediately be offered reinstatement and a promise that bygones shall be bygones'.[13] In such circumstances the unfair dismissal claim, even if upheld, could be penalised by a reduction in compensation.

The example of a rapid-fire dismissal followed by an offer to forgive and forget seems to envisage some official encouragement for a style of personnel management which most professionals would regard as slapdash and even whimsical. Moreover the tribunal would make its finding only several months after the dismissal. Research indicates that some dismissed employees are reluctant to return to work for the same employer, not because of the lure of 'easy' money by way of unfair dismissal compensation, but rather because of doubts about the possibility of re-establishing a viable employment relationship.[14] A similar logic helps to explain why the tribunals only rarely order reinstatement. The Employment Act has in effect introduced a version of the duty to mitigate loss in order to reduce the basic award. The mitigation duty is however inappropriate in respect of the basic award, which is supposed to recompense the employee for the deprivation of his job 'property'.

Secondly, the basic award must be reduced or further reduced, as the tribunal considers just and equitable, to take account of the employee's conduct before the dismissal, *other* than conduct which contributed to the dismissal (EPCA s.73(7B), inserted by EA s.9). Given that conduct contributing to the dismissal is already taken into account in assessing the basic award, why was it necessary to make special provision covering other conduct? The explanation is to be found in certain utterances of the Law Lords in the leading case of *Devis* v. *Atkins* (1977). A manager of an abattoir was dismissed on grounds that he refused to carry out his employer's orders. After the dismissal new facts came to light which led the employer to believe that the former manager had defrauded the company. It was held that the employer could not justify the dismissal by reference to the conduct of the employee which was not known at the time of the dismissal. This had to be the case because the fairness of the dismissal was determined by reference to the employer's reason for it and whether he acted unreasonably in relation to it, not subsequently, but at the time of the dismissal. It also followed (though the Law Lords omitted to make express reference to this) that any behaviour by the employee contributing to the dismissal, which could be used by the tribunal to reduce or even eliminate compensation, also had to be known by the employer at the time of the dismissal. Nevertheless all was not lost for the employer. It was further held that misconduct discovered after the act of dismissal could still be taken into account by a tribunal, either in assessing compensation generally or to deny re-engagement, because the remedies for unfair dismissal were entirely subject to what the tribunal considered to be equitable.

Fair enough, one might say, but there was a further twist to the tale. *Devis* v. *Atkins* was in 1977 the first unfair dismissal case to reach the House of Lords and it was clear that their Lordships were unhappy to discover that certain of the new-fangled statutory principles conflicted with their own notions of fairness. In particular the Employment Protection Act had introduced the basic award. It seemed that an employee who was found to be unfairly dismissed but whose true misconduct came to light only after the dismissal might still automatically be given a basic award as this was not dependent on the tribunal's 'just and equitable' discretion (which could still effectively block a compensatory award). In situations of the kind illustrated by *Devis* v. *Atkins* the basic award might thus become, in the words of Lord Diplock, 'a veritable rogue's charter'.

This moral indignation was clearly shared by the architects of EA s.9, which amends EPCA s.73 in order to allow the tribunals to reduce the basic award on account of the conduct of the employee leading up to the dismissal but which the employer discovers afterwards. Indeed the Employment Bill as first published envisaged that the reduction of the basic award would take account of the employee's conduct not only prior to but also after the dismissal. That amendment, which might have encouraged the continuing surveillance of employees after dismissal, was dropped. The section as drafted is restrictive enough. It discounts the fact that the dismissal in question is unfair, an unlawful act for which the basic award is supposed to compensate. It also arguably encourages a poor system of personnel management where it would be unnecessary for the employer to carry out the fullest inquiry at the time of the dismissal, providing he can discover some alleged facts prejudicial to the employee afterwards.

The third blow is the most important of all. It is the abolition of the irreducible minimum basic award of two weeks' pay (EA s.9(5) repealing EPCA s.73(8)). The minimum was, according to the government, an unfair burden on small employers. It was also argued that there was no justification for automatically giving an unfairly dismissed employee a minimum of two weeks' pay when he might be entitled to less under the statutory redundancy payments scheme. The small firms argument has been examined elsewhere, though it should be emphasised that the abolition of the minimum basic award applies to all unfairly dismissed employees not just to those who work for small firms. While it is doubtful whether employers guilty of unfair dismissal were inconvenienced by a sum as modest as two weeks' pay, the abolition of the minimum must have a significant impact on the compensation awarded to the unfairly dismissed individual. In 1978 three quarters of all basic awards consisted entirely of the minimum of two weeks' pay. It is the shorter service employees who may now get a basic award of less than two weeks, assuming they get any basic award at all and assuming also that they have the requisite service qualification to make a claim in the first place. The rationale of the irreducible minimum basic award was that it acknowledged that an unfairly dismissed employee suffered a loss of security and an injustice as well as any other non-quantifiable loss not covered by the compensatory award. By providing a minimum penalty against the employer who perpetrated unfair dismissal it underlined the public policy of encouraging employers to adopt fair dismissal procedures. The legal support for that policy has clearly been eroded.

So what is left of the unfairly dismissed employee's entitlement to a basic award? Assuming he has not received a redundancy payment cancelling the basic award, the unfairly dismissed employee has to jump the following hurdles: (a) Is he guilty of contributory fault known to the employer at the time of the dismissal? If so his basic award like his compensatory award may now be reduced to zero. (b) Is he guilty of any other conduct prior to the dismissal but coming to light after it which would prompt a tribunal to reduce the basic award? Once again the reduction can wipe out the basic award altogether. (c) Has he failed to mitigate his loss by unreasonably refusing an offer of reinstatement? In that case the basic award may also be reduced to nothing.

Before leaving the issue of compensation for unfair dismissal, EA s.10 should be noted. It inserts ss.76A–76C into the EPCA. These provisions enable an employer to join to proceedings on an unfair dismissal complaint those responsible for putting pressure on him by industrial action to dismiss an employee who is not a member of a union. They are intended and likely to apply mainly in the context of closed shop employment and are discussed fully in chapters 3 and 4. But they are nevertheless of general application in all cases of unfair dismissal. For example, if an employee claims that his selection for redundancy because he is a non-unionist is in breach of customary arrangements and thereby automatically unfair under EPCA s.59, the employer may, in an appropriate case, join to the proceedings those responsible for putting pressure on him to dismiss the employee by threatening a strike unless non-unionists are made redundant. Those exerting the pressure might then be ordered by the tribunal to pay the employer an indemnity for compensation which he may have to pay to the dismissed employee.

PUNISHING THE UNEMPLOYED

Social security

Restraint on social security expenditure has a vital role in the overall scheme of public expenditure cuts. This is part of the rationale behind the proposals to transfer the responsibility for sick pay from the state to the employer.[15] In the belief that over-generous benefits could constitute disincentives for claimants to return to work the government has also aimed to strengthen the 'industrial discipline' function of social security. The legal centrepiece of this combined economy and deterrence policy is the Social Security (No. 2) Act 1980, which empowers the Secretary of State for Social Services to fix the levels of national insurance benefits below the levels of prices. This principle applies to the whole range of short-term contributory benefits for unemployment, sickness, and industrial injury plus the maternity allowance. Also earnings-related supplement to these benefits is being phased out and will be abolished in January 1982. Inevitably an ever larger proportion of the impoverished unemployed will be thrown back onto the means-tested supplementary benefit. In addition, under the Finance Act 1981, benefits for the unemployed and for strikers' families are to be subject to income tax from April 1982. The entitlement of strikers' families to supplementary benefit is reduced in other ways and these merit a brief explanation.

Those who participate or are directly interested in a trade dispute are not entitled to unemployment benefit, and the question is the extent to which their dependants may be entitled to supplementary benefit. On the one side, it is argued that welfare provisions should be 'neutral' and should certainly not be used by the state to support employers by in effect driving strikers back to work. On the other side, it is argued that the state ought not to fund industrial disputes, that welfare payments to strikers' dependants give too much power to trade unions and may have the effect of prolonging strikes (the so-called 'state subsidy' theory of industrial conflict). Clearly it is the latter arguments which underpin the highly restrictive Social Security Act 1980 (and regulations made thereunder) and section 6 of the Social Security (No. 2) Act.[16] The combined effect of these provisions is as follows. First all payments received during a stoppage of work are fully taken into account in calculating the entitlement to supplementary benefit; according to the DHSS *Supplementary Benefits Handbook* 1980 para. 8.18, 'income tax refunds available to the striker (whether or not he receives them) are taken into account in full with no disregard'. Second supplementary benefit is not paid if the weekly rate is calculated at £12 or less and, if calculated at more than £12, the weekly rate is the amount duly calculated less £12. In other words £12 is 'docked' from the supplementary benefit entitlement of strikers' dependants, whether or not a union (if there is a union) has actually paid out strike pay. The figure of £12 is to be up-rated regularly. Third the narrow entitlement of the striker himself to claim for urgent needs is abolished, although regulations now provide that payments may be made by way of emergency relief as strictly defined.

This approach to social security complements the changes in labour law. Many workers have been disenfranchised from their right to complain of unfair dismissal, and, as will be explained in the penultimate section of this chapter, new obstacles have been thrown in the path of mothers who wish to return to their jobs. As unemployment is increased so employment protection rights are decreased. Two other government measures touch directly on job and income security: changes in the entitlement to guarantee pay and in the consultation rights over redundancy.

Guarantee payments

The Employment Act seeks to narrow the basis of entitlement to statutory guarantee payments. Under EPCA ss.12—18 employers are liable to pay a minimum guarantee payment to their employees for a limited number of days on which work is not provided. Collectively agreed arrangements must not undercut the minimum payments but they may and frequently do improve upon them. It is also possible to contract out of the statutory payments if exemption is granted by the DE in respect of a collective agreement or a wages council order, and by early 1981 twenty-one exemption orders had been made. Statutory guarantee pay is subject to various exclusions, most notably for trade disputes: 'An employee shall not be entitled to a guarantee payment in respect of a workless day if the failure to provide him with work occurs in consequence of a trade dispute involving any employee of his employer or of an associated employer' (EPCA s.13(1)). This is a very broad formulation, wider indeed than the analogous trade dispute disqualification for unemployment and supplementary benefit. Provided the employee is not excluded, he is entitled to a guarantee payment of up to £8.75 (reviewed annually) per day for a maximum of five days in a three month period.

It is the computation of this period which has been changed by the 1980 Act. Previously the year was divided into four fixed quarterly periods beginning on the first day of February, May, August and November. Section 14 of the Employment Act abolishes the fixed quarters and substitutes a rolling three month period, that is, the maximum of five days entitlement now falls 'in any period of three months'.

The explanation of this apparently technical amendment is to be found in the industrial confrontations of the 'winter of discontent' of 1978–79, in particular in the lorry drivers' dispute. This happened to straddle two of the fixed quarters and, though the striking lorry drivers themselves were disqualified from guarantee pay, a few of the other workers who were laid off in consequence of the dispute were entitled to two tranches of five days of guarantee pay in rapid succession. The present government thought that this was too much of a burden for employers, especially small employers. The sums involved, which were substantially less than the level of supplementary benefit, were described as an unjustifiable 'windfall'.

It is doubtful whether employers were significantly inconvenienced by the fixed quarterly period. The surveys of both Daniel and Stilgoe and Clifton and Tatton-Brown found that only a miniscule proportion of employers were worried by the guarantee pay provisions. Fixed quarters had the merit of relative simplicity. Employers, whether large or small, did not have to keep any complicated records of payments to each individual employee but will have to now, as patterns of short-time working may vary from employee to employee. More disputed cases are by the same token likely to be taken to the industrial tribunals. The fixed quarter principle was also more convenient, in view of the off-set between state benefits and employers' guarantee payments, for the civil servants responsible for administering social security benefits. In fact the fixed quarters were originally defined so as to avoid the end of the periods coinciding with Christmas, Easter and the summer holidays when the employment offices have to cope with a large number of job seekers and students.

Some workers will end up with less guarantee pay than before. Those most adversely affected will probably not be higher status and salaried employees but the lower grade workers who are still liable to be laid off without notice and without pay. It was significant that the IPM opposed this change in so far as it would have the effect of worsening blue collar conditions of service compared with white collar conditions. The low paid are the most hard hit. Low pay and earnings instability tend to go hand in hand as low paid workers (including junior grade clericals as well as manuals) are especially vulnerable to spells of short-time working and unemployment. And because the low paid are less likely to be organised in trade unions the minimum legal entitlements are of correspondingly greater importance. 'Workless' days are caused by a whole variety of factors irrespective of whether there is a dispute. The government's determination to punish the lorry drivers' strike (the repeal of the Road Haulage Wages Act has the same motivation, see chapter seven) appears to have distorted its sense of proportion.

Redundancy consultation

The second of the two July Orders amends the legal framework under which trade unions have a right to be consulted over redundancies.[17] Under EPA ss.99–107 management has a legal duty to consult on proposed redundancies with the representatives of 'recognised' trade unions, that is, trade unions which the employer recognises for the purposes of collective bargaining, and also to notify the DE. The employer has to disclose to the union the reasons for his proposal, the numbers of employees involved, the method of selection, and the method of carrying out the dismissals (with due regard to agreed procedures) and the period over which the dismissals are to take effect. He must also give a reasoned reply to any representations made by the union. The consultation must begin 'at the earliest opportunity' (s.99(3)) and in any event must begin in advance of the dismissals taking effect. How far in advance? The law specifies minimum periods the length of which varies according to the number to be made redundant. Where an employer is proposing to get rid of 100 or more employees at one establishment within a time-span of ninety days, the consultation must begin at least ninety days before the first of the dismissals takes effect. But where an employer is proposing to shed between ten and ninety-nine employees within thirty days, the July Order reduced the minimum period of consultation (and the period of notification to the DE) from sixty days to thirty days.

The employer's duty to consult is underpinned by the possibility of compensation and this is also affected by the July Order. If the industrial tribunal upholds a union complaint that the employer has not consulted, it may make a 'protective award' ordering the employer to pay remuneration to the relevant employees for a 'protected period'. The maximum length of this period, which thus determines the maximum amount of the award, varies according to the size of the redundancy. If 100 or more employees are to be dismissed, the maximum protected period is ninety days but if between ten and ninety-nine employees are to go the July Order reduced the maximum from sixty to thirty days.

Notwithstanding the Order, which seeks to curtail the consultation right, the tribunals might still interpret the Employment Protection Act in such a way as to promote its objectives — here the encouragement of good industrial relations and of manpower planning. They could stress the fact that the consultation period which the Order has shortened is a minimum period. The employer's overriding duty is to consult 'at the earliest opportunity' once he has formed the proposal to make redundancies. Consequently an employer who is in this position, say, sixty days before the first redundancies are to take effect but, in mistaken reliance on the Order, does not begin consultation until thirty days before the first dismissal ought to be held to be in breach of the consultation duty. In order to arrive at this conclusion the tribunals will have to overcome their tendency, which is understandable in view of the union's difficulty in proving exactly when consultation might have started, to treat the statutory minimum periods as de facto maximum periods. Similarly, even though the July Order has reduced the maximum amount of the protected period, the tribunals must follow the EAT in recognising that the length of the protective period is dependent on the number of lost days of consultation with the union (*Spillers French Ltd.* v. *USDAW,* 1980). After this decision, the protective period ought to turn on the union's loss of opportunity to be consulted and not on the extra duration of employment (if any) that might have ensued if the employer had followed the correct consultation procedure.

The supposed justification of this Order was that the EPA's framework of redundancy consultation imposed too damaging a burden on employers, especially small firms. Not only is this argument in itself not sustainable but the Order applies to all redundancies of between ten and ninety-nine employees whether declared by small businesses or by the largest companies in the country. Indeed there is now an incentive for large firms to make employees redundant in a series of small parcels and so avoid the embarrassment of a genuine period of consultation or even notification to the DE. How extraordinary it is that, at a time when the government's own policies are necessarily increasing the level of unemployment, this Order reduces the period specifically designed for exploring ways of avoiding redundancies and of mitigating their consequences. Where fewer than 100 employees are to be made redundant in a single tranche, the employer is supposed to propose the redundancies and disclose to the unions the reasons and method of selection etc., and the union officials must prepare and put their counter-arguments, to which the employer must give a reasoned reply, all within a minimum statutory consultation period of thirty days. Within the same minimum period, the DE and the Manpower Services Commission (with its resources depleted by government cuts) are supposed to advise on job prospects and training. State encouragement to effective manpower planning whether at the level of the firm or the region is thus downgraded. But in defence of the Order it might still be argued that it mitigates the problems of an employer, especially a small employer, who, confronted with a sudden change of circumstances (e.g. loss of a market) is unable to carry out his consultation duties. This argument is also unsustainable. The EPA explicitly caters for an employer who experiences 'special circumstances'; he is not bound to adhere rigidly either to the process of consultation as defined by statute or to the minimum consultation periods but needs only take such steps towards compliance 'as are reasonably practicable in those circumstances' (EPA s.99(8)). By going for a blanket reduction of the minimum period rather than relying upon the Act's 'special circumstances' qualification, the government was perhaps indicating its real intention of ending serious consultation on dismissals of fewer than 100 employees. This policy could not be formally adopted because it would have required its own section in the Employment Act (rather than a quick statutory Order) and also because it would have involved a breach of the Common Market Directive on Collective Redundancies.[18]

MATERNITY RIGHTS

By the end of the 1970s nearly 40 per cent of the labour force in Britain were women and more than half the women between the ages of sixteen and fifty-nine were at work. The increasing participation of women in the workforce during the 1970s was accompanied by a significant development of legal rights for women in employment. The Equal Pay Act was passed in 1970 but only came into force at the end of 1975. It attempts to establish equality between men and women in pay and other contractual terms of employment in defined circumstances according to certain criteria, the limitations of which were fully exposed in the first five years of its operation. Greater potential is to be found in the Sex Discrimination Act 1975 which became effective at the same time. It renders discrimination on grounds of sex and marital status in employment generally unlawful, though the remedies for discrimination which it provides are of limited efficacy in eradicating unlawful practices. The year 1975 also saw the creation of some statutory protection for the employment rights of women in respect of maternity. In the EPA dismissal for any reason connected with pregnancy was designated automatically unfair in most circumstances and rights to maternity pay and to return to work after pregnancy or confinement were established. The maternity rights came into force in 1976 and 1977 and were consolidated in the EPCA in 1978.

It is these maternity provisions which the government considered to be in need of amendment. Given its commitment to general economic policies which, on its own admission, create unemployment at least in the short term, it is not disingenuous to suggest that the government was happy to alleviate or disguise the extent of unemployment by encouraging women to withdraw from the labour market. The most obvious target for such 'encouragement' was women with children, particularly children of pre-school age. The belief that these women should be at home looking after their children can be and was presented as something which is of itself desirable. 'Quite frankly', said the Secretary of State for Social Services, 'I don't think mothers have the same right to work as fathers. If the Good Lord had intended us to have equal rights to go out to work, he wouldn't have created men and women. These are biological facts, young children do depend on their mothers.'[19] However the ostensible justification for changes in the maternity rights of working women was that '[the] maternity pay and reinstatement provisions have not worked satisfactorily in practice' (Working Paper on Employment Protection). Indeed, although the right to return is considerably restricted by ss.11 and 12 of the Employment Act, these amendments were defended somewhat illogically on the grounds that they would create more jobs for women, particularly with small employers.

Time off for ante-natal care

The solitary addition to workers' rights made by the Employment Act is in s.13 which inserts s.31A into the EPCA. It establishes the right of a pregnant employee not to be unreasonably refused time off during working hours, paid at the appropriate hourly rate, in order to keep appointments for the purpose of receiving ante-natal care. Section 31A is drafted in terms which are generally consistent with the EPCA's other time off provisions. The right is subject to the condition that the employer may require the employee to provide both a certificate of pregnancy and evidence of an appointment for ante-natal care for all appointments except the first in respect of which time off is sought.[20] As with all time off rights disputes are referable to industrial tribunals. An employee may complain either that her employer has unreasonably refused her time off or failed to pay her the amount due in respect of time off allowed. The usual three month time limit applies, with a discretion for the tribunal to allow complaints to be made outside this limit where it is not reasonably practicable to do so within it. It is difficult to anticipate the circumstances in which the employer's refusal would not be unreasonable. The remedy for being unreasonably refused time off is compensation equal to the amount which the employee would have been entitled to receive had time off been allowed. As is normal with respect to statutory rights to pay, any contractual payment counts against the statutory right and vice versa.

A legal right to time off work for ante-natal care was contemplated but rejected as unnecessary during debates on the Employment Protection Bill in 1975. Concern at the extent of perinatal mortality and handicap expressed by and to the House of Commons Select Committee on Social Services prompted a change in government attitude which led to this provision being added to the Employment Bill. Infant mortality in the United Kingdom is among the highest in the EEC. One reason for this is considered to be the reluctance of some women to go for regular ante-natal check-ups. A legal right to time off work for this purpose is therefore a welcome and long overdue reform. Although many employers had already provided paid time off in these circumstances, the practice was far from universal. The new right may be of some assistance in reducing the extent of infant mortality and handicap, even though it is likely to amount to no more than six half-days off for women who stop work eleven weeks before the expected week of confinement. It could be of greater value to women who lack the two years' employment qualification for statutory 'maternity leave' and remain at work after the first six months of pregnancy. In any event however its beneficial effects are likely to be offset by cuts made and proposed in government expenditure on housing and health care in general.

Pregnancy and unfair dismissal

A special provision, which is now s.60 of the EPCA, was added by the EPA to the law of unfair dismissal. It provides that the dismissal of an employee because she is pregnant or for any other reason connected with her pregnancy (e.g. miscarriage) is automatically unfair. This principle is subject to two exceptions: where the employee is incapable of doing her job adequately because of her pregnancy and where her continued employment would contravene a statutory restriction or duty. Even in these circumstances her dismissal is automatically unfair if a 'suitable available vacancy' exists and the employer fails to offer it to her. Any such offer must be of a new contract of employment taking immediate effect, suitable in relation to the employee and appropriate for her in the circumstances and be such that the provisions of the contract as to capacity, place and other terms and conditions are not substantially less favourable than those of her previous contract. On a complaint of unfair dismissal by an employee who alleges that no such offer was made, the onus is on the employer to show either that he made an offer satisfying these criteria or that no such suitable available vacancy existed.

There are several difficult problems of interpretation which arise under EPCA s.60. However it is clear that the minimum service qualification applies to complainants relying on it. The changes made to this have thus limited the number of women protected against, or, more accurately, provided with redress from dismissal for pregnancy and connected reasons. After the July Orders of 1979 and the Employment Act 1980, a woman cannot complain of unfair dismissal and rely on s.60 unless she has been continuously employed for at least fifty-two weeks, and the qualifying period becomes two years if during that period her employer, together with any associated employers, has not employed more than twenty employees.

An attempt to avoid the impact of the minimum service qualification by making a complaint under the Sex Discrimination Act 1975, for which no service qualification is necessary, failed in *Turley* v. *Allders Department Stores Ltd.* (1980). The Court of Appeal refused leave to appeal against the majority EAT decision that dismissal of a woman because she is pregnant is not sex discrimination since there cannot be a man in comparison with whom the woman was unfavourably treated. The combined effect of this interpretation of the law and the 1979–80 statutory amendments is to reduce the extent to which the policy behind the original enactment of s.60 is fulfilled. This was that the decision about continuing to work during pregnancy should be taken by the woman herself unless her employer could show that she was or would become unable to perform her normal duties.

Maternity pay, allowance and grant

Similarly, although the EA did not amend the statutory provisions on *maternity pay*, in so far as more employees are vulnerable to dismissal because of pregnancy without any redress for unfair dismissal, fewer women will build up the necessary service qualification for entitlement to it. Although the qualifying conditions for both maternity pay and the right to return to work were the same before the EA, an employee's right to claim maternity pay from her employer is not in any way conditional on her returning to work after maternity leave. A woman who has been continuously employed for at least two years by the beginning of the eleventh week before the expected week of confinement and who informs her employer that she will be absent because of pregnancy or confinement, in writing if requested and at least twenty-one days before her absence begins or if that is not reasonably practicable, as soon as reasonably practicable, is entitled to claim maternity pay from her employer for the first six weeks of her absence. The weekly amount is nine-tenths of a week's pay, minus the maternity allowance payable under the Social Security Act 1975 whether or not she is entitled to claim this allowance. The employer can claim a 100 per cent rebate from the maternity pay fund which is financed by a small percentage of employers' social security contributions. As with other statutory rights to pay, any contractual payment counts against the statutory right. Disputes over entitlement to maternity pay and the employer's right to a rebate are referable to the industrial tribunals.

Women who can satisfy the contribution conditions are entitled to claim a weekly *maternity allowance* from the state for the eighteen weeks from the eleventh week before to the sixth week after the expected week of confinement. A woman must stop work before she can claim it. The amount of this benefit is reviewed annually and in November 1981 it was increased to £22.50 per week. It is one of the social security benefits which carries with it an earnings related supplement which is shortly to be abolished (above p. 40). It is nevertheless to be hoped that the real value of maternity allowance will be safeguarded at least at its present level.

Many women do not qualify for maternity pay and/or maternity allowance. The third entitlement, a *maternity grant* of £25, has like maternity allowance been dependent on certain social security contributions being satisfied, in this case by the claimant or her husband. From April 1982 it has been made in effect a non-contributory benefit by the Social Security Act 1980 s.5. However the government has resisted attempts to raise the derisory level of the maternity grant, a 'one-off' payment, which was last increased in 1969. At £25 it is worth less in real terms than the £1.50 paid when it was first introduced in 1911.

More radical amendments to the financial entitlement on maternity generally were mooted in a DHSS consultative document produced in October 1980.[21] This made clear that while the government was prepared to consider any amendment to the three existing maternity benefits, including the abolition of one or more of them, this was subject to the overriding constraint that the current level of expenditure would not be increased. The three options suggested were a single lump sum payment to all expectant mothers, maternity grant plus a weekly allowance paid by the employer combining resources at present devoted to maternity allowance and maternity pay, and maternity grant plus a weekly allowance paid by the DHSS. The second option would broadly align maternity benefits with the amendments to financial entitlements during periods of absence from work because of sickness proposed in the Green Paper on sickness benefits (above p. 40). The general response to the consultative document on maternity benefits was as hostile as that to the Green Paper and in January 1981 it was announced that no major amendments to maternity benefits were to be made.[22] Whatever the relative degree of responsibility of the state and employers it is clear that the government have no intention of improving the financial security of women during pregnancy and after childbirth, a policy which conflicts with the recommendations of the EOC's study of maternity rights.[23]

Right to return to work

The basic condition for the right to return to work is that the employee's absence was wholly or partly because of pregnancy or confinement. As originally enacted there were three further qualifying conditions in EPCA s.33. The first two of these remain unchanged: the employee must have been continuously employed for at least two years by the beginning of the eleventh week before the expected week of confinement and she must continue in employment, whether or not actually at work, until immediately before this time. Section 11 of the EA has modified the third condition and added a fourth. Both concern notices by the employee to her employer. In the first notice she must inform him in writing at least twenty-one days before her absence begins or, if that is not reasonably practicable, as soon as reasonably practicable[24] (a) that she will be (or is) absent from work wholly or partly because of pregnancy or confinement, (b) that she intends to return to work, and (c) of the expected week of confinement or, if it has already occurred, the date of confinement (EPCA s.33(3)(d) as added by EA s.11(1)). This third item is new. So is the stipulation that the notice must be in writing. The new notice requirement, in EPCA s.33(3A) inserted by EA s.11(2), is written confirmation of her intention to return given within fourteen days of her employer's requesting it. Such a request may not be made until at least forty-nine days after the week or date of confinement referred to in the original notice. This request must also be in writing and be accompanied by a written statement of the effect of failure to comply with the notice requirement (s.33(3B)). This is intended to ensure that employers inform their employees that the right to return will be lost if they do not provide the confirmation sought.

If these conditions are satisfied, the employee may exercise her right to return at any time within twenty-nine weeks of the week in which the actual date of confinement falls (EPCA s.45(1)). To do this she must give her employer notice of the day on which she proposes to return (s.47(1)). Section 11(3) of the EA has both made it mandatory for this notice to be in writing and extended the necessary period of notice by two weeks to twenty-one days. Her return may be postponed by her employer for up to four weeks for any specified reason, and she herself may postpone it for up to four weeks if she has a medical certificate stating that she will be incapable of returning on the date notified or at the end of the twenty-nine week period (s.47(2)(3)). It may also be postponed where an interruption of work (whether due to industrial action or some other reason) makes it unreasonable to expect her to return on the notified day or, where no date has been notified, within the twenty-nine week period (s.47(5)). She may then return as soon as reasonably practicable after work resumes if she had notified a day of return or, if she had not, within twenty-eight days — extended from fourteen days by EA s.11(3) — of the resumption of work (s.47(6)).

These changes to the notice requirements, in particular the introduction of the new 'confirmation' notice in s.33(3A), were ostensibly intended to protect employers from the irritation of women who give the initial notice but fail to return. However the complexity of the notice provisions makes it even more likely than before that there will be two classes of working women so far as the right to return is concerned. There will be those who understand the provisions and give the required notices even if they are not certain that they will want to return since there is no penalty for failure to return having notified an intention to do so.[25] On the other hand there will be an almost certainly greater number of women who are not aware of all the notice requirements. Unless they are well advised by their union representatives or possibly their employers, who may of course refrain from insisting on the new 'confirmation' notice, they will fail to fulfil these requirements and so forfeit their rights.

The most fundamental of the changes made to maternity rights by the EA are contained in s.12. Their effect is heavily to qualify the substance of the right to return. As enacted in 1975 this was a right to return to work with her employer or his successor in the job in which she was originally employed on terms and conditions not less favourable than those which would have been applicable to her if she had not been absent. This meant that as regards seniority, pension and other similar rights periods of employment prior to her absence had to be regarded as continuous with employment after her absence (EPCA s.45(1)(2)). As defined in EPCA s.153(1) 'job' in relation to an employee means the nature of the work she is employed to do in accordance with her contract and the capacity and place in which she is so employed. Thus if under her contract an employee is required to be mobile or flexible, return to a different place of work or type of work may still satisfy the statutory requirements. If it is not practicable for the employer to permit an employee to return to work by reason of redundancy, then under s.45(3) and (4) the right to return becomes a right to be offered alternative employment by the employer or his successor or an associated employer. Such alternative employment must be both suitable in relation to her and appropriate in the circumstances under a contract not substantially less favourable than if she had returned to her original job. If no such 'suitable alternative vacancy' exists then, provided the employee exercises her right to return in accordance with s.47, she is treated by EPCA s.86 as dismissed for the purposes of a redundancy pay claim.

The Working Paper on Employment Protection announced the

government's intention to extend this modification of the right to return in s.45(3) and (4) to situations other than redundancy where it was not reasonably practicable for the employee to return to work in her old job. But instead of amending the terms of s.45(3) and (4), EA s.12 has adopted the somewhat complex technique of limiting the circumstances in which an employer's failure to permit an employee to return is treated by EPCA s.56 as a dismissal for the purposes of a complaint of unfair dismissal. Section 56 is made subject to a new s.56A, subss.(2)–(4) of which provide that where an employer can show that it is not reasonably practicable for a reason other than redundancy for him to permit an employee to return to her original job, but that either he or an associated employer offered her alternative employment, suitable in relation to her and appropriate in the circumstances under a contract not substantially less favourable than if she had returned to her original job and she either accepts or unreasonably refuses it, she cannot complain of unfair dismissal. What this does in effect is to fundamentally alter the whole nature of the right to return. A woman who is not permitted to return to her original job can rarely be certain whether her return was not reasonably practicable and if so whether her refusal of any alternative employment offered will result in the loss of a potential remedy for being denied the right to return.[26] Its value is accordingly diminished.

The right to return may be effectively eliminated by the other provision in the new s.56A, which embodies one of the Employment Act's concessions to the small business lobby. It qualifies the employee's right to treat her employer's failure to permit her to return to work as a dismissal for the purposes of a complaint of unfair dismissal even further if, immediately before her absence began, he, together with any associated employers, employed five or fewer employees. If such a small employer can show that it was not reasonably practicable either to permit her to return to her original job or for her to be offered by him or an associated employer a 'suitable', 'appropriate', 'not less than favourable' alternative, he cannot be penalised under the unfair dismissal provisions for failing to permit her to exercise her right to return. If the employee nonetheless exercises her right to return in accordance with s.47, he could, by virtue of s.86, be obliged to pay her a redundancy payment in an appropriate case.

To understand the potential impact of s.56A it is necessary to appreciate the limitations on the employee's remedies where she is denied the right to return even where she can make a complaint of unfair dismissal.

Schedule 2 of the EPCA modifies the unfair dismissal provisions in order to apply them to such complaints, and its key provision is the substituted s.57(3). As amended by EA Schedule 1 para. 23 (consistent with the amendment made by EA s.6), this provides that 'whether the dismissal was fair or unfair, having regard to the reason shown by the employer [for not permitting her to return to work], shall depend on whether in the circumstances (including the size and administrative resources of the employer's undertaking) the employer would have been acting reasonably or unreasonably in treating it as a sufficient reason for dismissing the employee if she had not been absent from work; and that question shall be determined in accordance with equity and the substantial merits of the case'. The implications of the amendment to s.57(3) proper have already been discussed (p. 30). In this context it means that specifically the size and administrative resources of an employer and generally any circumstances may justify a decision not to permit an employee to return to work irrespective of both whether or not it was reasonably practicable and questions of offers of alternative employment. It is even open to a tribunal to find it reasonable not to permit an employee to return simply because a replacement has been engaged, although this would be contrary to the policy of the original provisions.[27]

What s.56A does is to enable any employer prepared to offer alternative employment to argue that such circumstances made it not reasonably practicable to permit her to exercise the right to return and that the employment offered was 'suitable', 'appropriate' and on 'not less favourable' terms and conditions. Employers with fewer than six employees can argue that it was not reasonably practicable to permit her to return in any capacity. Even if they fail, employers can still fall back on the general reasonableness argument under the substituted s.57(3), when as we have seen (p. 30) the onus of proof is no longer on them.

Legal policy versus the facts

These changes in the right to return to work were justified by the government with arguments which will by now be familiar: before the 1980 Act maternity rights were too much of a burden on employers and led to the employment of fewer women, a disincentive effect which was particularly serious in small firms. More specifically, the Act's notice requirements are intended to give employers greater certainty in anticipating who will return, and the greater scope for making job offers which are suitable, appropriate and not substantially less favourable is designed to make it easier for employers to accommodate the women who do return. If the employee fails to accept such an offer or fails to comply with the notices, the employer is free to resist reinstatement without worrying about having to pay compensation.

The assumption that the maternity rights are an impediment on management, especially in small firms, is contradicted by the factual evidence. When employers were asked, in the Clifton and Tatton-Brown investigation of small firms (above p. 24), whether any government measures had caused difficulties only one person (a fraction of 1 per cent) mentioned the maternity provisions; when then asked whether any specific employment protection laws had affected them only two persons mentioned maternity rights; and when subsequently given a list of twelve laws and asked to indicate which they had experienced and whether they had been troublesome, 4 per cent had experience of holding a job open for a pregnant woman but not a single respondent said that it had caused difficulties. The responses to further questions indicated that the supposed disincentive effect of the maternity rights on the willingness of employers to recruit women was simply non-existent. Another survey of employers, this one conducted by and for *Industrial Relations Review and Report*, found that 83 per cent of employers considered that the maternity provisions were working well in practice.[28] In both surveys the employers who expressed concern about the maternity rights were typically those who had no experience of them. The results of these surveys of employers were confirmed by W. W. Daniel's comprehensive survey on behalf of PSI of mothers who had been employed during pregnancy.[29]

Daniel found that little over half the women in his sample satisfied the conditions for statutory maternity rights, a startling indication of the prohibitive effect of the service qualifications. Small firms in fact employed the highest proportion of short-service employees. The survey posed questions which bear directly on the familiar criticism that women give notice to return just to keep their options open when they have no real intention of going back. The survey found that only about a quarter of the entire sample had given notice to return and the smaller the firm the less likelihood there was of a notice being given. The large majority of those who had no intention of returning refrained from giving notice. Generalising from his survey results, Daniel calculated that of all women leaving work to have a baby, only about one in six is likely to give notice to return but fail to do so, and in firms of fewer than ten employees the proportion is one in twenty. 'Small firms' he concluded 'were least likely to employ women who qualified for maternity rights, least likely to be subject to formal notification of return and least likely to have been subject to an unfulfilled notification.' Those who did return to work were disproportionately concentrated at the two poles of the socio-economic scale — among higher status and professional employees, who had a high degree of intellectual and material satisfaction in work, and unskilled manuals, whose opportunities arose through the availability of part-time work and flexible hours often in small firms. In practice these factors are usually more important than the framework of statutory rights.

The statutory right to return is however of some significance. It has helped at least a few individual women to regain their jobs and, more generally, it has helped to stimulate the development of arrangements giving pregnant employees additional benefits over and above the statutory minima. The reinstatement right and the publicity it has received may have increased women's awareness of the possibility of returning to work whether they are statutorily qualified or not. Equally the right may have served as a public symbol of the social acceptability of the practice. Certainly there is no justification for the Employment Act's restrictive and excessively technical provisions, which have dismayed not only the TUC but the EOC and the IPM. The Act in effect encourages employers to make less effort to keep jobs open and entrenches (along with the unfair dismissal changes) a two-tier status of employee rights with the inferior status attaching to employment in small firms. What is required of a future government is a strengthening of the right to return to enable women to go back to work on the basis of reduced working hours, a shorter service qualification and without the amazing complexities of a triple written notice system.

INDUSTRIAL TRIBUNALS' PROCEDURE

The expansion of the jurisdiction and consequent increase in the workload of industrial tribunals was outlined in chapter one. The rationale for these specialist labour courts is that they provide an expert, easily accessible, informal and inexpensive forum for administering industrial justice in individual employment disputes far more speedily than the ordinary courts. Their speed and accessibility comes in part from the relative simplicity of the procedure for initiating proceedings, essentially by filling in certain standard forms or otherwise providing the information which they require. The time taken for an application to come before a tribunal is normally measured in weeks, compared with the months or years which elapse before cases come before the ordinary civil courts.

Informality comes from the procedure both before and at tribunal hearings. Most of the issues over which the tribunals have jurisdiction are referred to ACAS conciliation officers who try to assist the parties to reach a settlement without the need for a hearing. About two-thirds of all applications stop at this stage either because a settlement is agreed or the claim is voluntarily withdrawn. The procedure at tribunal hearings is intended to minimise the necessary formalities, in particular so that the parties, in theory, do not feel the need to be represented by lawyers. This and the normal practice of not awarding costs against unsuccessful parties help to keep the proceedings relatively inexpensive. The framework for tribunal proceedings is provided by regulations which have been constantly modified in the light of experience. For example a 1978 amendment extended the power of tribunals to require a party to provide further particulars of the grounds he is relying on.

The government revised the regulations in 1980 principally to introduce three major changes.[30] The first and least contentious of these concerns the procedure at the actual hearing before the tribunal. The rules have always given tribunals power to regulate their own proceedings (rule 12(1) in the 1980 regulations). This is intended to maximise both flexibility and informality. However the Working Paper on Employment Protection referred to the growth of statute and case law having conduced to some tribunal proceedings becoming longer and more legalistic. Rule 8 of the new rules therefore includes for the first time an express instruction to a tribunal 'to conduct the hearing in such a manner as it considers most suitable to the clarification of the issues before it and generally to the just handling of the proceedings'. Express references have also been introduced to the need to avoid formality and the fact that a tribunal is not bound by the rules of law which apply to the admissibility of evidence before the courts.

This new direction only reflects the established practice of most tribunals. Indeed the EAT had already ruled that a tribunal was wrong to refuse to entertain hearsay evidence, although it could justifiably be given reduced weight (*Coral Squash Clubs* v. *Mathews*, 1979). The other change to the rules on procedure at hearings has removed the right of each party to make an opening statement. This was apparently considered by the Presidents of the tribunals in England and Scotland to be a particularly important step towards discouraging legalism.[31] By themselves these changes would no doubt have been generally welcomed without reservation. They are however arguably devalued by and possibly even inconsistent with other new provisions.

The Working Paper referred to 'a widespread belief among employers that many cases which reach the stage of a tribunal hearing are without merit and should have been sifted out earlier'. A new *pre-hearing assessment* stage has therefore been added to the procedure by rule 6. This enables a tribunal either on the application of one of the parties or of its own motion to consider the contents of an originating application and entry of appearance by the respondent before the hearing. If the tribunal considers that the application is unlikely to succeed or that any of a party's contentions have no reasonable prospect of success it may indicate that in its opinion costs may be awarded against the party concerned if the application or contention(s) are nevertheless pursued to a hearing. In view of the existing powers in rule 1 for the Secretary of the Tribunals to notify an applicant that his application appears to have no chance of success and rule 4 for obtaining further particulars, and the sifting out of unmeritorious claims at the pre-hearing conciliation stage, it may be asked whether this additional stage is really justified. An experimental use of pre-hearing assessment at one of ACAS's regional offices in 1979 apparently resulted in very few claims being dropped.[32] But under the new rule employees complaining of unfair dismissal in particular may be deterred from pursuing their claims after having received an unfavourable opinion at the pre-hearing assessment by the fear of having to pay substantial costs. The applicant who is however determined to have his day in court is unlikely to be deterred in any event (e.g. *Neefjes* v. *Crystal Products Ltd.*, 1973).

Before 1980 the power of tribunals to award costs was limited to cases in which a party acted frivolously or vexatiously. An employee acts frivolously if he knows that there is no substance in his claim and that it is bound to fail or if the claim is on the face of it so misconceived that it can have no prospect of success. If he brings a claim not with the expectation of receiving compensation but out of spite to harass the employer or for some other improper nature he acts vexatiously.[33] Rule 11 in the 1980 regulations extends the tribunals' power to award costs where a party acted 'otherwise unreasonably'. This may be compared with the power of the EAT to award costs where it appears that any proceedings were unnecessary, improper or vexatious or that there has been unreasonable delay or other unreasonable conduct.[34] In *Croydon* v. *Greenham (Plant Hire) Ltd.* (1978), although noting that this power was the only safeguard against irresponsible litigation, the EAT said that costs should only be awarded under this rule in exceptional circumstances. The Under Secretary of State for Employment may therefore have been correct when he forecast that the change would make little difference to the practice in industrial tribunals where hitherto costs had only been awarded in 2 per cent of the cases heard.[35]

However, when combined with the threat of costs in a tribunal opinion on a pre-hearing assessment, the indeterminate scope of 'unreasonable conduct' is an invitation to successful parties to ask for and tribunals to award costs on a wider basis than before. (It is to be hoped that the decision of the EAT in *Carr* v. *Allen-Bradley Electronics*, 1980, that a tribunal was wrong to award full costs against an employee because he was supported by a trade union will not be disturbed on the grounds that the 1980 rules have changed the basis for tribunals' awarding costs). Since costs are an aspect of lawyers' law par excellence, the incentive to use lawyers in tribunal proceedings is again increased and the likely effect of the attempt to make the procedure at the hearing more informal reduced. Similarly since parties must be notified of their right to make written and oral representations at the pre-hearing assessment stage, one thing the introduction of this stage clearly will not do will be to reduce the trend to legalism. One of the alleged disadvantages of the conciliation process as a detector of unmeritorious claims is that employers are easily persuaded to buy off the complainant rather than face the greater expense and inconvenience caused by a tribunal hearing where, before the 1980 regulations took effect, they had little prospect of obtaining an order for costs. There is now an incentive to use lawyers at the pre-hearing assessment stage to coerce a complainant into dropping his case by the threat of having to pay costs if he does not and loses.

The changes in industrial tribunal procedure are thus an integral part of the general erosion of the individual employee's statutory floor of rights. The government's philosophy is that the employer's traditional prerogatives to hire and fire should take precedence over individual rights. These are only to be encouraged if they can be exercised at the expense of trade unions, a point which we develop in some detail over the next three chapters.

3

The Right to Organise

One of the central commitments in the Conservative Party's 1979 election manifesto was to change the law on the closed shop. The Employment Act has indeed done this. What is much less widely appreciated is that it has also significantly modified the EPCA's limited provisions which are designed to protect the right of workers to organise in trade unions whether or not there is any form of closed shop. Specifically, the legal rights of workers to be members of or participate in the activities of independent trade unions are now severely qualified by the Employment Act's revival of the principle of a general right to dissociate.

BACKGROUND TO THE MODERN LAW

In order to explain the nature and possible effects of the changes made by the 1980 Act it is necessary to outline the previous development of the law concerning workers' organisational rights. Before the Industrial Relations Act was passed in 1971 there was virtually no statute law and very little judge-made common law which had a direct bearing on the right to organise. While trade unions had been recognised as lawful for 100 years, even if they were in restraint of trade (see p. 8), there was no positive legal recognition of a right for workers to organise in trade unions. This was very much in keeping with the traditional role of the law in collective labour relations in Britain: a negative immunity from common law doctrines to the extent required to enable unions to function but no positive legal rights. The social right to organise in trade unions was recognised only by the Fair Wages Resolution of the House of Commons (setting out industrial relations standards for government contractors), clause 4 of which still provides: 'The contractor shall recognise the freedom of his workpeople to be members of trade unions.' Apart from this statement of public policy, which is not legally enforceable at the option of the workers themselves, specific legal protection for the right to organise was considered to be unnecessary. In 1951 the United Kingdom ratified ILO Conventions No. 87 on Freedom of Association and the Right to Organise and No. 98 on the Application of the Right to Organise and to Bargain Collectively. The former provides that workers shall have the right to establish and join organisations of their own choosing. The latter requires that they shall have adequate protection against acts of anti-union discrimination in their employment. But the 'necessary and appropriate measures to ensure that workers ... may freely exercise the right to organise' (Convention No. 87 article 11) and 'machinery appropriate to national conditions ... for the purpose of ensuring respect for the right to organise as defined' (Convention No. 98 article 3) in Britain were not considered to involve the law.

The Donovan Report supported a very limited legal incursion into this area. It recommended that the 'yellow dog contract', under which a worker agrees as a term of his employment that he will not join a trade union, should be declared void (paras. 242–6). Generally however Donovan was adamant that there was no case for the enactment of a right *not* to belong (or dissociate) as a correlative to its proposed limited recognition of the right to belong: the 'former condition is designed to frustrate the development of collective bargaining, which it is public policy to promote, whereas no such objection applies to the latter' (para. 599).

The Industrial Relations Act adopted an approach to the right to organise which was fundamentally different from that of the ILO Conventions and the Donovan Report. Although the promotion of collective bargaining was one of its stated aims, the Act was more concerned to protect certain individual rights. Where these conflicted with collective interests, the IRA favoured the individual. Thus s.5 established rights for the individual worker enforceable against his employer to belong to and take part in the activities of a registered union, which apparently reflected collective interests, but also created the right not to belong to any union. The positive assertion of a legal right to dissociate was basically inconsistent with the aim of protecting the right to organise and promoting collective bargaining. This fundamental contradiction has been raised again by the EA's amendments to the laws enacted in 1974 and 1975. These provisions, originally in TULRA and the EPA and now consolidated in the EPCA, were intended primarily to deter employers from discriminating against or dismissing employees because of their membership of or participation in the activities of an independent trade union. They also sought to preclude employers from discriminating against or dismissing employees who refused to join non-independent unions. A limited right to dissociate in closed shops was recognised only in respect of employees who genuinely objected to membership of any trade union on grounds of religious belief.[1]

LEGAL FRAMEWORK OF WORKPLACE ORGANISATION

A preliminary point which is crucial to an understanding of the effect of the EA's amendments is the meaning of 'independent' trade union. This is defined as a union which is neither under employer domination or control nor liable to interference by employer(s) tending towards such control (TULRA s.30(1) and EPCA s.153(1)). The EPA's procedure for obtaining a certificate of independence from the Certification Officer was intended to separate genuine unions from 'house' unions established by employers or subject to employer influence to such an extent as to negate any claim they might have to be genuinely representative of organised workers. In practice the great majority of organisations on the 'list' of trade unions which have applied for a certificate of independence have received one and consequently the Certification Officer's interpretation of the statutory criteria of independence has been subjected to considerable criticism by the TUC.[2] Although it may not have been completely successful in achieving its intended purpose, the definition does serve to exclude at least the most extreme cases of house unions from the benefit of certain legal advantages. It is only the representatives of independent unions who are legally entitled to information for collective bargaining and to consultation on safety and redundancy. Independence is also the prerequisite for the individual legal rights in respect of trade union membership, that is, time off work rights under EPCA ss.27 and 28 supplemented by the ACAS Code of Practice on Time Off for Trade Union Duties and Activities and (what we are concerned with here) the rights to belong to and take part in the activities of a union.

EPCA s.58(1) provides that an employee's dismissal is automatically unfair if the reason for it was that he '(a) was, or proposed to become, a member of an independent trade union [or] (b) had taken, or proposed to take, part at any appropriate time in the activities of an independent trade union'. This protection against dismissal for such an 'inadmissible' reason is available regardless of how long the employee has been employed (EPCA s.64(3)). There are parallel rights for an employee 'not to have action (short of dismissal) taken against him as an individual by his employer for the purpose of (a) preventing or deterring him from being or seeking to become a member of an independent trade union, or penalising him for doing so; or (b) preventing or deterring him from taking part in the activities of an independent trade union at any appropriate time, or penalising him for doing so' (EPCA s.23(1)).

Various difficulties associated with the right to take part in union activities are common to both provisions. First the right is limited to participation in activities at an 'appropriate time', which is defined either as outside working hours or inside working hours in accordance with arrangements agreed with or consent given by the employer (EPCA ss.23(2) and 58(2)). Since 'working hours' is stated to mean any time when the employee is required to be at work under his contract of employment, it has been held by the House of Lords that meal breaks, tea breaks and the like are outside working hours. The right is therefore exercisable on the employer's premises without his consent during these times: *Post Office* v. *UPW* (1974), which concerned a similar definition in IRA s.5(5). This decision was the culmination of a series of individual complaints by workers belonging to the unrecognised Telecommunications Staff Association in respect of union activities on Post Office premises, which the Post Office discouraged or refused to allow, although equivalent activities were in many instances permitted on behalf of the recognised UPW. It has also been acknowledged by the Court of Appeal however that the employer's consent to taking part in union activities inside working hours may be implied, though in what circumstances is less clear. Established practice at the particular workplace appears to be a crucial consideration (*Marley Tile Ltd.* v. *Shaw,* 1980). But what are 'activities of an independent trade union' and when is an employee taking part in them?

In the *Post Office* case the House of Lords limited permitted activities to those not requiring the employer's assistance in the form of facilities, or which only required facilities normally available to employees, or which only required the employer to submit to trifling inconvenience. The Law Lords declined to be more specific, saying that disputed cases could be determined by industrial tribunals on the facts. The EAT has shown an inconsistent approach to this difficult problem. In a helpful decision (*Dixon* v. *West Ella Developments Ltd.,* 1978) it acknowledged that 'activities' should not be subject to a restrictive interpretation which would confine them to members' meetings and activities involving their status as trade unionists. However, perhaps not surprisingly, taking part in industrial action has been excluded (*Drew* v. *St. Edmunsbury B.C.,* 1980). Further in *Chant* v. *Aquaboats Ltd.* (1978) a trade unionist organising and presenting a petition to management concerning safety at work was held to be acting as an individual and, therefore, not taking part in the activities of an independent trade union.

Under the 1980 Act not only do all these difficulties remain but a further one is made worse. This is the encouragement given to inter-union competition and disputes by an unlimited right to take part in union activities. In the light of the problems illustrated by the *Post Office* case, s.23 of the EPCA as originally enacted sought to reduce the potential for inter-union strife in respect of employment which was subject to the practice of a 'union membership agreement' (UMA). The right to take part in activities *on the employer's premises* was limited to the activities of a 'specified' union. There was therefore no sanction against an employer who prevented or deterred an employee from, for example, seeking to recruit members for an independent union which was not specified for the purposes of the UMA or penalising him for doing so if the activity took place on the employer's premises. To *dismiss* an employee for such activities was though, and still is, automatically unfair since no parallel limitation was placed on that category of unfair dismissal (see chapter four). Although the provision has been redrafted, EPCA s.23(2A)(a) (inserted by EA s.15(2)) broadly preserves this limitation in respect of action short of dismissal. It is however subject to a new qualification. This flows from the requirement introduced by s.7 of the EA that, in order to be recognised for the purpose of limiting individual employment rights, UMAs taking effect after 14 August 1980 must have been approved by a ballot in accordance with the new EPCA s.58A. The redrafted limitation on the right to take part in union activities therefore only applies in respect of a UMA taking effect after 14 August 1980 if it has been so approved: EPCA s.23(2B). Thus if a closed shop takes effect after this date without such ballot approval it is vulnerable to disruption by employees taking part in the activities of another independent union on the employer's premises during breaks between working hours and claiming legal protection for their right to do so.

In respect of alleged action short of dismissal the employee may complain to an industrial tribunal. Once he proves that the action complained of was taken, it is for the employer to prove the purpose for which it was taken, but s.15(3) of the EA has deleted the previous express statutory obligation to prove that it was not a purpose relating to union membership or activities. Although it does not appear to have made any major change, it seems probable that the true reason for this repeal was a desire to align the burden of proof on such complaints with that on complaints of unfair dismissal as amended by the 1980 Act (see above p. 30). If the complainant wins his case he may be entitled to certain legal remedies. In addition to a declaration that the complaint is upheld, a tribunal may award compensation which is just and equitable in all the circumstances having regard to the infringement of the complainant's right and any loss sustained which is attributable to the employer's action (EPCA ss.24(3) and 26). It has been accepted that this may in principle include compensation for frustration of the employee's desire to join a union or to see his union recognised (*Brassington* v. *Cauldron Wholesale Ltd.*, 1978).

Apart from seeking the normal remedies for unfair dismissal (see p. 35), an employee who alleges that his dismissal was unfair because the reason for it was his membership or his taking part in the activities of an independent trade union may also apply to an industrial tribunal under EPCA s.77 for 'interim' relief in advance of the determination of his unfair dismissal complaint. Such an application must be made within seven days of the termination of his employment and be accompanied by a certificate from an authorised union official stating that he was or proposed to become a union member and that there appeared to be reasonable grounds for supposing that the reason for his dismissal was one alleged in his complaint. If the tribunal finds that this is 'likely' it will make an order for the continuation of his employment if agreement on reinstatement or re-engagement pending determination of the complaint cannot be reached. In practice tribunals are very reluctant to uphold applications for interim relief. In any event an order for continuation of employment does not oblige the employer to permit the dismissed employee to return to work but only requires him to treat the employee as still employed for the purposes of pay and other benefits. The potential impact of interim relief as a measure reinforcing the right to organise is therefore very limited.

It should be noted that the management prerogative to decide who to engage is unaffected by any provision concerned with trade union organisational rights. This was confirmed in the *Beyer* case (1977), an unsuccessful unfair dismissal claim by a trade union activist who had been blacklisted by major employers in the building industry. He was taken on at one of the appellant's sites where the agent did not know him, but he was sacked two hours later when his identity was discovered. While the reason for his dismissal may have been his trade union activities, s.58(1)(b) only makes a dismissal automatically unfair where the reason was trade union activities during the period of employment with the employer who dismissed him. As the EAT put it in a memorable passage 'there is no place on earth where it is correct to say that a man has a right to a job. . . . Until there is work available for all, obviously the employer must have a vested right to pick and choose. There is nothing in the legislation . . . which lays down that an employer may not refuse to employ a man. . . .'[3]

This contrasts in formal terms with s.5 of the IRA which did provide redress for a worker who was refused employment because of his membership or taking part in the activities of a union which had registered under the Act. But this right was worthless in view of the overall content of the section, including the right not to belong, and the fact that TUC affiliates did not register. However the right to organise is reinforced in one other respect. Under EPCA s.58(1)(c) an employee is provided with redress if he is dismissed for non-membership of a union which is *not* independent.

A RIGHT TO DISSOCIATE

In its original form, EPCA s.23(1)(c) was an extension of the reinforcement for organisational rights provided by s.58(1)(c). Whereas that section makes dismissal for non-membership of a non-independent union automatically unfair, s.23(1)(c) established a parallel right for an employee 'not to have action (short of dismissal) taken against him as an individual by his employer for the purpose of . . . compelling him to be or become a member of a trade union which is not independent'. By deleting the last four words − 'which is not independent' − EA s.15(1) has turned a legal right for trade unionists into a severe limitation. EPCA s.23(1)(c) as amended now affords legal recognition for a general right to dissociate unless (by virtue of EPCA s.23(2A)(b) inserted by EA s.15(2)) there is a statutorily approved form of closed shop. The Employment Act drastically reduces the scope of that approval. Thus, in employment where it is the practice to belong to a specified union in accordance with a UMA, the right to dissociate is available only to employees who fall within one of the Act's three exempted categories, which we discuss in detail in chapter four. In this respect the law on dismissal and action short of dismissal in UMA employment are the same.[4] But the government's claim that all the amendments made to EPCA s.23 by EA s.15 only align the law on action short of dismissal with that on unfair dismissal, after the amendments to the latter made by EA ss.7 and 10, is demonstrably false.

The potential impact of the new right to dissociate is uncertain for various reasons. In the first place the failure to make a similar amendment to EPCA s.58(1)(c) means that the non-unionist who is dismissed (rather than subjected to action short of dismissal) because of his reluctance to join a union has no automatic remedy, unless there is a closed shop and he falls within one of the three exempted categories. If he has the requisite qualifying period of fifty-two weeks continuous employment he may complain of unfair dismissal. Under the general unfair dismissal provisions it will be for the employer to show that his non-membership was a 'substantial reason of a kind such as to justify the dismissal of an employee holding the position which that employee held' (EPCA s.57(1)(b)). If that is established it will then be for the tribunal to determine in accordance with equity and the substantial merits of the case 'whether in the circumstances (including the size and administrative resources of the employer's undertaking) the employer acted reasonably or unreasonably in treating it as a sufficient reason for dismissing the employee' (s.57(3) as amended by EA s.6). A tribunal might read the policy behind the amendment to s.23(1)(c) into the law on unfair dismissal and thus hold the dismissal to be unfair. Conversely it might do the opposite because of the absence of any similar amendment to the parallel provision in s.58(1)(c). There is moreover some authority prior to the enactment of the EA for the view that dismissal of an employee for non-membership of a union outside a closed shop may at least in some circumstances be fair.[5]

The scope of the new EPCA s.23(1)(c) depends on three indeterminate factors: what is the ambit of 'action short of dismissal'? when is such action taken against an employee 'as an individual'? and when is it taken 'for the purpose of compelling him to be or become a member of a trade union'? Action short of dismissal is not defined in the EPCA. Case law has established that it covers transferring an employee to less desirable work and disciplinary action.[6] Whether it covers a threat of action as distinct from the action itself was questioned by the EAT in *Brassington* v. *Cauldron Wholesale Ltd*.[7] One can but speculate on whether it would include non-disciplinary suspension on full pay where the opportunity to earn bonuses might be lost, being deprived of the opportunity to work overtime or to do particular work, or being denied access to a grievance procedure negotiated between management and unions. Such matters are often within the control of shop stewards who naturally enough do not tend to go out of their way to protect non-unionists in discharging their 'helper' functions.[8]

Assuming, as is likely, that all these instances do fall within 'action short of dismissal', the circumstances in which such action would not be taken against the non-unionist employee 'as an individual' are hard to foresee. In *CEGB* v. *Coleman* (1973), a case concerning IRA s.5, the NIRC drew a distinction between detriments suffered and benefits enjoyed by a worker as an individual in the context of his contract of employment and benefits enjoyed by workers qua trade union representatives. The court held that confining eligibility for election to a works committee to members of recognised unions was discrimination *between* trade unionists and non-union employees, but not discrimination against the latter. It is thus arguable that it is not action taken *against* a non-unionist *as an individual* to deny him the same facilities as trade unionists, for example, with respect to grievances. But the reasoning of the NIRC is not wholly convincing and clearly did not impress Lord Denning in the Court of Appeal in the *Post Office* case where he declared: 'When you discriminate between two workers you almost invariably discriminate against one and in favour of the other.'[9] In all probability the non-unionist will have little difficulty in persuading a tribunal that action taken to compel him to belong to a union was taken against him as an individual. But attempts by members of unrecognised unions to use the amended EPCA s.23(1)(c) in the same way as members of the unrecognised Telecommunications Staff Association in the Post Office attempted to use the Industrial Relations Act are perhaps more likely to give rise to the sort of nice distinction which appealed to the NIRC in the *Coleman* case.

The greatest difficulty is identifying action which will be held to be for the purpose of 'compelling' an employee to be a union member. No one can be confident that a tribunal or one of the appellate courts will not see, for example, the denial of overtime to a non-unionist as designed not merely to discriminate against him because of his non-membership, which s.23(1)(c) does not proscribe, but to compel him to join. Indeed if the logic of the Employment Act is to establish an effective right to dissociate, tribunals may be inclined to protect it without regard to the precise point at which mere discrimination stops and compulsion begins. That being so, a wide range of established practices are vulnerable to attack by non-unionists and members of unrecognised unions relying on the new right to dissociate. Certainly any attempt to confine the benefits of collective bargaining to union members only now runs the risk of illegality.

The law reports however contain only limited evidence of experience of the previous general right to dissociate provided by the Industrial Relations Act. The notable exception is the saga of Joseph Langston, whose prolific litigation conclusively showed that a non-unionist's legal rights were of little practical utility against a well-entrenched closed shop.[10] But most of the reported disputes concerned members of unrecognised registered unions asserting their right to take part in the activities of their own union. Assertion of the similar right in EPCA s.23(1)(b) on the employer's premises is at least limited to where membership of recognised unions is not the practice according to a UMA and on that basis employers have an incentive to agree to UMAs. But after the Employment Act members of unrecognised unions might also try to rely on EPCA s.23(1)(c) if, for example, they were assigned to less desirable work or denied opportunities for overtime on the grounds that this was intended to compel them to belong to a recognised union. It is clear that the EA's right to dissociate may have more impact as a spur to inter-union disputes than as a source of protection for the individual non-unionist.

JOINDER: THE EMPLOYER'S CLAW BACK

Rather than trying to limit the right in EPCA s.23(1)(c) not to be compelled to join a trade union by the negotiation of UMAs, some employers may prefer to take advantage of the crucial addition to the provisions on remedies where an employee complains of infringement of this right. EA s.15(4) inserts s.26A into the EPCA. This enables an employer against whom such a complaint is made to join to the proceedings 'a trade union or other person' who he claims induced him to take the action complained of by 'calling, organising, procuring or financing a strike or other industrial action' (hereafter referred to simply as 'organising' industrial action) or threatening to do so. If the industrial tribunal finds this claim well-founded, it may order that person to pay a contribution of up to 100 per cent of any compensation awarded. In order to appreciate the potential effect of this provision, it must be read with some of the EPCA's other sections dealing with the enforcement of legal rights in respect of union membership, non-membership and activities. Section 25(2) requires any pressure on the employer by way of organising industrial action to be ignored in determining whether the action complained of was taken by the employer and the purpose for which it was taken. Section 26(4) requires compensation as against the employer to be assessed as if no such pressure had been exercised.

The combined effect of these sections, which are applicable whether or not there is a closed shop, is that the right to dissociate may in practice be exercised at the financial expense of trade unions, union officials, shop stewards and individual workers. It should however be stressed that this is not an automatic consequence. It requires that the employer does not take any action short of dismissal against a non-unionist until subjected to some pressure by industrial action or threat of it unless he does so. It then requires the non-unionist to complain to a tribunal that his right under s.23(1)(c) has been infringed by his employer. The employer must then join the union, official(s) and/or workers allegedly responsible for the pressure to the proceedings. If the tribunal upholds the complaint it must then award compensation to the employee assessed as against the employer. Finally it must exercise its discretion to order any of those joined to make a contribution to the compensation awarded. As under the IRA the potential is there. Only time and experience will tell if it is to be realised.

The joinder principle not only reinforces the right to dissociate at the expense of trade unionists, but it is a significant dilution of the right to organise. Parallel provisions in the law of unfair dismissal have been made by EA s.10 which inserts ss.76A–76C into the EPCA. Section 76A corresponds directly to s.26A. It applies where an employer claims that he was induced to dismiss the employee who is complaining of unfair dismissal by pressure exercised by a trade union or other person organising or threatening industrial action because the complainant employee was not a member of any trade union or a particular union. The employer may then join the union or other person as a party to the proceedings before the complaint is heard. If the unfair dismissal complaint is upheld and the tribunal awards compensation,[11] it may then, if it finds the employer's claim of pressure well-founded order the union or other person to pay a contribution of up to 100 per cent of the compensation awarded.

Double joinder

Whether or not there is a closed shop, the joinder principle is also applicable to the practice of main contractors stipulating that work on subcontracts must be performed by union labour (EPCA ss.76B and 76C). Where the practice is a term of the subcontract and the subcontractor dismisses a non-union employee because the main contractor refuses to relax the requirement of union membership and the subcontractor has no other suitable work for him, s.76B enables the subcontractor against whom the dismissed employee has made a complaint of unfair dismissal to join the main contractor as a party to the proceedings before the complaint is heard. If the tribunal makes an award of compensation for unfair dismissal and upholds the subcontractor's claim, it must order the main contractor to pay the subcontractor an amount equal to that compensation.

If the main contractor claims that a union or other person induced him to withhold consent to permitting the complainant non-unionist to do work under the contract by pressure exercised by organising or threatening industrial action, he in turn may under s.76C join the union or other person as party to the proceedings before the hearing of the unfair dismissal complaint. If the tribunal upholds this claim it may order the union or other person to pay a contribution of up to 100 per cent of the amount which the main contractor has to pay to the subcontractor under s.76B, that is, the compensation awarded for unfair dismissal.

The government's dislike for this practice of union labour only contract clauses is underlined by paragraph 41 of the Closed Shop Code, which states that where a UMA is agreed there 'should be no attempt, by formal or informal means, to impose a requirement of union membership on the employees of contractors, suppliers and customers of an employer'. This is further emphasised by EA s.18 (withdrawal of trade dispute immunities for acts to compel union membership, see chapter nine). Moreover the Green Paper *Trade Union Immunities* raised for discussion various additional proposals for curbing union-only clauses (paras. 296–302). These included the enactment of a general provision making such discrimination unlawful. This would in effect be an extension of the right to dissociate established by the amended EPCA s.23(1)(c) in two respects. Firstly, it would no longer be confined to protecting only against action short of dismissal taken to compel an employee to join a trade union but would be more general in scope like

IRA s.5(1)(b). Secondly, the right would become actionable not only against an individual employee's own employer but also against parties to commercial contracts with his employer. This would establish a position similar to that which existed under the Industrial Relations Act. Section 5(2) of the IRA made it an unfair industrial practice for an employer to take action infringing the s.5(1) rights of a worker, that is, any worker and not just one employed by him. Since under IRA s.33(3)(a) it was an unfair industrial practice to organise industrial action to induce an employer to commit such an unfair industrial practice, an employer who as a result of such pressure required other employers to employ only union labour on their contracts with him could recover compensation payable to workers thus discriminated against from those responsible for organising or threatening the industrial action. When read with the Green Paper, EPCA ss.76B and 76C may become but the first steps to restoring yet another aspect of the IRA.

Making the union pay

The Working Paper on the Closed Shop only envisaged provisions for an employer to join a trade union to unfair dismissal proceedings arising out of closed shop employment. Apart from the fact that EPCA ss.76A–76C are not confined to complaints of unfair dismissal from UMA employment but apply generally to any unfair dismissal complaint, they also enable an employer to join any person who he claims was responsible for inducing him to dismiss an employee for non-membership by organising industrial action. Where the action in question, actual or threatened, was or would have been unofficial, it may well be difficult for an employer to identify which persons 'called, organised, procured or financed' it. Even if he can do so, their ability to meet any contribution to compensation ordered might well be in doubt. In these cases an employer minded to join anyone might well therefore prefer to join the employee's trade union and allege that it was responsible for whatever action was threatened or occurred. One of the major issues raised in the courts under the Industrial Relations Act was the circumstances in and extent to which a union could be made vicariously liable for the acts of its officials and members in organising and taking industrial action.[12] Under the joinder sections of the 1980 Act this matter is once again a major issue.

The introduction of provisions enabling trade unions to be joined to proceedings because of pressure brought to bear by industrial action or the threat of it also makes it easier to argue that the immunity of trade unions as such from liability in tort in respect of industrial action under TULRA s.14(1) is no longer appropriate. Why should such responsibility be confined to industrial action directed at non-union employees or employees who belong to rival unions? This argument is in fact raised by the Green Paper (paras. 104–137) and we shall return to it in chapter nine. Whether or not this idea is ever legislated, EA ss.10 and 15(4) have added to the list of 'unlawful means' for the purposes of tort liability. Any industrial action in which the employer's enforcement of payment of a contribution ordered under the new law was at issue would probably involve unlawful means arising from breach of statutory duty, which would fall outside the ambit of any protection provided by s.13 of TULRA.[13]

The joinder provisions are inconsistent with a major principle concerning the role of the law in industrial conflict. The belief that industrial tribunals should not be required to investigate and pronounce on the merits of industrial action was part of the philosophy underlying the original provisions of the EPCA. It is reflected in s.62, which excludes tribunals from hearing complaints of unfair dismissal by employees dismissed during industrial action or lock-outs, except cases of victimisation, as a matter of jurisdiction. It is also the basis for the sections which provide that pressure from industrial action or the threat of it must be ignored in determining the purpose of the employer's action short of dismissal (s.25(2)) and, in unfair dismissal complaints, the reason for dismissal and whether the employer acted reasonably in dismissing (s.63). Sections 26(4) and 74(5) reiterate this requirement in the context of assessment of compensation. The tribunals are now in the bizarre situation of having to determine the substance of complaints of unfair dismissal and action short of dismissal to compel union membership and where necessary assess compensation against the employer without regard to any pressure on him from industrial action, and then to determine the amount of any contribution to the compensation solely on the basis of such action. The amount of contribution up to 100 per cent is moreover such as the tribunal considers to be just and equitable in the circumstances (EPCA ss.26A(3) and 76A(3)). This not only destroys the basic principle of not requiring tribunals to pronounce on the merits of industrial action. It also enables a tribunal to absolve an employer from any responsibility for his acts in dismissing an employee for non-membership of a union or taking action to compel him to join that union in response to industrial pressure. The tribunals are thus being required to discharge a function for which they are arguably ill-fitted and which may well destroy their credibility in the eyes of trade unions and their members.

The impact of the joinder provisions has to be considered in three contexts: complaints of unfair dismissal generally (to which only EA s.10 is relevant), employment subject to union membership in accordance with the practice of a UMA; and union membership disputes arising outside such employment. If their potential is fully exploited they could make the right of workers to organise, that is, to assert their collective interest, exercisable only at a prohibitive financial cost to the workers themselves and their trade unions. The aim of financial deterrence is indicated by the fact that these sections expressly refer to the possibility of the tribunals awarding 'a complete indemnity', that is, a 100 per cent contribution to the employer, which in some unfair dismissal cases may run into thousands of pounds. The beneficiaries will be those who exercise the right to dissociate, a right explicitly recognised by the Employment Act. Part of the 'moderate' image of the Act is that it is designed to deal merely with the worst abuses of the closed shop, but it has laid the foundations for legal restraints on the right to organise almost as constricting as those of the Industrial Relations Act.[14]

4

The Closed Shop

There is no more emotive issue in British industrial relations or politics than the closed shop. Many of the opinions held concerning it are propounded as articles of faith rather than rational conclusions from empirical evidence. Any appreciation of the impact of the law must proceed from an attempt to understand the nature of prevailing practices which are generally identified under the closed shop umbrella.

SOME FACTS AND ARGUMENTS ABOUT THE
CLOSED SHOP

In 1964 McCarthy defined the closed shop as 'a situation in which employees come to realise that a particular job is only to be obtained and retained if they become and remain members of one of a specified number of trade unions'.[1] However the research project on the closed shop which was conducted in 1978–80 at the London School of Economics (hereafter referred to as the LSE project) suggested that this definition is not universally accepted by employers and trade unions.[2] Practices taken to be closed shops for the purposes of the LSE survey were not always perceived as such by those in industry and conversely the fact of 100 per cent union membership at a particular time was not automatically accepted as sufficient evidence of closed shop employment. While this difficulty should be kept in mind it does not fundamentally affect the adequacy of McCarthy's definition for an understanding of the role which the law has played and now seeks to play. It is also usual to subdivide the different types of closed shop into two broad categories: the post-entry shop where workers must join a particular union or one of several unions within a certain time of obtaining employment; and the pre-entry shop where union membership is a precondition for obtaining a particular job. This distinction, which is very important from the point of view of industrial relations, had legal relevance while the Industrial Relations Act was in force but it has no legal significance in the context of the modern statutory law.

McCarthy's study, the LSE project, and research undertaken in the 1970s by the Industrial Relations Research Unit at Warwick University[3] provide a reasonably complete picture of the development of the closed shop in the two decades preceding the introduction of the Employment Act's amendments to the law. In 1964 McCarthy estimated that approximately three and three quarter million workers (40 per cent of union members and 15 per cent of all workers) were in closed shop employment, three quarters of a million of these being in some form of pre-entry shop. Four years later Donovan concluded that the decline in the number of workers employed in traditional closed shop industries had probably been offset by growth of the closed shop elsewhere so that McCarthy's statistics were still generally accurate (para. 589). Both the Warwick study on the effects of the Industrial Relations Act and the LSE project found evidence of increased coverage between 1968 and the time when the relevant provisions of that Act came into force.

The attempt at detailed legal regulation of closed shops made by the IRA, which is outlined below, was not successful. Indeed the effect of the IRA as revealed by the Warwick study was almost diametrically opposed to that which the legislature intended. Operation of existing closed shops was found to be little affected, which pointed to the management interest in preserving the practice. The statutorily approved forms of closed shop – the agency shop and approved closed shop – were little used, but the Act did deter the negotiation of new formal closed shop agreements outside its framework. After its repeal in 1974 there was a big increase in the number of formal agreements concluded. The LSE project indicated that this trend reached its peak in 1976–77. One of the main contrasts between the practice up to the 1960s and that developed in the 1970s was in the use of formal agreements. These have tended to become quite detailed in contrast to the single sentence in a works collective agreement which might have been found before 1968. The LSE project concluded that in 1979 a minimum of approximately 5.2 million workers were in closed shop employment, 837,000 of these being in some form of pre-entry shop. Thus it can be said that when the Employment Act came into force about one in four of the working population and about half of all union members were in closed shops. Moreover it appeared that the closed shop was a growing feature of white collar as well as manual trade unionism in both the public and private sectors.

The main arguments for and against the closed shop were debated throughout the 1960s and 1970s. Donovan found the most convincing arguments in favour to be those related to the efficacy of collective bargaining: that in some industries such as merchant shipping and entertainment it was difficult for trade unions to establish effective and stable organisation without the help of the closed shop, and that even where members could be obtained and retained without the closed shop there were instances where it was needed for the effective deployment of workers' bargaining strength (para. 592). In fact the closed shop has historically been a union objective, a method of consolidating membership and bargaining strength and so of defending 'hard won terms and conditions and security of employment from being undermined by persons willing to work for worse terms and conditions' (TUC Guide *Trade Union Organisation and the Closed Shop* para. 6). The most commonly used argument by unions in favour of the closed shop is that based upon objections to the 'free rider'. The trade unionist in the closed shop claims his individual right to work alongside only those who contribute to the union that bargains for the workforce as a whole. Hence the union disapproval of free riders who pocket the benefit of union efforts (collective agreements normally apply for the benefit of non-members) without the costs and responsibilities of membership. Furthermore, both the Warwick and LSE research confirmed that such workers do not generally attract management sympathy. Management support for the closed shop increased and became more visible in the 1970s. In negotiations with unions in respect of closed shop employment management has the advantage of knowing that they are dealing with organisations which represent all the workers, the unions' disciplinary power is accordingly increased, agreed procedures cover all the workers and relationships are stabilised. Keeping out competing unions and avoiding the potentially disruptive effect of non-members accord with management's interest in maintaining an orderly framework. Closed shops in conjunction with the TUC's 'Bridlington' principles on inter-union disputes (discussed in chapter five) are indispensable means for avoiding or at least containing multi-unionism. As the TUC Guide (para. 3) states: 'in this context, the existence of non-unionists may be positively harmful to good industrial relations and can undermine the stability of established negotiating and consultative arrangements'.

Part of the government's argument against the closed shop is that it erodes individual liberty by destroying a person's freedom to choose not to belong to a trade union. Further it subjects the individual to the exercise of arbitrary discretion by trade unions and effectively destroys the right to express disagreement with the union by leaving. Undoubtedly individuals and sometimes minority groups may experience difficulties under the closed shop. This however is one of the justifications for providing safeguards — legal and extra-legal — against abuse rather than an argument against the practice of the closed shop as such. The allegedly adverse economic effects of the pre-entry closed shop, which is stigmatised as a restrictive labour practice, are also used as an argument against any form of closed shop. Indeed the Green Paper *Trade Union Immunities* does just this (para. 265). But there are no concrete facts to demonstrate why the much more frequent post-entry closed shop creates inefficiency.

Judicial attitudes and public policy

There were no statutory provisions concerning the closed shop before 1971. Judicial attitudes towards the practice have varied. In 1924 a trade union's pursuit of 100 per cent membership was held by the Court of Appeal to be a legitimate interest for the purposes of civil liability for conspiracy to injure (*Reynolds* v. *Shipping Federation*) and in the early days of the Second World War the House of Lords adopted a similar line of reasoning (*Crofter Harris Tweed* v. *Veitch*, 1942). In *Faramus* v. *Film Artistes Association* (1964) the House of Lords recognised the justification for a closed shop in the employment of film extras. In this case the court refused to strike down a union rule which precluded a person with a criminal record from belonging to the union. Despite his apparent membership for several years Faramus (who had been convicted of offences at the age of seventeen) had in law never been a member. Notwithstanding their sympathy for the individual, the Law Lords acknowledged the need for the sort of regulation of the employment of film extras which the union's rule book and closed shop arrangement provided.

Not surprisingly judges who seek a reputation as champions of individual liberty have taken a less charitable view. Lord Denning in particular has since the 1950s sought to establish a common law right to work which would at least enable the courts to strike down union rules which in their view give the union an unfettered discretion to exclude individuals from membership. Thus in *Edwards* v. *SOGAT* he said:

> [A man's right to work] is now fully recognised by law. It is a right which is of special importance where a trade union operates

a 'closed shop' or '100 per cent membership'; for that means no man can become employed or remain in employment with a firm unless he is a member of a union. If his union card is withdrawn, he has to leave the employment. He is deprived of his livelihood. The courts will not allow so great a power to be exercised arbitrarily or capriciously or with unfair discrimination, neither in the making of the rules, nor in the enforcement of them. ... A trade union exists to protect the right of each one of its members to earn his living and to take advantage of all that goes with it. ... If the union should assume to make a rule which destroys that right or puts it in jeopardy — or is a gratuitous and oppressive interference with it — then the union exceeds its powers. The rule is ultra vires and invalid.[4]

Contrary to popular opinion Lord Denning's views do not automatically achieve the status of accepted law. This particular view is clearly inconsistent with the House of Lords' decision in the *Faramus* case, a decision which does establish a binding precedent. Further the support which Lord Denning has attracted from other judges has been noticeably limited. Indeed in 1978 Vice Chancellor Megarry pointed out the difficulties which the notion of a legal right to work must necessarily involve: he raised the awkward question of who was under a duty to provide the work and hoped that the catch phrase 'right to work' would not be accepted as an example of a true legal right.[5]

Nevertheless the government clearly had Lord Denning's views in mind when it included in paragraph 45 of the consultative 'draft' Code on the Closed Shop published in August 1980 the remarkable assertion that pre-entry closed shops 'may infringe the right to work'. Modification of this to 'may infringe the freedom of individuals to work' in paragraph 46 of the Code finally issued scarcely affects the extent of the misrepresentation of the law involved. No doubt the government hopes that Lord Denning's views will be developed, at least in the context of control of union rules and the practice of the closed shop. As yet though they remain in legal terminology 'obiter dicta', the limitations of which need to be fully emphasised.

The issue of the closed shop was further analysed by the Donovan Royal Commission but against a background of closed shop practices which were at the time (1965–68) still largely informal. Donovan argued that there should not be any attempt to ban the closed shop but that its importance and justification should be recognised and legal safeguards for individuals introduced. These included protection via proposed legislation on unfair dismissal for conscientious objectors to union membership and when closed shops were introduced for existing employees who objected to joining a union on reasonable grounds. The establishment of an independent review board as the ultimate appellate body for disputes over refusal of admission to and expulsion from unions was also proposed. It is noteworthy that Donovan expressed the hope that in time trade unions would come to feel that the closed shop was no longer necessary because of the extension of union organisation and collective bargaining consequent on other proposals which it made (para. 602). However, it is clear from the Warwick and LSE research that not only has this not happened but that the closed shop has rather tended to become a concomitant of the development of comprehensive industrial relations practices and procedures of the kind which Donovan itself recommended. The closed shop has often been introduced in the post-Donovan era as part of the management-initiated reform of collective bargaining.

The Industrial Relations Act and the closed shop

The IRA adopted a different approach to the law from the one recommended by Donovan. The right conferred by the Act not to belong to any union put all closed shops in legal jeopardy. Moreover pre-entry agreements were declared to be void and a worker refused a job because of such an agreement could seek a declaration from the NIRC. In the absence of such a declaration however there was no sanction which could be invoked against the specific practice of pre-entry closed shops, the continued operation of which limited the opportunities for workers to get into a position whereby they could successfully establish that an employer had committed an unfair industrial practice by infringing their right not to belong. For the same reason post-entry closed shop practices could continue to operate by limiting the opportunities for workers to challenge them. There was therefore relatively little attraction for trade unions in the agency and approved closed shop provisions of the Act. They were only open to registered organisations and the few unions which did register were ultimately expelled from the TUC with the consequent loss of the protection of the TUC procedures regulating inter-union competition. Equity and the NUS took advantage of the approved closed shop agreement procedure which was enacted for their benefit and enabled them to continue to operate closed shops as long as they allowed conscientious objectors to pay contributions to charity instead of union dues. But, apart from NUBE and the Bakers' Union, few trade unions which remained registered actively pursued agency shop agreements where the right of workers to pay contributions to the union while remaining non-members also had to be recognised.

One effect of the IRA was to develop an awareness particularly in management of the need to operate tight closed shops to avoid the potential disruption which workers who did not belong to closed shop unions could cause by asserting their legal rights. This awareness has inevitably been carried over into post-IRA practice because of the continued presence of the law, albeit very different law from the IRA. The evidence suggests that both management and unions would have liked to have revived the previous relaxed attitude towards the operation of closed shops, but retention of the law on unfair dismissal made this impossible.[6] Because the sanctions of unfair dismissal operate against management (subject now to the joinder provisions of the Employment Act) it was in management's interest to have an efficiently run closed shop in order not to have to face and lose complaints of unfair dismissal by employees dismissed because they did not belong to closed shop unions. Since the closed shop is generally seen as a practice which is primarily for the benefit of unions, this apparent paradox needs to be borne in mind in analysing the development and impact of the law after 1974.

THE CLOSED SHOP AND UNFAIR DISMISSAL: 1974—1980

There is not and never has been a legal requirement to operate a closed shop: it is purely a question of voluntary arrangement and negotiation. In fact the modern law which is relevant to the closed shop is to be found mainly in the statutory provisions on employment protection. The rights of employees to complain of unfair dismissal and action short of dismissal are qualified in certain respects where employment is subject to the practice of membership of one or more specified unions in accordance with a union membership agreement (UMA). The provisions originally enacted in 1974 and 1975 were significantly amended in 1976 and the resulting position consolidated in the EPCA 1978. The Employment Act has made further extensive amendments of a very different nature to those passed in 1976. It has also added in ss.4 and 5 a new right for an employee who is or wishes to be in UMA employment. This is exercisable against a specified trade union which has excluded him from membership. It thus forms a novel addition to that aspect of internal trade union law concerned with the rights of members and individuals excluded from membership and it is considered separately in the next chapter.

Under the unfair dismissal provisions originally enacted in the IRA, the dismissal of an employee because he did not belong to a trade union as required by a closed shop practice was automatically unfair unless the closed shop was an agency or approved closed shop and the dismissed employee was not a conscientious objector prepared to pay contributions to charity or, in the case of an agency shop, a non-member prepared to pay contributions to the union. In 1974 TULRA made express provision that where membership of a specified union was the practice for all employees of the relevant class in accordance with a UMA, dismissal for non-membership of a specified union was fair. This was subject to exceptions for employees who genuinely objected on grounds of religious belief to being a member of any union or on any 'reasonable' grounds to being a member of a particular union: their dismissal was automatically unfair. UMAs were defined as agreements or arrangements having the effect of requiring the terms and conditions of employment of every employee of the relevant class to include a condition that the employee must be a member of a union party to the agreement or arrangement or of another appropriate union.

This position was an unhappy compromise between the intentions of a minority Labour government and the combined forces of the main opposition parties. It was difficult for employers and unions to operate closed shops which were consistent with these requirements for various reasons. First establishing the existence of a practice for all employees of the relevant class to belong to a specified union was bound to cause difficulties in large areas of closed shop employment, even though the EAT acknowledged that the legislation did permit some very small degree of tolerated non-membership (*Home Counties Dairies* v. *Woods,* 1977). In the celebrated 'Ferrybridge Six' case (*Sarvent* v. *CEGB,* 1976), the employers could not rely on the fair dismissal provision because they could not establish the practice of membership of one of the four closed shop unions in the face of evidence that some 1,000 out of 39,000 employees did not belong. Therefore the CEGB had no defence against the allegation that the highly selective dismissals of activists in the breakaway Electricity Supply Union was unfair. Second the 'other appropriate union' which UMAs had to permit employees to belong to was not defined, although it was held not to extend to *any* independent trade union. Third the basis for objection to membership of a particular union on any reasonable grounds was not established, a fact of some significance in relation to the changes in the law made by the Employment Act. Indeed in the 'Ferrybridge Six' case the tribunal expressly declined to make public their views on the point on the grounds that it was a 'political and sociological' issue and therefore not suitable for an industrial tribunal to resolve.

These difficulties were all removed by amendments made in 1976. As re-enacted in EPCA s.58(3) the law on unfair dismissal provided that dismissal for non-membership of a specified union was fair if it was the practice in accordance with a UMA for employees for the time being of the same class as the dismissed employee to belong to a specified union or one of several specified unions. This was subject to an exception where the dismissed employee genuinely objected on grounds of religious belief to being a member of any trade union, in which case the dismissal was unfair.

The Labour government was prepared to concede a right to dissociate on the grounds of genuine objection to membership of any trade union based on religious belief because it was thought to be relatively easy to ascertain whether the beliefs of a particular creed or faith precluded trade union membership. There are, for example, certain Christian sects which prohibit association with non-Christians (believers must 'not be unequally yoked with unbelievers', 2 *Corinthians* VI. 14) and whose adherents are therefore unable to join any external organisation whatsoever. As interpreted by the EAT though, the statutory exception was given a much wider ambit. It was held to extend to any employee whose own subjective interpretation of the requirements of his religion meant that he genuinely believed that he should not join a trade union even if adherence to this particular creed did not of itself preclude union membership (*Saggers* v. *British Railways Board*, 1977 (No. 2) 1978). This made the exception somewhat open-ended even to the extent of substituting personal conscience for religious belief.

Meaning of UMA

The definition of UMA has remained in TULRA s.30 as amended and it has not been altered by the Employment Act. It covers agreements or arrangements between independent unions and employers or employers' associations relating to employees of identifiable classes. The effect of the agreement or arrangement must be to require employees for the time being of the class to which it relates (whether as a formal condition of their contracts of employment or not) to belong to a union party to it or to another specified union, that is, a union specified in it or accepted by the parties to it as equivalent to a union so specified. With reference to this definition it is provided that employees are treated as belonging to the same class if identified as such by the parties to the UMA and that they can be so identified by reference to any characteristics or circumstances whatsoever.

The definition embraces informal 'arrangements' as well as formal agreements. This no doubt reflects the fact that up to 1974 closed shops were typically informal though the LSE project revealed that most closed shops established or renegotiated since then have been embodied in formal agreements. It is clear that the UMA definition does not include all closed shop practices and it may be a matter for argument in a suitable case whether a practice which satisfies the other requirements of the definition is an 'arrangement' which 'exists between' the employer(s) and independent unions concerned. Only independent trade unions can be parties to UMAs (on the meaning of independence see p. 62).

One of the most important changes made in 1976 was the rider to the definition which enables the class of employees to whom the practice of union membership applies to be identified 'by reference to any characteristics or circumstances whatsoever'. This was designed in particular to meet fears vociferously expressed in 1974–76 that the UMA provisions as a whole were a threat to the freedom of the press. Complete flexibility in defining the class of employees covered enables specified employees such as editors or even named individuals to be expressly excluded from the scope of the UMA. In the same way employees who objected to union membership on grounds of religious belief could be excluded from the requirement of membership by the terms of the UMA. The LSE project confirmed that religious objection has been widely accepted by unions and management as a legitimate ground for avoiding union membership.

Further elements of flexibility were introduced in 1976 by limiting the requirement of union membership to a matter of practice irrespective of whether or not it was a term of the individual contract of employment, and by removing the reference to membership of *all* employees. The significance of this change was recognised by the EAT in *Taylor* v. *Co-operative Retail Services Ltd.* (1981) where it was held that no particular percentage of employees in membership was required; in a disputed case it was a question of fact for the tribunal to decide whether the required practice existed. However, as already noted, one effect of the 1970s legislation generally has been to encourage a tighter operation of closed shops. Where too great a degree of tolerance of non-membership is shown there will always be the risk that the practice of membership is not sufficient to satisfy the UMA definition and in that case the employer will be unable to rely on the 'fair dismissal' provision in s.58(3).

Finally it should be noted that the specified union of which membership is required need not necessarily be a party to the UMA or even expressly specified in it. Thus if, for example, certain existing employees are allowed to retain their membership of a union not party to the UMA when it takes effect or certain skilled workers are permitted to belong to an appropriate craft union although in a class of employees to whom a UMA between their employer and other unions applies, the requirements of the UMA definition may still be satisfied.

What the employer has to prove

In order to be able to rely on the fair dismissal provision in EPCA s.58(3) the employer must prove that the reason for dismissal was that the employee was not a member of a specified union. If the employer believes this to be the case but it later transpires that his belief was mistaken, whether or not he can rely on s.58(3) will depend on the circumstances. While it has been established that he may be able to rely on information from union officials that the employee is no longer a member he is required nevertheless to investigate the matter at a responsible level. What this is will depend on the industrial relations realities of the particular situation.[7]

A further judicial gloss has been placed on the words of s.58(3) where the UMA contains procedures for processing disputed cases of individuals who refuse to join or who lose their membership. Over half of the UMAs covered by the LSE project contained special procedures for dealing with issues arising out of the operation of the agreement. Where these include conditions which have to be fulfilled before dismissal for non-membership occurs it is incumbent on the employer to show that he has satisfied them before he can rely on s.58(3),[8] unless the procedural deviations were very minor or insignificant or unless it was for the employee to initiate the procedure but he failed to do so.[9] Other attempts by employees to avoid the impact of s.58(3) have been unsuccessful. It still applies where the UMA requires non-members to pay dues to charity and the employee was dismissed for failing to do so, and it overrides inconsistent provisions in individual contracts of employment.[10]

THE LAW AFTER THE EMPLOYMENT ACT 1980

Although the Conservative government elected in 1979 was hostile to any form of closed shop practice, the Employment Act did not remove the main provision in EPCA s.58(3): that the dismissal of an employee of a class to which a UMA applies because he does not belong to a specified union is fair. Instead EA s.7 has attempted to emasculate it by creating three new excepted categories; the dismissal of employees who are not members of specified unions and who fall into one of these categories is automatically unfair. First the religious belief exception has been expanded to cover genuine objection 'on grounds of conscience or other deeply held personal conviction' either to union membership in general or to membership of a particular union (EPCA s.58(3A)). The second category covers employees who were in the relevant employment before the UMA took effect and have not belonged to a specified union while it has been in effect (s.58(3B)). The third category comprises non-members where the UMA took effect after 14 August 1980 without the approval of 80 per cent of the relevant class of employees who were eligible to vote in a secret ballot (s.58(3C)). Where such a ballot does give the necessary 80 per cent approval, those who remain non-members after the ballot are still within the exception.

The retention of EPCA s.58(3) in any form was the subject of criticism from some quarters on the grounds that the government was thereby recognising the legitimacy of the closed shop. The government justified not attempting to outlaw the closed shop by reference to the failure of that approach in the IRA. The new excepted categories, the joinder provisions, the Closed Shop Code, and the restriction by EA s.18 of acts to compel union membership (see chapter nine) were presented as a pragmatic approach, which recognised the realities of industrial practice and limitations of the law but sought to establish the protection for individual rights necessary to deal with abuses. At the same time employers were to be supported in adopting a firm and responsible approach towards closed shops. This justification is a key part of the posture of moderation which the government projected for the Act as a whole. But if the EA is but the first step of a step-by-step approach, its goals appear to be in many respects and certainly as regards the closed shop essentially the same as those of the IRA. Although the structure of section 58(3) is retained, the real intention of the amendments made by EA s.7 can be seen as establishing a position in which 'for all practical purposes existing union membership agreements can be undermined and future union membership agreements will be virtually impossible to negotiate'.[11]

Conscience or deeply-held personal conviction

The extension of the religious belief exception to genuine objection 'on grounds of conscience or other deeply-held personal conviction to being a member of any trade union whatsoever or of a particular trade union' (EPCA s.58(3A) inserted by EA s.7(2)) has revived the debate carried on at length both inside and outside Parliament from 1974–76. The Working Paper on the Closed Shop indicated that the government was uncertain whether or not to restore the original 1974 position when the exception covered employees who objected to membership of a particular trade union on any reasonable grounds. In the event this was rejected on the grounds that it would have imported an objective test into something essentially subjective and was not sufficiently precise. The phrase 'deeply-held personal conviction' was considered appropriate because judicial interpretation of 'conscience' had held it to have necessary connotations of religion.[12] It was moreover taken to be axiomatic that conscience or deeply-held personal conviction should not be limited to unions in general but included objections to particular trade unions. Whether or not 'reasonable grounds' would import an element of objectivity into the issue, the admission that this category of exception is essentially subjective is the most damning criticism that can be made of it as a basis for successfully assimilating the law into closed shop practice. The subjective construction placed on the religious belief exception was open to the same criticism but at least it still required some link, however tenuous, to be established between the employee's subjective views and a creed of religious beliefs. By itself conscience might be similarly confined. But the possible range of other deeply-held personal convictions must be unlimited. Although the Closed Shop Code offers no guidance on this particular exception, the Lord Chancellor conceded in debate that it could embrace objections to the political purposes of a union.[13] This is moreover just one aspect of the potential of EA s.7 as a whole for increasing inter-union conflict. Employees may

develop deeply-held personal convictions against unions specified for
the purposes of a UMA because of their support for the political stance
of competing unions. One of the perceived advantages of closed shops
as a basis for stability in industrial relations is thus threatened in a way
which the religious objection exception did not permit.

Another basic criticism that can be made of a legally recognised right
to dissociate on grounds of conscience or other deeply-held personal
conviction is that there is no social consensus about what are legitimate
grounds for objecting to trade union membership. As the LSE project
revealed, a variety of acceptable grounds for non-membership of a
specified union are written into UMAs as a matter of practice: religious
beliefs, conscience including moral grounds and deeply-held personal
conviction and 'reasonable' grounds are among the most common. But
while management and unions may agree on the ambit of these exclusions in the context of their own voluntary arrangements, it does not
follow particularly after the experience of the IRA that they can be
satisfactorily adopted as criteria for legal rights. If however the aim is
rather to make closed shop practices as difficult as possible to operate
and so to undermine their efficacy, then the new open-ended criteria
are admirably suited to their purpose.

Existing employees

The case for legal recognition of the right of existing employees who
are not members of a specified union to remain free from an obligation
to join when a UMA takes effect is no doubt also a reflection of the
best prevailing practice.[14] The LSE project found that two thirds of the
UMAs surveyed made such a provision without further qualification.
Others allowed existing employees who were members of non-specified
unions to remain outside membership of any of the UMA unions. One
of the dangers of tolerating members of other unions is the risk of inter-
union conflict. The new legal right exacerbates this risk, particularly if
members of other independent unions try to exercise their legal right to
take part in union activities *on the employer's premises*. While in a
closed shop they have no protection against action by the employer
short of dismissal to prevent or deter them from doing this or penalising
them for it, it is an inadmissible reason for dismissal and automatically
unfair under EPCA s.58(1)(b).

An equally fundamental point is that the existence of a significant
number of employees who do not belong to a specified union, whether

because they were non-members when the UMA took effect or because to dismiss them would be unfair under the deeply-held personal conviction exception, could preclude the possibility of the employer proving the requisite 'practice' of union membership. This is as we have seen essential if he is to take advantage of EPCA s.58(3), that is, to avoid liability for unfair dismissal of any employee for non-membership of a specified union.

UMAs agreed after 14 August 1980

The introduction of the third category of exception in respect of closed shops agreed after the commencement of the 1980 Act is based on the premise that many people are forced into closed shops against their wishes. The Working Paper on the Closed Shop envisaged that the legislation would require 'overwhelming' support in a secret ballot and that advice as to the exact percentage would be provided in the forthcoming Code. In the event, EPCA s.58A stipulates the need for support from 80 per cent of those eligible to vote. But the Closed Shop Code states that 80 per cent is a 'minimum' figure 'to furnish employers with a defence against possible future unfair dismissal claims or complaints of action short of dismissal', and that the employer might decide that there should be a higher percentage in favour before agreeing to 'such a radical change in his employees' terms and conditions of employment' (para. 35). This is misleading in so far as it implies that if an employer only agrees to establish a UMA after a higher percentage is achieved he may not be able subsequently to rely on the fair dismissal provision in s.58(3) if this higher level of support is not forthcoming. An employer can rely on s.58(3) (subject to the two other exceptions) in respect of any UMA practice taking effect after 14 August 1980 where a ballot held in accordance with s.58A has demonstrated the support of 80 per cent of the employees eligible to vote for the introduction of the practice. Encouraging employers to require a higher percentage is but a thinly disguised expression of a government policy opposed to the creation of any new closed shops.

The new regime for post-14 August 1980 UMAs is in fact generally short on statutory detail and leaves many questions unanswered. For one thing it seems to leave no scope for informal arrangements which 'exist between' employers and independent trade unions. Since the required level of support is 80 per cent of those eligible to vote, precise definition of the constituency is of paramount importance. Section

58A(2) defines this as all employees of an employer of any class to which a UMA would apply on the day on which the ballot is held. Since it is for other purposes possible to define that class by reference to any characteristic or circumstances whatsoever, s.58(3E) provides that for this purpose it cannot be defined by reference to union membership or objection to membership. But clearly there might be scope for argument as to the ambit of the relevant class or classes, as to who was in the relevant employment on the day in question and indeed as to which members of the class were 'employees'. Similarly s.58A(3) provides general guidance as to the conduct of a ballot under the section stating only that so far as is reasonably practicable all those entitled to vote must have an opportunity of voting and doing so in secret. The guidance in the Closed Shop Code on secret ballots (paras. 33–36) does not resolve the many difficulties that may arise. For example, paragraph 34(iii) suggests that employees should be aware of the intention to hold a ballot, the terms of the UMA and 'any other relevant information'. Could this include a statement of the case against a UMA from persons opposed to it? Could a ballot be invalidated on the grounds that all relevant information was not provided? Paragraph 34(iv) suggests that the ballot form should be confined to a single question. Could the presence of other questions invalidate the ballot? What is the position if, despite the advice of paragraph 34(v), no arrangements are made for those absent from work and therefore unable to vote in a workplace ballot?

These questions may all be hypothetical if unions and management choose not to use the ballot procedure to sanctify closed shop practices. But the point is fundamental. If the government wishes to move to regulation of UMAs by ballot – and paragraph 45 of the Closed Shop Code suggests extending the practice to *existing* UMAs (see below) – then there is logically no escape from the sort of detailed supervision and regulation once provided for by the Industrial Relations Act. Ballots were an integral part of the IRA's elaborate agency and approved closed shop procedures. However the IRA did enable such agreements to take effect without a ballot where employers and unions were agreed and, in the case of approved closed shops, a favourable report from the CIR had been received. Twenty per cent of the workers covered by such an agreement could require a ballot to be held and it could then continue only if 50 per cent of those eligible to vote or two thirds of those actually voting supported it. A union could also request a ballot on whether an agency shop should be established where the employer would not enter into a voluntary agreement. If one or other of the above-mentioned support levels (which are less stringent than the 80 per cent requirement of the EA) was achieved, an agency shop could be imposed on the employer. Although the intricacies of these procedures with their attendant sanctions were barely touched on in practice,[15] the IRA provisions demonstrate the extent of the technicalities necessarily involved in any serious attempt to make closed shop practices subject to systematic regulation by ballot. Such are the implications of paragraph 45 of the Code and also paragraph 277 of the Green Paper *Trade Union Immunities,* which indicated that some form of mandatory review by ballot is under consideration.

It must be remembered that in industrial tribunal proceedings adherence to the statutory requirements on ballots can only become an issue on a complaint of either unfair dismissal or action short of dismissal to compel union membership. At that stage many disputed points will be beyond proof unless detailed records of any ballot held are retained. Since it is for the individual employee to bring his case within EPCA s.58(3C) he might possibly seek to establish this in advance by a High Court challenge to any ballot in fact held. If this happened it could introduce the worst kind of legalism into closed shop practices. Moreover it is probable that any serious attempt to comply with the statutory ballot requirements would involve ACAS in efforts to resolve disputed issues. The Closed Shop Code expressly refers to the availability of ACAS's conciliation services where there are disagreements in the arrangements for secret ballots (para. 36). In view of the controversial nature of the provisions, it is unlikely that this is a task which ACAS would relish since it could place its reputation as a neutral conciliator at risk.

If the legal regime for new UMAs is not observed, operation of closed shop practices taking effect after 14 August 1980 could be seen as in some way unlawful. It is possible that an individual adversely affected could succeed in civil proceedings for an injunction or damages against the union officials and employers concerned on the argument that non-observance of these provisions provided the ingredients of 'unlawful means' for liability in tort (see chapter nine). One way or another the introduction of new closed shop practices could become difficult to achieve without the risk of some legal penalty, though it is probably true that both sides of industry will do their best to contrive the continuance of most existing closed shops.

COMPENSATING THE UNFAIRLY DISMISSED NON-MEMBER

As was explained in chapter three, a complaint of unfair dismissal arising from employment governed by a UMA is now subject to the joinder provisions introduced by EA s.10 (under which the union or other person applying industrial pressure can be ordered to indemnify the employer for compensation paid to the unfairly dismissed non-unionist). While it is important to stress again that the application of the joinder principle is not confined to cases of dismissal from UMA employment, it is in this area that it is most likely to be invoked. This is because pressure to dismiss an employee because of his non-membership of a union is to be expected in employment subject to some form of closed shop practice; most closed shop practices fall within the ambit of EPCA s.58(3) and thus of the Employment Act's three exceptions when dismissal from UMA employment for non-membership of a specified union is automatically unfair.

There can be no doubt that the joinder provisions provide an incentive to the employer to resist dismissing employees who refuse to belong to trade unions even if subjected to pressure to do so by the threat of industrial action. But what if he does succumb to the pressure? If the employment is subject to the practice of membership of a specified union in accordance with a UMA and the employee falls within one of the permitted exceptions so that his dismissal is automatically unfair, the employer can then invite the industrial tribunal to order the union, officials or workers responsible for organising the industrial action to make a contribution of up to 100 per cent in respect of the compensation award. The same is true of course if the relevant closed shop practice is not in accordance with a UMA but the reason for dismissal is still found to be the employee's non-membership and the dismissal is held to be unfair.

In the previous chapter it was suggested that the joinder provisions make the right to organise exercisable only at a high cost to workers and their unions. The risk that the integrity of closed shop practices can only be maintained against non-unionists at the expense of the closed shop unions and workers who belong to them is more patent and even greater. Indeed the Employment Act's encouragement to employers to resist the dismissal of non-unionists should be viewed as a step towards the ultimate objective of completely undermining closed shop practices.

ACTION BY EMPLOYERS SHORT OF DISMISSAL

Employees' rights in EPCA s.23 in respect of action short of dismissal taken against them by their employers on account of their union membership and activities or non-membership were analysed in the previous chapter. It is convenient here to summarise the modifications to these rights which apply where the relevant employment is subject to the practice of membership of a specified union in accordance with a UMA.

An employee's right not to have action short of dismissal taken against him by his employer because of his union activities is limited to the activities of a specified union so far as activities on the employer's premises are concerned. This modification was in the original EPCA s.23. As redrafted and amended by EA s.15(2) however it only applies in respect of UMAs taking effect after 14 August 1980 where they were approved by 80 per cent of those eligible to vote in a secret ballot. The absence of any similar modification to the parallel provision in respect of dismissal for taking part in union activities (EPCA s.58(1)(b)) is part of a wider inconsistency in these statutory provisions both before and after amendment. The Employment Act's amendment appears to limit the potential use of legal rights to promote inter-union rivalry and conflict. In practice the qualification in respect of closed shops taking effect after 14 August 1980 combined with the unqualified 'right' not to be dismissed for taking part in the activities of *any* independent union on the employer's premises means that the significance of this ostensible support for closed shop practices is minimal.

The same comment applies to the modification of an employee's right not to have action short of dismissal taken against him by his employer for the purpose of compelling him to belong to any trade union (EPCA s.23(1)(c) as amended by EA s.15(1)). Where employment is subject to a UMA, this right is confined to employees who fall within one of the three excepted categories of non-membership. The uncertainties surrounding the circumstances when s.23(1)(c) is infringed and the indeterminate ambit of these three excepted categories make the extent and importance of the differences between the right to dissociate inside and outside UMA employment virtually impossible to assess.

Finally there is the joinder provision (which also applies outside UMA employment). Where an employer takes action short of dismissal to compel an employee to join a UMA specified union as a result of pressure from industrial action, those responsible for this pressure may be joined by the employer to proceedings on any complaint by the employee for the purpose of seeking an order that they make a contribution to any compensation awarded (EPCA s.26A added by EA s.15(4)). The comments made above with respect to EA s.10 apply equally to joinder in this context.

CODE OF PRACTICE ON CLOSED SHOP AGREEMENTS AND ARRANGEMENTS

The Closed Shop Code forms an essential complement to the changes in the law made by the Employment Act. The government recognised the limitations of the law as such in bringing about 'the far-reaching changes in the procedures and institutions of collective bargaining which we all know are essential if there is to be any improvement in our industrial performance'.[16] One of the stated aims of the Code is to explain the law in layman's terms and to illustrate the standards of the statute. It is however the other stated aim, providing guidance as to good industrial relations practice, which will help to achieve 'far-reaching changes'. Indeed the Code must be seen as guidance towards the reduction and eventual elimination of closed shop practices, a point on which both its supporters and its critics would agree.

The explanation of the law for the layman is contained in Section B which is headed 'Legal Rights of Individuals'. Its scope is in fact confined to the rights of individuals who either do not want to join or are excluded from a union of which membership is required in accordance with a closed shop. The rights of trade unionists who support closed shops are not mentioned although the law has not yet been changed so that they have none. Nor of course is there any reference to the rights of trade unions. McCarthy described this aspect of the Code as so partisan, confused and incomplete that the trade union movement would be forced to provide its own rather different version of the law.[17]

Practical advice

The general guidance on closed shops is to be found in Section C.[18] It begins with advice to employers and unions on matters to be taken into account before 'there is any question of negotiating on proposals for a closed shop'. This part contains the first group of forty or more ob-

stacles, conditions or exceptions intended to induce employers to pre-
varicate. The guidance is essentially confined to suggestions limiting the
circumstances in which employers should agree to and unions should
press for closed shops, though the underlying assumption that employers will be generally disposed to oppose closed shops and only concede them under trade union pressure hardly reflects the reality of the
management interest in the practice. The anti-closed shop tone is equally strong in the Code's guidance on the scope and content of closed
shop agreements, which includes the advice that a UMA should provide
that an employee will not be dismissed if expelled from his union for
refusal to take part in industrial action (para. 30(v)).

Perhaps the most provocative and dubious part of the Code is the
suggested provision for periodic review of existing closed shops and a
procedure for their termination (paras. 30(vii) and 42—46). The consultative draft Code's treatment of this issue met with considerable
opposition from employers' organisations as well as the TUC. This led
the House of Commons Select Committee on Employment to suggest
that this proposal should be deleted.[19] Modifications to the suggested
occasions for review were in fact made to meet the reservations expressed by the CBI. The final version of the Code in paragraph 43 proposes
reviews every few years or more frequently where there is evidence that
the support of employees has declined, where there has been a change
in the parties to the agreement, where there is evidence that any part of
it is not working satisfactorily or where 'there is a change in the law
affecting the closed shop, such as the Employment Act 1980'. The
express reference to the Employment Act presumably means that all
closed shops in operation prior to the summer of 1980 should be reviewed. After the review the Code envisages that either party might give
notice to terminate, or, if the continuation of the closed shop is jointly
favoured, there should be a secret ballot 'to test opinion' (para. 45). In
suggesting regular ballots and also that no new pre-entry shops should
be introduced because they may infringe 'the freedom of individuals to
work' (para. 46), the Code is attempting to legislate by the backdoor. It
may of course be trailing possible future legislative changes but there is
no law in the EA or elsewhere which requires closed shops to be period-
ically approved by ballot to retain their validity. Nor does the law
impugn the validity of pre-entry shops, however much the government
might desire the courts to develop the common law so that it did. If the
government wish to make regular ballots compulsory and to outlaw the
pre-entry shop it is incumbent on it to propose legislation to this effect.

Freedom of the press

The most curious passages of the Closed Shop Code are contained in
Section E (paras. 56–61) on 'The Closed Shop and Freedom of the
Press'. Section E replaces s.1A of TULRA which was repealed by EA
s.19(a) on 22 December 1980, just after the Code came into operation.
The insertion of s.1A into TULRA by the Amendment Act of 1976 was
the unhappy compromise resulting from an extensive two year debate
over whether and if so to what extent the legislation on unfair dismissal
and the closed shop posed a threat to the somewhat ill-defined freedom
of the press.[20] The fears expressed concerned the possibility of a closed
shop for journalists, including editors, leading to the unions dictating
the editorial content of newspapers and circumscribing an editor's freedom to decide what and what not to print. This it was argued could
occur because if an editor resisted the union's wishes he would put his
union membership at risk. If he lost this he could be dismissed, fairly
under the terms of the legislation.

Section 1A of TULRA required the Secretary of State to prepare a
charter on the freedom of the press providing guidance on these issues
if, as proved to be the case, employers, editors and unions had not
agreed one. The charter would have been admissible in court and tribunal proceedings in much the same way as failure to observe the
provisions of a code of practice. Although proposals were made, no
charter was ever presented to Parliament for the requisite approval.
Section E of the Closed Shop Code may be taken to be the present
government's views on what it should have contained.

The gist of these six paragraphs is that the freedom of the press to
publish information, comment and criticism is in potential conflict with
the actions of trade unions and 'in particular any requirement on
journalists to join a union creates the possibility of such a conflict'
(para. 57). Thus employers and unions should respect the feeling of any
journalist that union membership is incompatible with his professional
freedom (para. 58), and a journalist should not be disciplined by a
union for anything written or any research carried out according to
'generally accepted professional standards' (para. 59). An editor must
be free to decide whether or not to become or remain a union member
(para. 60) and needs to be free from improper pressure seeking to influence how he exercises his final responsibility for contents 'within the
agreed basic policy' of his publication (para. 61).

A lot of this is so vague as to be capable of a wide range of interpretation. Who can claim to be an editor? What are 'generally accepted

professional standards'? Does freedom of the press extend beyond freedom from any collective pressure from journalists? For example, the Code is resoundingly silent on the issue of proprietorial monopoly and the drastic effect that may have on the content and bias of newspapers. Overall, perhaps it would not be sensible to take this part of the Code too seriously. Its relatively quiet reception suggests that a lot of the fears expressed in 1974—76 lacked any real substance. The present state of the law certainly makes bizarre provisions such as those in Section E of the Code superfluous.

THE SURVIVAL OF THE CLOSED SHOP

By seeking to erect obstacles going beyond those created by the Employment Act itself the Code clearly demonstrates the government's intention to make it as difficult as possible to maintain and develop closed shop practices. McCarthy described its non-legal guidance as written from the point of view of a 'bigoted and ignorant opponent of the closed shop' essentially addressed to employers and industrial tribunals, both being invited to make it as difficult as possible for trade unions to obtain and enforce closed shops.[21] This rhetoric may be colourful but the essential point is valid. It may be suggested that the changes made in 1980 are likely to lead to the same degree of involvement with the law as under the IRA and with the risk of the same result. That is not only that the law fails to eliminate closed shop practices other than those statutorily approved. Legal recognition for the right to dissociate did not in practice benefit individual dissenters. It served rather as a catalyst for inter-union rivalry which the stability provided by closed shops helps to limit. Stability and order in industrial relations are goals generally espoused by the supporters of a general right to dissociate. To achieve the latter at the expense of the former is not on the face of it a good bargain let alone a fair one.

A similar lack of perspective was implicit in the majority opinion of the European Commission on Human Rights.[22] This was to the effect that the individual right to 'freedom of association with others, including the right to form and join trade unions for the protection of his interests' in Article 11 of the European Convention on Human Rights necessarily implies the right to choose which trade union to join. It was given on complaints by three former employees of British Rail who were dismissed because they refused to join one of the three rail unions as required by the closed shop agreement between British Rail and the unions. Because the pre-EA law on unfair dismissals as applied to UMA employment did not recognise the freedom to choose which union to join, the majority concluded that Article 11 had been violated. Final resolution of these complaints depends on the decision of the European Court on Human Rights. If it follows this majority opinion, any changes made to the domestic law to bring it into line with Article 11 as so interpreted would further extend the scope for inter-union disputes.[23]

It is not yet clear whether the Employment Act and the Code will achieve the disruption of closed shop practices which the government so clearly desires. The January 1981 Green Paper *Trade Union Immunities* contemplated the possibility of further legal changes: voiding closed shop agreements; making the periodic review of closed shops either mandatory in order to attract protection against unfair dismissal complaints by dismissed non-members, or available at the request of a fixed percentage of the employees covered; and a general right of complaint to an industrial tribunal against unreasonable operation of the closed shop. The Green Paper acknowledged the obvious limitations and disadvantages of all these steps (paras. 273–281). There is little doubt that they would politicise the industrial tribunals and discredit them in the eyes of trade unions and their members. Uncertainty as to whether legal regulation would achieve its goals was also expressed by the Green Paper with reference to attempts to proscribe the practices of refusing to handle work from non-union companies, refusing to work with non-union labour and union labour only contract clauses (paras. 287–302). But memories of the IRA experience seem to be short-lived and if the EA and Code leave the more vociferous opponents of the closed shop unsatisfied, such steps may be taken.

5

Trade Union Membership

The relationship between the individual member and his union has historically been governed by the contract of membership embodied in the rules of the union. The Employment Act introduces in ss.4 and 5 a new jurisdiction which cuts across this traditional legal pattern. The Act's novel remedies are in addition to and interact with the common law rights of individuals based on the rule book, and it is the common law position which we consider first.[1]

INDIVIDUAL RIGHTS AND THE COMMON LAW

British trade unions have the legal status of voluntary unincorporated associations: they have no corporate legal personality independent from that of their members.[2] The legal definition of a trade union embraces any (even temporary) organisation of workers whose de facto principal purposes include the regulation of relations between workers and employers (TULRA s.28(1)). Further, the procedures for entry in the list of trade unions and certification of independence are not obligatory and a body of workers which is in law a trade union may legitimately refrain even from the purely administrative process of listing. With certain exceptions, trade unions may draw up their rule books in accordance with the normal freedom of contract.

A key aspect of trade unions' voluntary character is their freedom to determine their own rules governing applications for membership. It follows that rejected applicants have only limited rights at common law to challenge the union's refusal to admit them. The courts will construe the rules strictly as respects both substantive and procedural requirements, but they will not strike down union admission rules simply because they appear to be arbitrary. In the *Faramus* case (above p. 78), it was said that with more than four times as many people seeking

99

employment as film extras as there were jobs available 'the rules as to admission of membership must inevitably be in some degree arbitrary'.[3] Some judges however would like to exert a wider controlling power to strike down rules which infringe what Lord Denning has long championed as the 'right to work'.[4] But there are as yet no authoritative grounds for saying that such control exists. Indeed if there were the government might have thought twice about the need for introducing the new rights for individuals in the Employment Act. (It should however be noted that both the Sex Discrimination Act 1975 s.12 and the Race Relations Act 1976 s.11 prohibit discrimination by trade unions on grounds of sex, marital status and race in respect of admission and also disciplinary action including expulsion.)

An individual member has far greater common law rights against a union than an applicant for membership. The basis of most of these rights is the contract in the rule book, a contract between all the members and, to the extent that a trade union is an independent entity even though not a corporation, a contract between each member and the union. The content of the rules is subject to little statutory regulation, the most important provisions being those in the Trade Union Act 1913 concerning political fund rules; also the financial administration of unions is subject to fairly detailed control under the supervision of the Certification Officer.[5]

The member's right to enforce the contract in the rule book is the basis of the common law safeguards in respect of discipline, of which the ultimate and most important sanction is expulsion. Although the disciplinary rules and procedures have not been subject to direct statutory regulation, strict construction of union rules by the judiciary has given the courts a very wide measure of control in this area. This is particularly evident with regard to discipline for contravening such general rules as 'action contrary or detrimental to the aims and interests of the union or its members'. The LSE closed shop project, which included a survey of the rule books of seventy-nine TUC-affiliated unions with a membership of just under twelve million (99 per cent of the TUC's total membership in 1979), found such general provision in the rule books of sixty-nine unions with a combined membership of 11.2 million. In most rule books there was a list of specific offences and then a blanket rule to cover unforeseen circumstances, though 900,000 members were in unions which had only the blanket rule.[6]

Members who wish to contest any disciplinary sanction imposed on them may and most probably will have rights of appeal within the union. The rules of seventy-five unions with 11.6 million members were found to provide a right of appeal. The use of internal appeals procedure is at the option of the individual member, and the courts now seem reluctant to recognise the enforceability of rules which require the exhaustion of the internal procedure prior to any High Court litigation against the union.[7] Any rule book provision which actually purports to oust the jurisdiction of the courts is ineffective and void at common law. When disciplining a member a union must strictly adhere to its own rules and the principles of natural justice. The latter broadly require that an individual be informed of the charges against him, given an adequate opportunity to prepare and present his defence, given a fair hearing and that a bona fide decision is reached. The LSE project found considerable diversity in the extent to which formal procedures were laid down in detail in the rules and embodied these standards. Whether or not the rules of natural justice are expressly written into disciplinary procedures, the courts will grant relief to an individual who has been subjected to disciplinary action without their having been observed.

The extent of the member's common law rights may be illustrated by some of the leading cases. The House of Lords decision in *Bonsor* v. *Musicians' Union* (1956) is the classic illustration of the need for strict observance of the rules. According to the rule book in this case, a member twenty-six weeks in arrears with his subscriptions could be expelled by his branch committee. Bonsor, who was fifty-two weeks in arrears, was expelled by the branch secretary. That technical defect was enough to enable him to obtain the remedies of an injunction and damages against the union. Strict construction of a blanket disciplinary rule is exemplified by *Esterman* v. *NALGO* (1974). Esterman, a NALGO member, who defied a union instruction not to co-operate in additional duties concerning local elections, was summoned to a disciplinary meeting by the branch committee. The relevant rule stated that any 'member ... who is guilty of conduct which, in the opinion of the [branch] executive committee, renders him unfit for membership, shall be liable to expulsion'. In advance of the meeting the judge granted an injunction restraining the union from all disciplinary action because he thought that no reasonable tribunal could possibly conclude that such disobedience to a union instruction demonstrated any unfitness to be a member.

Some of these cases reveal an inability on the part of the judges to hold a fair balance between the interests of the individual on the one hand and the interests of the union and the majority of members on the other, a proposition which may be supported by reference to decisions touching on inter-union relations. In *Spring* v. *NASD* (1956) the union expelled Spring in order to comply with an award of a Disputes Committee of the TUC. But it had no rule which expressly allowed for this and had to argue therefore that there was an implied power in the rules for it to expel members in accordance with the TUC's 'Bridlington' principles and procedures (on which see below p. 114). Because the individual member, Spring, had not heard of the Bridlington Agreement when he joined the union, the court held that there was no such implied power. The union's institutional interests, indeed, the interests of the union movement as a whole and of management in the orderly settlement of inter-union disputes could not prevail against this individualist approach. A similar moral may be drawn from *Rothwell* v. *APEX* (1976), a case which arose from an inter-union dispute in an insurance company. ASTMS was in competition for membership with an internal staff association, which then merged with APEX. ASTMS took the matter to a Disputes Committee of the TUC which awarded that APEX was in breach of the Bridlington principles and should therefore expel its members recently acquired from the staff association. Rothwell, the general secretary of the association, went to the High Court alleging that the decision of APEX to expel him was contrary to the union's own rule book, despite the fact that APEX had adopted the so-called 'model' rule which allows unions to expel in accordance with a decision of a TUC Disputes Committee under Bridlington. His expulsion was held to be in breach of the rules of APEX because the TUC award was itself void as a mistaken interpretation of its own principles. Thus the assertion of individual legal rights to enforce a rule book of one particular union led to an adverse judicial pronouncement on the TUC's procedures and mode of operation.

The enforcement of the contract of union membership may culminate in the legal remedies of declarations and injunctions (which normally involve reinstatement of membership) and also damages in order to provide financial compensation. A leading case on the measure of compensation is *Edwards* v. *SOGAT* (1971). The plaintiff, a Guyanese skilled printer, worked for a firm with a closed shop and a 'check-off' arrangement with SOGAT. He gave the necessary authorisation for his employer to check-off his union subscriptions from his wages but the union failed to arrange this by reason of an administrative muddle. He therefore fell into arrears and, under a rule providing for automatic forfeiture of membership in cases of six weeks of non-payment, he apparently ceased to be a member. In consequence the employer gave him notice and he lost his job. Because SOGAT operated a labour supply shop he could not obtain other work in the industry in the district. He was eventually readmitted and the union conceded that he had been expelled in breach of the rules. The question at issue was damages. The union was liable to compensate him for all the loss flowing from its wrongful act subject to his duty to mitigate the loss. The mitigation duty in the circumstances of this case did not require the plaintiff either to give up his occupation as a printer or to move from the district, and the Court of Appeal awarded him £3,500 damages.

It must be emphasised that the provisions of the Employment Act do not, to quote paragraph 18 of the Closed Shop Code, 'in any way detract from existing rights under the common law' (a point which is also clear from EA s.4(3)). Indeed the Closed Shop Code itself augments the common law rights of the individual member and applicant for membership. The legal effect of the Secretary of State's Codes under the 1980 Act (as will be more fully explained in chapter seven) is that they are admissible in evidence in proceedings before courts as well as tribunals and are, if relevant to a question, taken into account in determining that question. Many provisions in the Closed Shop Code are likely to be taken into account in common law cases brought by individuals against unions. For instance, according to Section D of the Code 'Union Treatment of Members and Applicants', in handling admissions 'unions should adopt and apply clear and fair rules covering: who is qualified for membership; who has power to consider and decide upon applications; what reasons will justify rejecting an application, the appeals procedure open to a rejected applicant; the power to admit applicants where an appeal is upheld' (para. 48). Paragraph 49 then specifies some of the criteria for admission. In handling discipline, 'unions should adopt and apply clear and fair rules covering: the offences for which the union is entitled to take disciplinary action and the penalties applicable for each of these offences; the procedure for hearing and determining complaints in which offences against the rules are alleged; a right of appeal against the imposition of any penalty; the procedure for the hearing of appeals against any penalty by a higher authority comprised of persons other than those who imposed the penalty; the principle that a recommendation for expulsion should not be made effective so long as a member is genuinely pursuing his appeal' (para. 50).

Suppose a union in the opinion of court has failed to 'adopt and apply clear and fair rules' on any of these matters. Or suppose that the case involves a UMA which has not been subjected to the test of a secret ballot contrary to paragraph 45 of the Code (see above p. 95). Suppose again that there is a pre-entry closed shop which infringes 'the freedom of individuals to work', which is now no longer purely a figment of Lord Denning's imagination since it appears in black and white in paragraph 46 of the Code. Numerous other paragraphs could be quoted, including the provision (see below p. 120) discouraging unions from taking disciplinary action against members who refuse to take part in industrial action. Clearly breach of the Code may be centrally relevant to many questions in cases involving the assertion of common law rights against unions. It will be taken into account by the court and will no doubt affect decisions on the interpretation of the express and implied terms of the contract of union membership and on the grant of legal remedies. However the court's decision is still tied to the issue of whether or not the rules have been observed. As we shall see, no such limitation applies to the individual rights under s.4 of the 1980 Act where the sole criterion is 'reasonableness'.

FROM DONOVAN TO THE EMPLOYMENT ACT

The Employment Act's regulation of trade union membership is comprehensible only in the light of earlier developments including not only the common law position but also the Donovan Report, the Industrial Relations Act 1971 and the Trade Union and Labour Relations Acts 1974–76. The Donovan analysis of union admission and expulsion was part of its consideration of the closed shop. Donovan rejected proposals for abolition of the closed shop but considered that safeguards for individuals were required inter alia in respect of admission and expulsion. Although concluding that 'there is little evidence that applications for membership are dealt with unfairly, or that membership is capriciously refused' (para. 610), it recommended that a union should make provision in its rules for a right of appeal by rejected applicants to its executive committee and thence to a proposed new independent review body. This body would also be the forum for appeals by those expelled from unions.[8] The TUC opposed legislation but in 1969 circularised affiliated unions with a series of proposals on rules and procedures as guidelines for voluntary reform. These stressed the need for clarity in the detail of rules on qualifications and procedures for admission, including a right of appeal, and also for disciplinary offences and procedures to comply with natural justice. The LSE project found that the rules of most of the larger unions affiliated to the TUC did not meet these standards but qualified all its findings by emphasising that conclusions as to actual practice in trade unions could not be drawn solely from a survey of formal rules.

The Industrial Relations Act made extensive additions to both the substantive and procedural aspects of the law concerning admission to and expulsion from trade unions, but these were not confined to closed shop employment. Unions which registered under the Act had to have rules on a wide range of issues (IRA Schedule 4). These included eligibility for membership, admission procedures including a right of appeal, conduct which could give rise to disciplinary action, disciplinary procedures, and 'any body by which, and any official by whom, instructions may be given to members of the organisation on its behalf for any kind of industrial action, and the circumstances in which any such instructions may be so given'. All unions whether registered or not could be obliged to comply with the 'guiding principles' in s.65 of the Act, which required that no appropriately qualified worker be excluded from membership by way of arbitrary or unreasonable discrimination. It proscribed disciplinary action that was unfair or unreasonable in general and action against a member for refusing to take part in industrial action which involved unfair industrial practices, or was organised other than in contemplation or furtherance of an industrial dispute (when it would almost certainly have been unlawful). And it required all union disciplinary procedures to conform with the rules of natural justice.

Overall these provisions caused very little change in either union rules or practices, though changes were made in the rules of some unions which remained registered. The relatively short period for which the Act was in force may partly explain this. That apart, although some of the requirements might have been of themselves unobjectionable, they were inextricably linked with the controls which the Act sought to impose on industrial action and were therefore unacceptable to the trade union movement. In any event the very small use made of the individual rights of complaint to industrial tribunals, the NIRC and Registrar of Trade Unions supported Donovan's conclusion that it was 'unlikely that abuse of power by trade unions is widespread' (para. 622).[9]

When the IRA was repealed in 1974, ss.5, 6 and 7 were inserted into

TULRA against the wishes of the minority Labour government. Section 7 provided that every union member would have the right to terminate his membership. Section 6 contained a list of mandatory subjects for trade union rules similar in many respects to IRA Schedule 4. Section 5 established a right for every worker not to be excluded or expelled from a union by way of arbitrary or unreasonable discrimination. Exclusion or expulsion of a worker because he was of a different description from the majority of the relevant part of the union or did not possess appropriate qualifications for such membership was expressed to be not of itself arbitrary or unreasonable. While s.5 gave the individual a right to seek a declaration that he was entitled to membership from an industrial tribunal, it was left to the High Court to award an injunction or such other relief as it thought just and expedient where a tribunal declaration was not 'implemented'. The deficiencies in the drafting of s.5 were not exposed by the small number of applications made to tribunals during the year and a half that it remained in force.[10]

In 1976 the Trade Union and Labour Relations (Amendment) Act repealed ss.5 and 6 but retained s.7 in modified form. It provides for an implied term in union rule books conferring a right on the member to terminate his membership on giving reasonable notice and complying with any reasonable conditions. Although this statutory right is not to be regarded as a bar on the enforcement of closed shops or on the operation of 'Bridlington', its existence ought not to be overlooked or forgotten particularly by union officers. As an alternative to the statutory regulation of admissions and expulsions, the TUC agreed to establish a three man Independent Review Committee (IRC) whose members were appointed by the TUC in consultation with the Secretary of State for Employment and the chairman of ACAS. Its function was (and is) to consider appeals from individuals who had been dismissed or given notice of dismissal as a result of having been expelled from or refused admission to a union in a situation where union membership was a condition of employment. The IRC, which is in some respects similar to the independent review body proposed by Donovan, was set up in April 1976 after the repeal of TULRA s.5. Before considering an appeal the IRC must be satisfied that the individual has exhausted internal union procedures and it will only make a recommendation about whether or not he should be admitted or readmitted if it cannot resolve the matter by agreement. Where a recommendation is made the IRC's terms of reference state that there is a clear responsibility on the part of the union involved to act on it. In his 1980 report to the TUC, the chairman of the IRC (Professor Lord Wedderburn) stated that in no case where it had made a recommendation had the union(s) failed to comply. By the end of June 1980, forty-seven complaints had been received, of which seventeen were outside the IRC's terms of reference. In nineteen of the remaining thirty a formal hearing was held. No recommendation was made in five of these. Recommendations for admission or readmission or for sympathetic consideration to be given to the possibility of admission or readmission were made in the remaining fourteen cases which involved twenty-one complainants.[11]

The establishment of the IRC and the TUC's 1969 proposals for reform of rules and procedures may be taken to be the voluntarist answer to the problems caused by refusal of admission to and expulsion from trade unions, both in the context of closed shop employment and outside it. The experience of the 1970s confirms the Donovan conclusion that there is little evidence of abuse of power by unions in this area. It was however predictable that a Conservative government would not be content to leave the extent of legal control over trade union admission and expulsion to the common law and anti-discrimination statutes referred to above.

UNREASONABLE EXCLUSION AND EXPULSION

The government's original proposal for a new right for individuals excluded or expelled from trade unions was made in the Working Paper on the Closed Shop, which envisaged that the right would apply to any worker whether in a closed shop or not. This curious inconsistency reflected the tendency of the media, politicians and judges of treating all cases of refusal of admission or expulsion as if they inevitably carried with them the consequence of loss of employment. What was contemplated was a right not to be unreasonably excluded or expelled which would be added to the common law jurisdiction of the High Court. The Working Paper also stated that there would be a strong affinity between the proposed new right and 'the long standing principle of the common law that a man should not be prevented from practising his trade or selling his labour'. In so far as this is a reference to the doctrine of restraint of trade, it is noteworthy that Parliament had to exclude its impact from trade union law in 1871 in order to ensure the basic legality of trade unions. In so far as it referred to the 'right to work' (see p. 78) any analogous statutory jurisdiction would give the courts carte blanche to control trade union actions.

An outline of Sections 4 and 5

In the event ss.4 and 5 of the 1980 Act confer the jurisdiction not on the ordinary courts but on the industrial tribunals and EAT. Unlike Donovan though, whose proposed independent review body would have been composed of a legally qualified chairman and two trade unionists, the government were not prepared to exclude employers' representatives from sitting on tribunals while they heard these cases. In its view the matter was not a purely internal union affair; the closed shop meant that it had consequences for the individual beyond his membership or non-membership of a union. Any risk to the credibility of industrial tribunals and the EAT in exercising their jurisdictions over matters between employer and individual employee if they are given the more controversial role of determining disputes between unions and members was discounted. Furthermore the ordinary courts still come into the picture because appeals on points of law lie from the EAT to the Court of Appeal and ultimately to the House of Lords.

The rights created by EA ss.4 and 5 also differ from the Working Paper in that they are confined to employees and persons seeking to be in employment with respect to which it is the practice for employees to be members of a specified union in accordance with a UMA.[12] These individuals have the right under s.4 not to have an application for membership of a specified union or a branch or section of it 'unreasonably' refused, and not to be 'unreasonably' expelled from such a union, branch or section.

A person may make a complaint to an industrial tribunal that one of these rights has been infringed within six months of the date of the refusal to admit or of the expulsion. This time limit may be extended by the tribunal by such period as it considers reasonable in a case where it is satisfied that it was not reasonably practicable to make the complaint within the six months' period. The tribunal has to determine whether the union acted reasonably in accordance with equity and the substantial merits of the case but in particular must not regard a union as having acted reasonably only because it acted in accordance with its rules or unreasonably because it acted in contravention of them. Where it finds a complaint to be well-founded the tribunal must make a declaration to this effect. An appeal may be made to the EAT on any question of law or fact arising from any decision of or in proceedings before an industrial tribunal under s.4.

Where a complaint has been declared to be well-founded the successful complainant may make an application for compensation under s.5.

Any such complaint must be made within the period from four weeks after the date of the tribunal's declaration to six months after that date. If he has been admitted or readmitted to the union at the date of the application, it is made to an industrial tribunal. The basis for compensation is what the tribunal considers appropriate for the purpose of compensating him for the loss sustained in consequence of his original exclusion or expulsion from the union up to a maximum of the combined current maximum basic award and compensatory award compensation for unfair dismissal (£10,150). An appeal may be made to the EAT on any question of law arising from any decision or in proceedings before an industrial tribunal under s.5. If at the date of the application he has not been admitted or readmitted to the union, the application is made to the EAT. Its award of compensation must be what it considers just and equitable in all the circumstances up to a maximum of the current maximum unfair dismissal basic award, compensatory award and additional award compensation (£16,910). The common law duty to mitigate applies to any award of compensation under s.5 and, if the industrial tribunal or EAT finds that the applicant's exclusion or expulsion was to any extent caused or contributed to by his own action, it must reduce the compensation by such proportion as it considers just and equitable having regard to that finding.

The preconditions

The restriction of the new rights to employees and would be employees in UMA employment makes them more limited in scope than either IRA s.65 or TULRA s.5. However, given the extent of closed shop practices, the limitation is not as great as it might appear. The admission and expulsion rules and procedures of virtually all major unions are potentially open to scrutiny under the EA. While the Act gives rise to the absurd possibility of different legal rights for two individuals whose treatment by a union is otherwise identical because the one is (or seeks to be) in UMA employment while the other is not, unions will hardly wish to operate two different sets of standards in these matters. Moreover Section D of the Closed Shop Code, which must be read with ss.4 and 5 of the Act, has implications which go beyond the closed shop. In particular the lists of contents for rules on admission in paragraph 48 and discipline in paragraph 50 (see p. 103) are analogous to the IRA's general attempt to control internal union administration. The government evidently wished to establish some form of legal control over the content of union rules without legislating directly on the matter. The criticism of the Secretary of State's Codes as a species of backdoor and arguably unconstitutional legislation is discussed in chapter seven.

While it may be legitimate to confine the operation of a voluntary procedure such as the TUC's IRC to cases where union membership is a condition of employment, it is less defensible to delimit legal rights by reference to this criterion. Apart from the anomaly of different legal rights for two identically treated individuals, its operation may be limited by an internal contradiction. If a group of workers are excluded or expelled from specified unions but not immediately dismissed, that may be sufficient to destroy the required 'practice' of membership of a specified union in accordance with a UMA which is an essential precondition for the existence of any right under s.4.

It should be noted however that under s.4 (in contrast to the jurisdiction of the TUC's IRC) a person can assert his right whether or not he has lost, is likely to lose, or has any prospect of employment in a job where membership of the union from which he has been excluded or expelled is the practice in accordance with a UMA. The right is available to 'every person who is, or is seeking to be, in employment to which this section applies' (s.4(2)), that is, UMA employment. It is one thing to allow someone who is in UMA employment but is expelled from a specified union to assert his s.4 right before he has been threatened with the loss of his job because without a union card he is always vulnerable to such loss. But it is quite another to extend the right to a person 'seeking to be' in UMA employment. The government resisted amendments which would have required a person to be actually offered or refused such employment because of his exclusion from a specified union. It argued that if the right was limited in this way it would not then extend to a situation such as that in merchant shipping where apparently no one can get on the register of seaman without an NUS card; an individual applying to get on the register would not necessarily have sought or been offered any particular engagement as a seaman. The government was content to rely on the good sense of tribunals to identify cases of people 'trying it on' by applying for membership of a union even though they had no real intention of seeking or prospect of obtaining a relevant job.

Reasonableness

Section 4 of the 1980 Act makes reasonableness the sole criterion in assessing a union's decision to refuse admission or to expel. Reasonableness is to be determined in accordance with equity and the substantial merits of the case and independently of whether or not the union's rules were complied with (s.4(5)). This creates a vast discretion for the tribunals and a whole range of uncertainties for trade unions.

In the first place it is uncertain what regard tribunals will give to stipulations in union rules concerning qualifications for membership. All except one of the unions surveyed in the LSE project had some form of entry requirement. While some unions such as the TGWU, APEX and ASTMS recruit in broad, loosely defined occupational groups and others are open either to all workers in a particular industry, such as the NUM and NUR, or particular grades within an industry, such as the CPSA and IPCS, the rules of craft unions were found to be fairly precise in elaborating the occupational groups eligible for membership and necessary qualifications, frequently including an indentured apprenticeship. An opposition amendment to the effect that absence of the necessary qualifications, skill or capacities would be a reasonable basis for exclusion was resisted by the government on the grounds that such a provision would be included in the Closed Shop Code. Paragraph 49 of this Code does indeed refer to possession of the appropriate qualifications for the type of work done by members of the union or section as a factor to which unions might have regard in deciding whom to accept into membership.

Another factor referred to in paragraph 49 is whether the number of applicants for membership is likely to pose a serious threat of undermining negotiated terms and conditions of employment. The Code cites acting as an example where this may be so. Notwithstanding this guidance it remains open to tribunals to impose their own value judgments in interpreting this criterion and it is possible that they will disapprove of pre-entry closed shop practices in particular. Critics of the original Working Paper doubted whether the High Court would handle such issues of labour supply and manpower planning satisfactorily and noted that even if the courts did not attempt to transfer entry control from the union to employers they would still be evaluating the union's methods of control according to the open-ended criterion of reasonableness. It may be hoped but it cannot be confidently expected that the industrial tribunals and EAT will be more satisfactory bodies than the High Court in this respect, though there remains the daunting probability that such issues will be resolved eventually by the Court of Appeal.

This is but one of several problems which flow from the explicit dissociation of reasonableness from adherence to union rules. Although, unlike the IRA, the EA has not sought to exercise any direct control over the content of union rules, it has done so indirectly via paragraphs 48 and 50 of the Closed Shop Code (above p. 103). Of course under the common law jurisdiction, the ordinary courts take the Code into account in deciding whether the rules have been observed. It is nevertheless possible to visualise a case where the Code is breached but the rules of the union are observed. The inference is that where exclusion or expulsion is carried out in accordance with union rules which do not satisfy the requirements of the Code, a tribunal should normally find that the exclusion or expulsion was unreasonable and therefore unlawful.

Any such decision could place the union in an impossible position. Section 4(3) expressly provides that an individual's rights under s.4(2) are in addition to and not in substitution for any right which exists apart from the section. That is a clear reservation in favour of his rights at common law as paragraph 18 of the Closed Shop Code confirms. What neither the Act nor the Code do is to clarify the relationship between the common law and the new statutory rights. The point was raised in Parliament more than once. It may be that the danger of inconsistent decisions by the High Court on an action for wrongful expulsion and a tribunal on a complaint of a contravention of EA s.4 in respect of the same facts could be overcome by the exercise of powers to stay proceedings (on the analogy of unfair and wrongful dismissal actions in respect of the same dismissal). But no explanation was offered for how a union could avoid the Scylla and Charybdis of a tribunal decision that an exclusion or expulsion was unreasonable and contrary to s.4 and a subsequent High Court decision in a case brought by a member to enforce the contract in the rule book that it had, in order to comply with a tribunal decision, acted in breach of its rules in admitting or readmitting the person in question (e.g. because he was not qualified for membership as in *Faramus* v. *Film Artistes Association*).

Section 4(9) extends the notions of exclusion and expulsion in two important respects. Section 4(9)(a) enables an applicant to regard his application for membership as having been refused if it has not been granted by the end of the period within which it might reasonably have been expected to be granted if it was to be granted. This is designed to prevent a union from avoiding the impact of the law by simply ignoring an application for membership. It could however apply also where a union gave an applicant a holding reply while quite properly investigating whether he was qualified for membership.

The more important provision is s.4(9)(b) which treats cessation of membership on the happening of an event specified in the rules as expulsion. This is aimed at the practice of 'lapsing' whereby membership ceases when subscriptions have not been paid for a specified period. The LSE project revealed that virtually all the major unions have such a provision. While termination is automatic in most unions some provide for advance notification, or the member has an opportunity to state his case or a right of appeal. The government's argument for s.4(9)(b) rested on this variety and the need to avoid inconsistency between individuals depending on whether the rules provided for automatic lapse (as in *Edwards* v. *SOGAT*) or treated arrears of subscription as grounds for expulsion. It also wanted to prevent unions from redrafting their rules to provide for automatic termination of membership rather than expulsion as a way of avoiding the Act. Against this it has to be pointed out that to equate lapsing with expulsion flies in the face of industrial realities. A lapsing provision is essential for unions with members in industries with a relatively high turnover of labour. Without it union membership statistics would be unrealistically inflated. The need for legal controls over lapsing beyond the common law requirement of strict adherence to the rules as in the *Bonsor* case was not made out. This is one instance where the Employment Act goes further than the Industrial Relations Act: action against a member for arrears of payment of dues was excluded from the statutory requirement of natural justice in disciplinary proceedings under IRA s.65(8), although prior notice of termination of membership for this reason was required by s.65(9).

VOLUNTARY PROCEDURES AFTER THE 1980 ACT

Paragraph 53 of the Closed Shop Code starts by saying that in general voluntary procedures are to be preferred to legal action and that all parties should be prepared to use them. The government view was that EA ss.4 and 5 were nevertheless necessary to ensure that adequate safeguards were available to individuals if voluntary self-regulation failed to provide them. It was not though prepared to write into the Act any requirement to exhaust extra-legal remedies before making a complaint under s.4, or that the tribunals should have regard to voluntary procedures and decisions under them, or even any express reservation as to their validity. Moreover EA s.4(11) states that any provision in an agreement which purports to exclude or limit the operation of or preclude any person from making a complaint under s.4 or 5 shall be void. The only limitation on the scope of s.4(11) is that it does not apply to an agreement made following action taken by an ACAS conciliation officer (under EPCA s.132(2) and (3) as amended by EA Schedule 1 para. 17). A provision in union rules requiring internal appeals to be exhausted before any legal proceedings are initiated must thus be rendered void so far as ss.4 and 5 are concerned, and it might be difficult for a tribunal to take internal proceedings and decisions reached under such rules into account in assessing reasonableness.

Inter-union agreements about membership may also be at risk in so far as they may require a union to expel or refuse to admit particular individuals. The principal inter-union agreement is of course the TUC's 'Disputes Principles and Procedures' which for convenience is referred to as 'Bridlington'.[13] As we saw from cases such as *Spring* v. *NASD* and *Rothwell* v. *APEX* (p. 102), Bridlington may require a union to expel members in order to comply with a decision of a TUC Disputes Committee on a complaint that the principles and procedures have been infringed. The LSE project found that sixty-one of the largest TUC affiliated unions with a combined membership of 10.7 million members had either the TUC's model rule or a similar rule enabling them to expel members in these circumstances. While Bridlington does not expressly purport to limit or exclude the operation of the EA provisions, it might be construed as having that effect. The likelihood of this is somewhat reduced by paragraph 49 of the Closed Shop Code which refers to the need for a union to have regard to whether the TUC's principles and procedures or the findings of a TUC Disputes Committee are relevant in determining whom to accept into membership. The Code also includes a general reference in paragraph 52 to the need for TUC–affiliated unions to bear in mind TUC guidance on 'these matters' and to inform individuals of the appeals procedure the TUC provides for those expelled or excluded from membership. But if the government really had as it professed no intention of undermining Bridlington it would have inserted a provision in the Act requiring industrial tribunals to take account of it, which would not have prevented a tribunal from finding an exclusion or expulsion nevertheless unreasonable.

The Independent Review Committee

The IRC is the apex of the voluntary procedures for regulating individual exclusions and expulsions from trade unions in the context of the closed shop. The case for legislation despite the fact that it covers much the same ground as the TUC procedure was that the IRC had no power to compel admission or readmission or to award compensation and that too long a period of time elapsed before its decisions were reached. The time factor was given as a reason for refusing to limit the right of complaint under s.4 until after this and other voluntary procedures were exhausted. The most the government was prepared to do was to extend the time limitation for s.4 complaints from three to six months to allow more time for voluntary procedures to operate, but there is no obligation on an individual to defer making a complaint for this reason. Indeed paragraph 53 of the Closed Shop Code states that it would be unreasonable to expect him to do so. This paragraph contains the Code's only explicit reference to the IRC stating that unions should take its decisions fully into account. But it is anyway part of the IRC's terms of reference that TUC affiliates have a clear responsibility to act on its recommendations and the IRC reported in 1980 that this had always happened (above p. 107). Criticism of the IRC on the grounds that it has no power to compel re-admission is to this extent undermined. Indeed it may be a far more effective mechanism for securing admission and re-admission than a declaration by an industrial tribunal. But while tribunals do not have power to compel re-admission either, they do have power to award compensation. The law can thus make the union pay for its 'unreasonable' actions though it does not attempt to overcome another limitation of the IRC: its inability to secure the employment or re-employment of those who have lost job opportunities or jobs because they had no union card.

In his 1978 report the IRC's chairman identified two issues of particular interest to an appraisal of ss.4 and 5. First he stressed that while if the IRC considered that a union had infringed its rule book it felt bound so to find, the main criterion it used was whether the union's action was reasonable in the circumstances. Not surprisingly the government used this statement to rebut criticism of the principle of EA s.4(5) that observance of the rule book of itself is not necessarily reasonable and therefore lawful. It should however be noted that the reports of the IRC's hearings do not disclose any instance of a recommendation which would have either condoned or required action by a union in breach of its rules. If a tribunal had been asked to decide some of these cases it might well have reached a different decision in the light of the express wording of s.4(5).[14] The second issue is the IRC's development of 'post-hearing' conciliation. This is undertaken after the IRC has reported its findings on a hearing only if all parties agree. Its aim is to explore the possibility of finding an agreed solution to the dispute. The details of post-hearing conciliation given in the chairman's reports for 1978—80 show that unions are often willing to help the complainant to find a way back to gainful employment. A survey in 1979 could however find no instance where a complainant had got his job back or had got a new job because of union help (even though it found that the IRC was highly effective in securing the admission or re-admission of complainants into membership).[15] As noted tribunal proceedings under ss.4 and 5 do not offer the individual any greater prospect of success in this respect. Further while a tribunal must under s.4 either grant or refuse a declaration the IRC can and does look for more flexible and pragmatic solutions. For example, its desire to give a decision favourable to one applicant on his complaint against ACTT, while not obliging the union to act in breach of its rules which it would have had to do in order to comply with a recommendation that he be admitted, was met by an agreed solution under which the union offered to give him a document stating that he was to be treated as a full member of good standing on any application for a job and that when he obtained employment he should be admitted on reasonable terms.[16]

That case also illustrated an important issue with which tribunals may be confronted under EA ss.4 and 5: the operation of a closed shop as a means of controlling entry to jobs. The reports of the IRC's hearings reveal others. Adherence to Bridlington is obviously one. Since EA s.4(10) (reference to a trade union in ss.4 and 5 includes reference to a branch or section) effectively makes the right not to be unreasonably excluded one which can be asserted against a particular branch of a union, one may ask how tribunals will resolve situations where it is not practical industrial relations for the individual to be re-admitted to the same branch (or to return to the same job if re-admitted) because of the antagonism between himself and the branch members. In one case the IRC refused to recommend re-admission of workers who had crossed a picket line and left the union voluntarily, only seeking re-admission when a UMA was concluded, because the members of the branch would resist it. In the light of paragraphs 54 and 55 of the Closed Shop Code (below p. 120), it is easy to see that a tribunal might grant complainants a declaration in a comparable case, the effect of which would probably be that the union would be liable to pay substantial compensation under s.5. The IRC however was able to recommend that the union should use its best endeavours to secure admission if any of the complainants applied to join a different branch.[17]

Critics of the enactment of statutory rights have suggested that it would be better to develop the work of the IRC, possibly by extending its terms of reference so that it could entertain cases before any threat of dismissal occurred and perhaps before internal procedures have been exhausted. It is however already evident that the IRC has attempted to assist in resolving some disputes which have come to its notice before they have reached a stage where they would be within its terms of reference. With its flexible approach to securing acceptable solutions, the IRC fits in well with the modern development of collective bargaining: the LSE project found that it is specified as the final stage of appeal in a third of the UMAs agreed since 1976. Although the small number of complaints made to it in its first four years is not surprising, there may still be a considerable lack of awareness of its existence among those who might wish to avail themselves of its assistance. For individuals genuinely interested in achieving a solution satisfactory to all parties that is a pity. Those whose main objective is short term financial reward at the expense of unions will in any event resort to the Employment Act.

LEGAL PROCEDURE

The government decided to give jurisdiction over the new rights to the industrial tribunals and EAT rather than the High Court because of their industrial experience. While the procedure has some similarities to those which apply to complaints by individuals against their employers, there are some striking points of difference. The first concerns the time limits within which individuals can enforce their rights. The original Bill proposed the standard 'three months plus tribunal discretion' time limit for complaints under s.4, but would have permitted applications for compensation under s.5 to be made at any time between four weeks and twelve months after a declaration under s.4 had been obtained in order to allow a sufficient period for voluntary procedures to operate. As already noted the three months period in s.4 was extended to six months for this reason, but unaccountably the twelve months proposed for s.5 was reduced to six months. The critical development that may occur within the limitation period is that the individual may be admitted or re-admitted to the union, which would restrict him to an application to an industrial tribunal for a lower maximum amount of compensation.

A major difference between ss.4 and 5 and any of the procedures in the EPCA concerns the role of the EAT. This is novel in two respects. First under s.4, but not s.5, there is a right of appeal from an industrial tribunal decision on questions of fact as well as questions of law. Second s.5 gives the EAT an original jurisdiction for the first time. It is true that under EPCA s.136(3) a trade union can appeal to the EAT on a question of fact arising out of a decision of the Certification Officer on an application for entry in the list of trade unions or for a certificate of independence. But the CO is an administrative agency while industrial tribunals are judicial bodies. It is unclear whether the government's justification for establishing a right of appeal under s.4 on questions of fact was based on principle or on expediency. The argument based on principle is that there is no more important issue than loss of or failure to obtain a union card in UMA employment. The expediency point is that while it might be equally desirable to have a right of appeal on questions of fact in cases of unfair dismissal, this would not be practicable because of the number of complaints of unfair dismissal heard by industrial tribunals. Either way the government's determination to maximise the rights of the individual against trade unions is manifest, although the right of appeal on questions of fact under s.4 is of course equally available to respondent trade unions.

Creation of an original jurisdiction for the EAT is more serious in that it alters its fundamental nature. Although the EAT has a status equivalent to the High Court, the essential reason for its success is that unlike the NIRC, which had a similar status, it was established with only an appellate jurisdiction. Moreover with the exception of hearing appeals from the Certification Officer, the appropriateness of which is in any event questionable, its jurisdiction had been confined to employment protection issues between individual employees and their employers (though trade unions are the initial complainants under the EPA's redundancy consultation procedure). Its original jurisdiction under s.5, although apparently a narrow one limited to assessing compensation, may well involve it in making judgments in situations where emotions run high as, for example, where trade unionists have refused to work with a non-member and may have threatened to take industrial action if he is readmitted to the union and consequently re-employed. Paradoxically the government advanced the difficult, delicate and sensitive nature of the issues as a reason for giving this jurisdiction to the EAT. In hearing both appeals on questions of fact under s.4 and applications for compensation under s.5 the EAT is assuming controversial jurisdictions which place its standing with trade unions at risk.

Various aspects of the procedure is ss.4 and 5 resemble that in the unfair dismissal provisions of the EPCA: the criterion of reasonableness as the ultimate determinant of whether the individual's rights have been infringed, the direction to tribunals to determine reasonableness in accordance with equity and the substantial merits of the case and the provisions on compensation. These compensation provisions in s.5 however are not identical with those for unfair dismissal in all respects. Under EPCA s.74(1) the compensatory award part of compensation for unfair dismissal is 'such amount as the tribunal considers just and equitable in all the circumstances having regard to the loss sustained by the complainant in consequence of the dismissal'. In the assessment of compensation awards for unreasonable exclusion or expulsion from a trade union, the EAT has a wide discretion to award what it 'considers just and equitable in all the circumstances' (EA s.5(4)(b)) — the first part of the unfair dismissal formula, whereas the industrial tribunals award an amount appropriate for compensating the applicant for loss sustained by him in consequence of his exclusion or expulsion — the second part of the unfair dismissal formula. Nor are the maximum amounts in s.5(7) and (8) fixed in the same way as for unfair dismissal. The amount of basic award compensation for unfair dismissal depends in the first place on the number of years for which the complainant has been employed and his age when dismissed. It can only reach the maximum of thirty weeks' pay if he had been employed for twenty years or more since he was aged forty-one. By contrast any applicant under s.5 may in principle obtain compensation up to the maximum basic award plus compensatory award and, if the application is made to the EAT, plus the maximum additional award.

One can but speculate as to what levels of compensation the tribunals are likely to award. What is clear is that the fact that a union admits or re-admits a complainant who has received a s.4 declaration will not necessarily limit the union's liability to the complainant's out of pocket expenses in the interim. If a tribunal is persuaded that, for example, he has lost the opportunity for UMA employment because he did not have a union card at the relevant time, it may decide to make the union pay for the loss of the benefits which it determines the individual would have received had he been able to take up the opportunity. If this is so, s.5 can be added to the joinder provisions (ss.10 and 15(4)) as demonstrations of the policy of making trade unions pay for establishing and maintaining closed shop practices. Indeed it is open to argument that since any reference to a 'trade union' in ss.4 and 5 'includes a reference to a branch or a section of a trade union' (EA s.4(10)), a complainant may possibly be able to direct his legal action at the local branch of a union.

CONTROL OF INDUSTRIAL ACTION

Sections 4 and 5 of the 1980 Act are of direct relevance to the legal regulation of industrial conflict. At first sight this seems strange because these provisions are ostensibly concerned only with the reasonableness of exclusion or expulsion from a trade union in closed shop employment. However the connection between the closed shop and the internal affairs of trade unions on the one hand and strikes and other forms of industrial action on the other was well established in advance of the Employment Act. In *Associated Newspapers Group* v. *Wade* (1979) Lord Denning equated the closed shop with the ability to mount effective industrial action, a point which was also made in the Working Paper on Picketing (below p. 154). And we have already seen how the court in *Esterman* v. *NALGO* used its power of construction of the union's rules so as to exclude from the ambit of permitted internal union disciplinary action a type of industrial action it thought undesirable. The potential for this type of legal control has been greatly expanded by the 1980 Act.

The most obvious link between EA ss.4 and 5 and industrial action is exemplified by the situation where the union takes what a tribunal regards as unreasonable and therefore unlawful disciplinary action against a member who has refused to participate in industrial action. The Closed Shop Code provides the tribunals (and also the ordinary courts so far as the common law jurisdiction is concerned) with fairly detailed guidance on the sort of industrial action it regards as undesirable. A union ought not to discipline a member because he has crossed a picket line 'which it had not authorised or which was not at the member's place of work' (para. 55, and Picketing Code para. 36). But discipline against a member who has crossed an authorised picket line is not necessarily to be condoned for the Code (para. 54) states:

> Disciplinary action should not be taken or threatened by a union against a member on the grounds of refusal to take part in industrial action called for by the union —
> (a) because industrial action would involve a breach of a statutory duty or the criminal law, would contravene the member's profes-

sional or other code of ethics, would constitute a serious risk to public safety, health or property; or
(b) because the action was in breach of a procedure agreement; or
(c) because the action had not been affirmed in a secret ballot.

The reference to ballots has a special significance in view of the liability of the union under EA s.4. Here is the 'stick' to complement the 'carrot' of funds for ballots which we discuss in the next chapter. But leaving ballots aside, this paragraph of the Code is of breathtaking width. It is clear that the intention is that a tribunal should regard expulsion on any of these grounds as unreasonable and therefore unlawful on a complaint under EA s.4. In other words, the tribunals are to decide the reasonableness of a union's discipline of a member who blacklegs on other members by reference to a list of factors which, in a given situation, could generate an explosive controversy. The neutrality of the tribunals in industrial disputes is in jeopardy. But government spokesmen were happy to acknowledge the link between ss.4 and 5 and the other sections of the 1980 Act dealing with industrial conflict; much of what the government was doing on secondary picketing (it was said) involved for its effectiveness these measures against unreasonable expulsion in closed shops.[18] One is inevitably reminded once more of the Industrial Relations Act. It was the use of provisions ostensibly concerned with the internal affairs of trade unions to effectuate government policies on industrial action that was such a disliked feature of the 'guiding principles' and registration requirements of that statute. It seems that the 1980 Act promotes a similar backdoor control of industrial conflict.

But that is not all. There is also the possibility of an expanded liability in tort based on contraventions of ss.4 and 5. For example, suppose there is a strike by workers to secure the dismissal of an employee held by a tribunal to have been unreasonably excluded from the union after he had refused to take part in industrial action. This action might provide the ingredients for the tort of interference with business by unlawful means, a liability which would not be protected by the immunities in TULRA. The government firmly resisted any amendment to exclude the possibility of an act in contravention of s.4 constituting unlawful means in tort (see further p. 217). It would perhaps be the employer rather than the excluded employee who would wish to bring an action for an injunction to restrain the strike, and his position would only be reinforced if he could quote a clause in a UMA providing that an employee would 'not be dismissed if expelled from his union for refusal to take part in industrial action' (Closed Shop Code para. 30(v)).

The ramifications of ss.4 and 5 of the Employment Act together with the Closed Shop Code should now be apparent. They provide a legal control mechanism over union discipline in industrial conflict. They erode union rules and policies on recruitment, discipline and other matters. They jeopardise the operation of the TUC's arrangements on inter-union relations. They are supposed to provide the individual with protection over and above the common law safeguards, but there is little evidence that unions abuse their powers in dealing with individuals. If the government was really in earnest about the position of the individual worker would it not have applied the logic of regulating union admission to job recruitment by the employer? The present law on unfair dismissals does not apply to unfair refusals to hire, even when the refusal is based on an 'inadmissible' reason like union activities or membership (*Beyer's* case, above p. 65). Nor is there any suggestion of providing an effective (as opposed to the present largely theoretical) right of reinstatement for those who have been unfairly dismissed. The ultimate rationale of ss.4 and 5 and of the other parts of the 1980 Act discussed in the previous two chapters is the government's detestation of the closed shop. While accepting that in the light of the experience of the Industrial Relations Act it is impossible to destroy it by a simple statutory prohibition, the Employment Act seeks to make the closed shop — and also the right to organise — maintainable only at a considerable cost for the unions, for their individual members and even for employers who favour the practice. It is indeed difficult to understand the claim that the Act's provisions affecting the closed shop strike any sort of fair balance.

6

Trade Union Ballots

The Employment Act contains two provisions on trade union ballots: s.1 provides for a state financial subsidy, which is at present confined by statutory regulation to postal ballots, and s.2 gives a legal right to hold workplace ballots on employers' premises. These measures reflect the fact that over recent years ballots have become a fashionable prescription. It is often argued that the union secret ballot has intrinsic democratic virtue and is the method of decision-making which is most conducive to sensible results. There is in fact wide diversity in trade union practice on the use of ballots for elections, in respect of industrial action and for other purposes. Indeed there is a live debate as to whether officers or certain officials should be elected or appointed, and, if elected, as to the method of election which should be used. In the 1970s great publicity was given to the controversy within the Engineering Section of the AUEW over the respective merits of voting at branch meetings and postal ballots in the elections of its president, seven member executive and full time officers. Postal ballots replaced branch voting in 1972. Another issue is the desirability of decisions on the taking and ending of industrial action being directly determined by the members concerned. In practice this overlaps with the question of submitting agreements to shop floor ratification.

So far as the common law is concerned, the role of ballots in internal trade union administration is essentially a matter for each union to decide. In accordance with the principle of freedom of contract, provision can be made in the rules for the holding and conduct of ballots for defined purposes. Where any such provision is made the individual member can assert his contractual right to enforce the rule book. Also it may be possible to control electoral malpractices by an action in tort as in the *cause célèbre* of *Byrne* v. *Foulkes* (1962) where ballot rigging in elections in the ETU amounted to a fraudulent conspiracy.

There are two exceptions to the general principle that a union is free to choose whether and in what circumstances to hold a ballot. Under the Trade Union Act 1913, if a union wishes to establish a political fund to finance party political objects it must obtain a simple majority of those members voting in a ballot conducted in accordance with standards laid down in the Act. This process is subject to the general supervision of the Certification Officer (CO). So are trade union mergers whether by way of amalgamation or transfer of engagements. The Trade Union (Amalgamations) Act 1964 requires a resolution to be passed on a vote by members of both unions in the case of an amalgamation, and members of the transferor union in the case of a transfer of engagements. Unless the rules make express provision to the contrary a simple majority of those voting is sufficient for the resolution to be passed. However the Act lays down in some detail the conditions which have to be satisfied for a valid vote and these cannot be displaced. It is noteworthy that although these require that every member must be allowed to vote without interference or constraint and must so far as is reasonably possible be given a fair opportunity of voting, they do not require a secret ballot.

DEVELOPMENT OF PUBLIC POLICY

Pressure for further regulation of internal union democracy in respect of elections and official industrial action in particular has been ostensibly motivated by three factors: the low level of participation in elections; election malpractices; and the damaging economic effects of industrial action in some major disputes. These issues were considered by the Donovan Royal Commission whose conclusions are still of considerable interest. Donovan came down very firmly against the notion of compulsory strike ballots (paras. 426–30). It found little evidence to support the belief that members are less militant than union leaders, noted that the necessary application of any law to major strikes only would exclude the overwhelming majority of stoppages which were small scale and unofficial, and pointed to the restriction on leaders' freedom of action that a vote in favour of a strike could cause, possibly delaying the settlement of the dispute. It therefore concluded that it was preferable that union leaders should bear and be seen to bear the responsibility for calling and calling off strikes and that the decision for any use of ballots should continue to rest with the unions.

Although concerned at the low level of participation in union elections Donovan observed that because of the cost involved unions might well consider the introduction of postal voting to be worthwhile only for senior posts or where there was reason to believe that perseverence with postal voting would progressively increase the size of the poll. It added that although some employers might be unwilling to provide the necessary facilities, workplace voting deserved to be encouraged and could be appropriately provided for in the factory level collective agreements which were an integral part of its reform strategy (paras. 635–36). No evidence was found of significant abuse in union elections but as a means of eliminating the scope for malpractices Donovan proposed that unions should define the method of holding elections in reasonable detail in their rules. A right of appeal to a proposed registrar of trade unions with redress obtained at a hearing before a new independent review body was suggested as a more satisfactory procedure for enforcing individual members' rights than actions in contract or tort before the ordinary courts.

While the Labour government's White Paper *In Place of Strife* accepted Donovan's general analysis it took a different line on strike ballots. It recommended giving the Secretary of State power to require unions to hold a ballot before a proposed strike which would involve a serious threat to the economy or public interest where there was doubt whether it commanded the support of those concerned. This was one of the controversial 'penalty clauses' that the government eventually dropped (see chapter 1).

Up to 1974 Conservative policy in this area concentrated almost exclusively on strike ballots. The IRA enabled the Secretary of State to apply to the NIRC for an order directing a ballot to be held where industrial action was causing or might cause an emergency situation as defined and there were grounds for doubting whether the workers were or would be taking part in accordance with their wishes. This provision had its origins in *A Giant's Strength* published in 1958 and *Fair Deal at Work* (1968) where the influence of the emergency provisions in the Taft-Hartley Act in the USA was acknowledged. The single use of this procedure in the rail dispute of 1972 only served to emphasise the strength of the case against any such provision so well summarised by Donovan.[1] Further the 1971 Act's principles on the internal management of all unions whether registered or not covered meetings and elections. The principles required voting in a ballot to be secret and every member to have a fair and reasonable opportunity of voting, but they did not make an election or ballot on any aspect of a union's internal affairs mandatory. By contrast under Schedule 4 of the IRA the rules of registered unions had to provide for the election of its governing body and the conduct of elections, though other officers and officials could be elected or appointed. But the limited experience of the Act indicated the very minor impact which it had on this aspect of union internal affairs. It also suggested that this was not one of the main priority areas which the Conservatives at that time saw as being in need of tighter legal regulation.[2]

The events leading to the February 1974 election changed this. Because it was felt that the government's pay policy was being challenged by union leaders rather than by the rank and file membership, the Conservative election manifesto proposed that it should be mandatory for the governing bodies and national leaders of unions to be elected by postal ballot. The idea of a financial subsidy for such elections was introduced in the manifesto for the October 1974 election and developed during the years of Labour government. Labour's policy was that if the TUC or individual unions were to request financial aid to facilitate the conduct of elections by postal ballot, the government would grant their request.[3] The thinking underlying Conservative policy however was that the leadership of trade unions was unrepresentative. Opening a debate on ballots in 1975 Mr. Prior cited the absence of any Conservative on the executives of the thirteen largest unions as a demonstration of this.[4] The political character of the trade union movement would be changed if the unrepresentative militants were removed from positions of power and replaced by moderates reflecting the wishes of the silent majority of members. The 'militant leadership dragooning a reluctant moderate membership' picture is the one usually painted as a justification for strike ballots. A proposal for state financial assistance for these ballots as well was added to party policy in early 1979, partly in response to the disputes in the 1978–79 'winter of discontent'.

An essential characteristic of the Conservative policy on ballots developed after the experience of the IRA and the 1974 election defeats was that there were to be no compulsory ballots. Financial assistance was to be available for certain ballots at the option of individual unions. This meant that the July 1979 Working Paper on Public Funds for Union Ballots had a very mild tone. While there was, it was said, wide public support for their more extensive use and growing recognition of their desirability inside the trade union movement it was not practicable for every decision to be taken this way and 'unions themselves must decide when ballots are appropriate'. The purpose of the proposed legislation was therefore to remove major financial constraints on unions holding 'important' ballots over such issues as elections to the governing body and posts as full time officers and the calling and ending of strikes. The scheme was to be administered by the CO from whose decisions no appeal would be possible.

Reaction to this Working Paper was muted. Those aspects of the proposal that were most likely to impinge on employers were not necessarily seen to be in their interests. In particular the CBI recognised that strike ballots could be used to strengthen the hands of union negotiators rather than as a means to reduce the extent of industrial action, and there was a division of opinion on the desirability of finance for workplace ballots. The trade union response was also cautious. The TUC was aware of the possible implications for trade union autonomy that accountability for use of public money would entail and therefore objected to government attempts to interfere in the internal democratic procedures of individual trade unions in general terms. It was always clear however that the ballots proposal carried with it the possibility of close supervision by the CO of the internal affairs of unions, especially if a disgruntled member could take the CO to the High Court for judicial review of his decisions. Other objections were based on industrial relations considerations. Ballots for 'ending' as well as for calling strikes in some circumstances could have the effect of prolonging rather than terminating disputes. Or where several unions are involved suppose one union was to favour a ballot and the subsidy and the other unions were opposed to both. Would the availability of the money help or impede the cause of industrial peace? Or again suppose a union were to request a subsidy for a ballot to call an official strike in breach of agreed procedure — should there be a subsidy for breaking agreements? It is difficulties such as these and the questionable assumptions underlying the policy of promoting ballots which need to be kept in mind in assessing the provisions ultimately enacted in EA ss.1 and 2 and the first scheme made under s.1.

STATE FINANCE FOR BALLOTS

Section 1 of the EA is an enabling provision. It empowers the Secretary of State for Employment to make regulations for a scheme providing for payments by the CO towards expenditure incurred by independent trade unions in respect of certain ballots. Any such scheme can only apply to ballots where the question or at least one of the questions to be voted on falls within one of the purposes set out in s.1(3). These are (a) obtaining a decision or ascertaining the views of members on the calling or ending of industrial action; (b) any election provided for in the rules; (c) electing a worker who is a member to be a representative of other members also employed by his employer; (d) amending the rules; and (e) obtaining a decision on a proposed merger in accordance with the 1964 Act. The Secretary of State may by order add to these purposes. The scheme must specify the circumstances in which and conditions subject to which payments may be made and the amount of the payments. It must restrict the cases in which payments are made to those in which the ballot is so conducted as to secure, so far as is reasonably practicable, that those voting may do so in secret.

In the event the Funds for Trade Union Ballots Regulations[5] establish a scheme which is more limited than the potential in s.1 in two respects. First it applies to postal ballots only where those voting have to do so by marking a voting paper and returning it individually by post to the union or another person responsible for counting the votes (reg. 6). Second it only applies to ballots where the question to be voted on falls within the purposes in s.1(3)(a), (d) or (e) referred to above (calling or ending industrial action, rules amendments and mergers), or concerns an election provided for by the rules either to the principal committee having the executive responsibility for managing the affairs of the union or to the positions of president, chairman, secretary, treasurer or any position held by the person elected as an employee of the union[6] (reg. 4). It must be emphasised that other elections under the rules and voting for shop stewards whether or not provided for in the rules are not included in the scheme. If there is more than one question to be voted on, the ballot will still come within the scheme if one or more of them falls within the specified purposes and each of the others relates to the same issue as a question falling within these purposes.

The scheme imposes several conditions in addition to the mandatory requirement of a secret ballot. Subject to certain qualifications the CO must not make any payment either if he is of the opinion that any of these have not been satisfied or if any assurance he requests from the union relating to them is not given (reg. 10). Except in respect of ballots on proposed mergers where special provisions apply (regs. 12(2) and 20), the holding of the ballot must not contravene union rules, and any requirements in the rules as the conduct of the ballot must be complied with unless the CO is satisfied that non-compliance had no significant effect upon the proper conduct of the ballot (regs. 11(a)(b) and 12(1)). Those entitled to vote must have been allowed to do so without interference or constraint and so far as is reasonably practicable have had a fair opportunity of voting. Any decision not to count votes must have been taken because of a change in circumstances which materially affected the issue to which the question related and which occurred after the first day on which voting papers were given or sent out. Where the votes cast have been counted they must have been fairly counted.

Payments may be made towards 'reasonable' expenditure on stationery and printing and postal costs. The latter are normally limited to the cost of despatch and return of voting papers by second class post or any cheaper method used. More expensive postal costs may be reimbursed where the CO considers them to have been reasonable; in his explanatory pamphlet[7] he cites a strike ballot where it is particularly important to obtain the result quickly as an example of where this might be the case.

Applications must be made to the CO on the prescribed form after the expenditure has been incurred, normally after the votes have been counted, and be accompanied by such other documents as he requires (reg. 8). Applications may be made in respect of arrangements to hold a ballot which would have qualified but was not proceeded with where voting papers had already been distributed (EA s.1(4) and reg. 19). The CO has indicated in his pamphlet that a sample of the complete package of voting papers, accompanying literature and envelopes distributed to voters must be provided together with documentary evidence of the expenditure incurred. Payment is made to the applicant union but not before six weeks have elapsed from the date of application or the date the votes were counted if that was later. If a postal ballot was held because the employer refused to make his premises available for a workplace ballot as required by s.2 (see below) and the union receives compensation from a tribunal in respect of that failure, any payment on an application under the s.1 scheme will be reduced accordingly (reg. 21).

The threat to union autonomy

A major issue in financial support for postal ballots is the extent of provision for associated activities, of which canvassing is the most important. One of the main criticisms of the postal ballot in elections for officials is that it may lead to excessive press influence by publicity

given to the political affiliations and leanings of candidates with open
support for those of the approved – usually 'moderate' – persuasion.
Nothing in the regulations enables the CO to exercise any control over
such interference. Nor has he a duty to see that there is any balance by,
for example, ensuring that subject to the union's rules all candidates are
entitled to have an election address distributed together with the voting
paper. It was apparently the government's intention that reimbursement would be provided for reasonable but not extravagent expenditure on such leaflets.[8] But while reg. 13 enables the CO to make payment towards what he considers to be reasonable expenditure incurred
on stationery and printing in respect of 'that part of any material enclosed with the voting paper which explains the matter to which the
question to be voted upon relates or the procedure for voting', his
explanatory pamphlet makes no reference to this. It does say however
that the costs of election addresses not enclosed with the voting papers
are not covered, implying that the cost of those distributed with the
voting papers may be.

The role of the CO could be crucial to how the scheme, if used, will
operate in practice. It was thought that s.1 schemes could appropriately
be put in the hands of a purely administrative officer who would not be
over-involved. Thus assurances were given in Parliament that the CO
would not be responsible for the way in which questions were framed,
the result of the ballot or for what happened afterwards.[9] Nevertheless
there may be a good deal of argument over the CO's administration of
the scheme. Although there is no provision for appeal from the CO, his
decisions on whether the conditions for making a payment are satisfied
offer considerable scope for 'judicial review'. This is the case, for
example, in respect of the requirements that in a strike ballot, so far as
reasonably practicable, all members likely to be called upon to participate or participating in the action are entitled to vote, and that they are
allowed to do so without interference or constraint (reg. 11(c)(d)). The
experience of ACAS of judicial review of its decisions under the now
repealed union recognition procedure in EPA ss.11–16 does not provide a happy augury (see chapter seven). The CO's role thus inevitably
involves decisions which go beyond simple administration and if they
did give rise to court actions would lead to internal union administration becoming subject to greater involvement with the law.

The same danger follows from the open ended scope of s.1(3) which
enables a s.1 scheme to cover ballots for any of the stated purposes and
such other purposes as the Secretary of State may specify. An assurance

was given that this power would not be used to enable a union to obtain reimbursement for action contrary to its rules. But there was no promise to limit s.1 schemes exclusively to ballots envisaged by the rules and the possible addition of ballots on major wage offers was expressly acknowledged.[10] Another possible addition would be ballots on union membership agreements. While the power could not be used to make ballots on any issue compulsory, its unlimited ambit understandably gives rise to fears that the real objective is to prepare the way for legislation which might make certain ballots mandatory. If, for example, the proposal for 'triggered' strike ballots raised in the January 1981 Green Paper and discussed below were enacted, it would be possible for the Secretary of State to bring such ballots within a s.1 scheme. Thus while s.1 can only be used in respect of expenditure incurred by independent trade unions, public funds could then be provided in effect to those within unions who forced the union to hold such a ballot although they were not empowered to require it by the rules and it was on an issue and in circumstances not provided for by the rules.

Whether or not this occurs the integrity of union rules is certainly threatened by s.1 and the regulations. As already noted the CO may disregard any irregularity in observance of union rules concerning the conduct of ballots if satisfied that it had no significant effect on the proper conduct of the ballot. The freedom given by s.1(5) to prescribe conditions subject to which payments may be made could obviously be the basis for further incursions, even to the extent of the CO prescribing some universal way for conducting ballots. It must be acknowledged that the provisions of the 1913 and 1964 Trade Union Acts on ballots already limit the freedom of trade unions to determine their own rules and procedures in certain ways.[11] However this has been done in respect of two specific issues and the limits are defined in the legislation itself. The objection to EA s.1 is that no such limits are written in to it. It would be unwise to rely on assurances from the government as to the intended ambit of the section given the commitment to a step-by-step approach to imposing restraints on trade unions by legislation. Seen in this light, the first scheme under s.1 may be a 'loss leader' (to adopt McCarthy's phrase) in relation not only to the rest of the 1980 Act but also to any future schemes and legislation on trade union ballots.

WORKPLACE BALLOTS

Although he has chosen not to do so in his first scheme, s.1 does enable the Secretary of State to bring workplace ballots within a future scheme under which public funds are available. If this were to happen the supervision by the CO would pose an even greater threat to trade union autonomy than the conditions to be satisfied under the first scheme for postal ballots. It is not clear whether extension of s.1 to workplace ballots is a serious possibility. The Secretary of State expressed the government's support for such ballots in strong terms but, perhaps significantly, in doing so he shifted the emphasis from unions to management. Workplace ballots, he argued, were 'good industrial practice'; he hoped that 'many more *companies'* would make full use of them as they were the 'most satisfactory way of increasing the number of people who took part in the affairs of their union, and the use of the postal ballot is perhaps a second best in this direction'.[12]

This enthusiasm for workplace ballots was channelled into support for a CBI initiative for a legal right for unions to hold secret ballots on employers' premises. To this end s.2, as it became, was added to the Bill during the House of Lords Committee stage. It applies where an independent, recognised union requests an employer to permit his premises to be used to give members of the union employed by him a convenient opportunity of voting on a ballot where the purpose of the question or one of the questions to be voted on satisfies the requirements of a s.1 scheme, and the union proposes to secure so far as reasonably practicable that those voting may do so in secret. Section 2(1) directs the employer to comply with such a request so far as reasonably practicable. If he fails to do so the union may make a complaint to an industrial tribunal. Such a complaint must be made within three months of the failure or such further period as the tribunal considers reasonable where it finds that a complaint within three months was not — yet again — reasonably practicable. Where the complaint is upheld, the tribunal must make a declaration to that effect and may award compensation of an amount which is just and equitable having regard to the employer's default in failing to comply with the request and any expenses incurred by the union in consequence of the failure. An appeal may be made to the EAT on a question of law arising from a decision of or in proceedings before an industrial tribunal.

The section raises various legal and practical difficulties. Like s.1 the right is confined to independent trade unions, but here they must also be recognised to some extent for the purposes of collective bargaining. Reported case law under EPA s.99 (duty on employers to consult with recognised trade unions on proposed redundancies) demonstrates that in many circumstances it is uncertain whether or not a union is recognised in the legal sense of the term.[13] Another restriction is that the obligation imposed by s.2 does not apply to an employer who together with any associated employers does not employ more than twenty 'workers' (a wider term as defined in TULRA s.30(1) than 'employees'). This is yet another aspect of the government's policy of relieving small employers from obligations imposed by legislation. Further the 'enforcement' procedure is similar to the standard one now used in respect of individual employment protection rights. But this issue involves a right given to a trade union. The only precedent for allowing unions to initiate industrial tribunal proceedings is the redundancy consultation procedure, and even there the ultimate beneficiaries of any tribunal award are individual employees. Here an award of compensation may be made in favour of the union. It is not clear what amount would be considered just and equitable over and above reimbursement of the expenses incurred in holding a vote elsewhere. The more fundamental point is that s.2 represents a novel extension of the jurisdiction of industrial tribunals to include collective rights. One of the effects of the EA is the increase in the direct involvement of trade unions in proceedings before industrial tribunals. Section 2 is in this sense the obverse of the Act's other provisions under which trade unions may be made respondents liable to pay substantial compensation to individuals (EA ss.5, 10, and 15(4)).

The thinking behind s.2 appears to be that while the government is at present reluctant to commit public finance for workplace ballots employers can justifiably be obliged to support them because it is in their interests to do so. Introducing the clause Lord Gowrie said that it was wrong that votes on strike action should be taken at 'mass meetings where the individual has no opportunity to cast his vote privately and may be, overtly or covertly pressured to vote one way or another'.[14] The inference is that a secret ballot, which is a pre-condition for the right to request use of employers' premises under s.2, is more likely to lead to workers voting against industrial action than mass meetings where 'moderates' may be reluctant to voice their dissent. The fact that a workplace ballot is much quicker than a postal ballot was no doubt also seen as an important factor. Whether s.2 in fact helps to achieve fewer strikes depends in the first place on whether those with the relevant executive authority within trade unions see the need to make use of it. Where workplace voting is not already the practice by agreement with the employer, a union might prefer to retain its freedom to find other venues at which members may express their wishes in whatever way the members determine.

STRIKE BALLOTS

Although the policy development behind the EA provisions on ballots may have been originally concerned primarily with trade union elections, the focus in Parliament shifted to the question of strike ballots. Despite Donovan's cogent statement on the case against any form of mandatory strike ballot and despite the experience of the Industrial Relations Act, backbench amendments were introduced to provide some mechanism for compulsory strike ballots in the belief that they would enable 'moderate' opinion to prevail. The government pursued a consistent line of argument against these proposals. While it acknowledged that it had the same goal as supporters of compulsory strike ballots, its strategy was encouragement rather than compulsion. It was confident that encouragement would work because there was a growing movement towards secret ballots. It was better to allow this to proceed than to risk jeopardising it by measures which would present opponents of ballots with the emotive argument that the government was going back to the Industrial Relations Act. If a compulsory ballot resulted in demonstrations of solidarity with the leadership, as in the 1972 rail dispute, ballots as a whole might become discredited and the long term strategy undermined.

Given the bandwagon in favour of ballots however it was inevitable that the government was obliged to give further consideration to proposals for compulsory strike ballots. The case in favour of them was put in the Green Paper *Trade Union Immunities*. It is apparently that ballots ought to be the basis of decision-making in trade unions just as they are an integral part of political democracy. But a significant extension of union ballots cannot be expected while those in power see them as a threat to their position. Government action is therefore required, though it should not be along the lines discussed in Donovan or proposed by *In Place of Strife* or enacted in the IRA where the compulsion came from the law or from the Secretary of State. Rather the compulsion should come from the members themselves, and a parallel with the right of shareholders to demand an extraordinary meeting of a company was suggested (paras. 255–56). Such 'triggered' ballots do not of course avoid the problems of the sanctions to be applied where such a ballot is nevertheless not held or the result of a ballot where the majority voting were against industrial action is not respected. The Green Paper assumed that the sanction would involve the withdrawal of the TULRA immunities against civil liabilities. However it pointed out some of the

difficulties, for example, the application of such provisions to unofficial strikes and the position with respect to immunities pending the
decision in a ballot (paras. 259–60). In general the Green Paper revealed a strong preference for continuing with the policy behind EA
ss.1 and 2.

A government genuinely concerned to encourage greater membership participation in trade union affairs might well consider strengthening the legal right to time off work to take part in trade union activities
in EPCA s.28. While this right may include attending meetings and any
voting which takes place at them, it would be possible and might be
desirable to make express provision for time off to vote in union elections or on other issues including industrial action. The beliefs however
that ballots are the only acceptable means of consultation and participation and that there should be no differentiation between members
who are active in union affairs and those who never go near a branch
meeting are not only simplistic and contentious. When made the basis
of legislation they mean that unions are singled out as bodies who
should not be able to determine their own procedures. Whether or not
the 'encouragement' in ss.1 and 2 does result in the 'right' type of trade
union leadership – 'moderate, favourable and responsible'[15] – and less
industrial action, they are unlikely to be regarded by the trade union
movement as a stimulus to internal democracy. Indeed the TUC's
policy as endorsed by its 1980 Congress is that affiliated organisations
ought not to avail themselves of the state subsidy.

7

Collective Bargaining

The Employment Act's repeal of EPA ss.11–16 and Schedule 11 and the Secretary of State's power under s.3 of the Act to issue Codes have major implications for the legal framework of collective bargaining. Traditional public policy towards collective bargaining was one of non-intervention: the sanctions underpinning collective agreements were economic rather than legal, there was no legally protected right to organise in unions and no legal duty on employers compelling them to recognise and bargain with unions. But, as explained in chapter one, the state gradually came to regard collective bargaining as the best method of settling terms and conditions and of securing industrial peace, order and stability. Successive governments sought to assist collective bargaining indirectly through initiatives such as the Fair Wages Resolution, voluntary conciliation and arbitration and wages councils legislation. These were 'props' to help to establish collective bargaining and to extend its benefits to the unorganised and the low paid. Since the mid-1960s controversy has centred on two interrelated issues: the contractual status of collective agreements, which is discussed by the Green Paper *Trade Union Immunities,* and the extent to which the state would assist collective bargaining, which is radically affected by the Employment Act.

COLLECTIVE AGREEMENTS

The non-contractual status of collective agreements has always been a distinguishing characteristic of the British system. *Ford* v. *AEF* (1969) confirmed that there was a rebuttable common law presumption, reversed by the Industrial Relations Act, that the parties to a collective agreement did not intend to create legal relations (above p. 8). TULRA s.18 in effect restores the common law position by enacting a conclusive presumption that the parties do not intend to make a legally enforceable contract, unless they agree in writing (however expressed) that they do so intend in respect of all or part of the agreement. Collectively agreed terms may however be incorporated into the legally enforceable individual contract of employment subject to TULRA s.18(4), which precludes incorporation of limitations on industrial action unless special conditions are satisfied. This provision is intended to eliminate the possibility of backdoor enforceability of collectively agreed 'peace' obligations or 'no strike' clauses, though industrial action nomally involves breach of the contract of employment irrespective of whether a collective agreement is violated (see chapter nine). But the basic principle is that the collective agreement as such cannot be enforced as a contract. If as in the *Ford* case there is a strike allegedly in breach of an agreement, the employer (whatever his other legal rights) cannot sue the union for breach of contract.

The basic principle was left undisturbed by the Employment Act but the Green Paper *Trade Union Immunities* again raised the issue of whether collective agreements ought to be legally enforceable contracts. It suggested that the prospect of damages and injunctions for breach of contract could help to stimulate the reform of collective bargaining by encouraging more formal and precise fixed term agreements, which would be conducive to a relatively predictable and less costly pattern of strikes (paras. 216–19). If legal enforceability also involved the vicarious liability of unions for the acts of their shop stewards they might be further induced 'to reform their structures and rule books and to turn themselves into more authoritarian organisations' (para. 125). But the document itself set out some of the main objections. First the courts would find it extremely difficult, given the characteristic informality of collective bargaining in Britain, to determine issues such as the existence and content of an agreement, the identity of the parties and whether or not the agreement was broken. These difficulties were in fact anticipated by Donovan (para. 233) and exemplified by the *Ford* case, where the main effect of the injunction was to put a halt to negotiations and thus to prolong the dispute.[1] Second, on the experience of the Industrial Relations Act, neither management nor unions would appear to want a legalistic system of collective negotiations. Third, if legal enforceability entailed the vicarious liability of unions, the attempt to secure more 'authoritarian' structures could easily backfire. Indeed those who advocate legal enforceability seem to assume that there is or ought to be some sort of 'chain of command' in trade unions. This assumption is misconceived for as the Donovan Report said: 'Trade union leaders do exercise discipline from time to time, but they cannot be industry's policemen. They are democratic leaders in organisations in which the seat of power has almost always been close to the members' (para. 122).

With regard to the other area of public policy controversy, the Employment Act has undermined the state's role of assisting collective bargaining. The rationale of this role was authoritatively stated in the Donovan Report

> Properly conducted, collective bargaining is the most effective means of giving workers the right to representation in decisions affecting their working lives, a right which is or should be the prerogative of every worker in a democratic society. While therefore the first task in the reform of British industrial relations is to bring greater order into collective bargaining in the company and plant, the second is to extend the coverage of collective bargaining and the organisation of workers on which it depends (para. 212).

These were the policy aims of the developments in collective bargaining law analysed in chapter one: the union recognition procedure, the extension of 'recognised' and 'general level' terms and conditions, the duty on employers to disclose information to and to consult with recognised unions on redundancy, safety and pensions, and the expanded role of ACAS including its power to issue Codes of Practice.

CODES OF PRACTICE

British industrial relations have always been regulated by 'codes' in the sense of voluntarily agreed rules: the collective agreement, the union rule book, the TUC's 'Bridlington' procedure and the more recent TUC 'Guides'. Statutory codes have also proliferated. Safety representatives function within a framework of regulations, codes and guidance notes.[2] ACAS, which is under a general duty to promote the improvement of industrial relations, is empowered by EPA s.6 to issue 'Codes of Practice containing such practical guidance as [it] thinks fit for the purpose of promoting the improvement of industrial relations'. ACAS Codes supersede the relevant part of the original Industrial Relations Code of Practice issued in 1972 under IRA s.3. ACAS has issued three Codes: *Disciplinary Practice and Procedures in Employment* (1977), *Disclosure of Information to Trade Unions for Collective Bargaining Purposes* (1977) and *Time Off for Trade Union Duties and Activities* (1978). Breach of an ACAS Code does not ot itself render a person legally liable, but a Code is admissible in evidence and, where relevant, must be taken into account by an industrial tribunal or the CAC (EPA s.6(11)). The ACAS Code on 'Disciplinary Practice' has been extensively used by the tribunals in unfair dismissal cases to develop standards of 'procedural fairness' (above p. 32).

Section 3 of the 1980 Act empowers the Secretary of State for Employment to issue his own Codes 'containing such practical guidance as he thinks fit for the purpose of promoting the improvement of industrial relations'. While breach of a Code does not ot itself render a person legally liable, in proceedings not only before an industrial tribunal and the CAC (as in the case of ACAS Codes) but also before a court, a Code 'shall be admissible in evidence' and its provisions, if relevant to any question, 'shall be taken into account in determining that question' (EA s.3(8)). 'Court' is not defined but would include all levels of civil and criminal courts. So far the Secretary of State has issued two Codes: *Closed Shop Agreements and Arrangements* and *Picketing*. Although the final drafts were approved by Parliament after only a few hours of debate,[3] earlier consultative drafts were the subject of an investigation and report by the House of Commons Select Committee on Employment.[4] We deal with the substantive content and legal implications of the Closed Shop Code in chapters four and five and the Picketing Code in chapter eight. Here we discuss just two questions: the impact of the Secretary of State's Codes on ACAS and their constitutional propriety.

The Employment Act envisages that a Secretary of State's Code may supersede the whole or part of an ACAS Code (s.3(7)) and, conversely, that an ACAS Code may supersede a Secretary of State's Code (EA Schedule 1 para. 4 amending EPA s.6). This apparent equality between the government and ACAS is consistent with the independence of the latter, which is not to be subject 'to directions of any kind from any Minister of the Crown as to the manner in which it is to exercise its functions under any enactment' (EPA Schedule 1, para. 11(1)). It is however clear from a reading of the 1980 Act in conjunction with the EPA that the Secretary of State has the whip hand so far as code-making is concerned. ACAS must have his approval to make a Code (EPA s.6(4)), whereas he needs merely to consult with ACAS (EA s.3(2)). In the case of the Closed Shop and Picketing Codes the consultation was purely nominal because the ACAS council, concerned to retain its credibility as an impartial tripartite body, simply refused to offer any comments.[5] Nevertheless, although ACAS is unable to recommend the Secretary of State's controversial Codes as good practice, they are an integral part of the legal framework on which it must advise management and unions and within which it conciliates. The Closed Shop Code specifically refers to ACAS conciliation on proposals for new closed shops (para. 29) and secret ballots (para. 36).

The Secretary of State's Codes are not 'consensus' documents on the analogy of the Highway Code. Nor are they in the same category as the ACAS Codes, the educative effect of which stems not only from their legal status but also from the fact that they are the agreed product of the representatives of employers and unions on the ACAS council. The refusal of ACAS to offer comments to the government only confirmed that the Secretary of State's guidance was unacceptable to unions and also (at least in relation to the closed shop) to many employers. Both the Closed Shop and Picketing Codes contain highly controversial provisions which (as we explain in detail in chapters four, five and eight) affect civil and criminal liabilities. Many of these provisions are not mentioned in the Employment Act itself, for example ballots for existing closed shops, restriction on unions disciplining members who refuse to take part in industrial action not affirmed by secret ballot and limitations on the number of pickets. But the Codes, unlike the Act, were not subject to line-by-line Parliamentary scrutiny. The affirmative resolution procedure permitted only a perfunctory debate on a 'take it or leave it' basis, that is, Parliament could accept or reject but could not amend them. The Codes then are arguably a 'species of unconstitutional legislation'.[6]

TRADE UNION RECOGNITION

The procedure in ss.11−16 of the EPA for dealing with union recognition was repealed by EA s.19(b). A union recognition procedure was advocated by the Donovan Commission as a means of promoting the peaceful and orderly extension of collective bargaining, particularly in respect of white collar employees who represented the largest potential growth area for union membership. It was seen as a way of encouraging a more systematic and positive attitude on the part of management towards recognition, which could help not only to extend the coverage of collective bargaining but also to minimise the problems of multi-unionism. Donovan's reform strategy had some influence on the Industrial Relations Act's procedure on 'bargaining units' and 'sole bargaining agents'. But a major effect of this measure, which was used by registered but unrecognised organisations including 'breakaway' unions and staff and professional associations, was to complicate inter-union quarrels. Further the procedure's excessive complexity was heedless of Donovan's warning that provisions on the North American pattern would invite 'detailed intervention by the courts in the processes of industrial relations' (para. 256). In fact the Act subjected the CIR to very close supervision by the NIRC and there was the additional possibility of judicial review by the High Court.[7]

Undue legalism was supposedly avoided by EPA ss.11–16. An independent trade union could refer to ACAS a recognition issue arising from a request for recognition by an employer or two or more associated employers.[8] The request could be for general recognition or for 'further' recognition, that is, for broadening the scope of collective bargaining (though further recognition claims were rare). ACAS was obliged to examine the issue and to encourage a voluntary settlement. If the issue was neither settled nor withdrawn ACAS had to prepare a written report setting out its findings, advice and recommendations if any for recognition. But it did not have to recommend recognition and nor was there any kind of general legal obligation on employers to recognise or bargain. There was however an enforcement procedure where the employer failed to comply with an ACAS recommendation. The union could complain that the employer was not taking such action by way of carrying on negotiations as might reasonably be expected to be taken by an employer ready and willing to negotiate. If at that stage ACAS conciliation failed, the union could ask the CAC for an arbitration award. The CAC award was statutorily incorporated into the individual contracts of employment of those covered by the claim. If the employer failed to perform his contractual obligation, the individual employee could in principle have sued him for breach of contract. It must be emphasised that the CAC could make awards only on terms and conditions of employment and would not award collective procedural terms obliging the employer to negotiate.[9]

ACAS v. The courts

Although there was no right of appeal from ACAS's decisions, its role in the recognition procedure was undermined by a series of court actions founded on allegations that it had exceeded its statutory powers. ACAS's discretion was drastically reduced by these cases, which provided the pretext for the repeal of EPA ss.11–16 and classically illustrated the judges' inability to comprehend the realities and values of collective labour relations.[10] At one extreme some of the judges characterised the procedure as an infringement of individual liberty. Browne-Wilkinson J. described ss.11–16 as 'procedures for the compulsory acquisition of an individual's right to regulate his working life'.[11] In *Grunwick* v. *ACAS* (1978) Lord Salmon in the House of Lords entirely agreed with Lord Denning in the Court of Appeal on the nature of an ACAS recommendation for recognition: 'such an interference with individual liberty could hardly be tolerated in a free society unless there were safeguards against abuse'.[12] The recognition issue in *Grunwick*[13] arose after dismissal and walkout incidents had led to a strike by well over 100 weekly paid staff. After most of the permanent workers who were on strike had joined APEX, the union made a formal request to the company for recognition. This was refused and the strikers were dismissed. APEX then referred the issue to ACAS under EPA s.11.

The House of Lords' decision that ACAS's report recommending recognition of APEX was void turned on the construction of ACAS's duty to ascertain workers' opinions in EPA s.14(1). This, in the majority opinion of the House of Lords given by Lord Diplock, required ACAS to 'ascertain and take into consideration [the opinions] that are held by every group of workers of any significant size that forms part of the workforce that could be affected by the recommendation'.[14] Thus while the correctness of ACAS's action in seeking the opinions of strikers who had been dismissed but were available for reinstatement was upheld, it had failed to discharge its statutory duty since the opinions of the remaining two-thirds of the affected workers who were still employed were unknown. This was because Grunwick refused to provide ACAS either with access to them or with their names and addresses.

Lord Diplock's 'legalistic' approach in *Grunwick* viewed the issue essentially as a straightforward question of statutory construction. Both this approach and the 'individualist' approach referred to above were also evident in the subsequent Court of Appeal decisions in *UKAPE* v. *ACAS* and *EMA* v. *ACAS* in 1979. In *EMA* the union challenged ACAS's decision not to proceed on a reference in respect of certain categories of engineering staff employed by a company which belonged to the EEF. Consistent with the national agreement between the EEF and the CSEU, a TUC disputes committee had ruled in favour of TASS on its complaint that EMA was infringing the Bridlington procedure in seeking to organise these workers. EMA then initiated legal proceedings against the TUC challenging this decision.[15] ACAS, which felt obliged to take account of decisions under Bridlington, decided to defer its inquiries until it knew the outcome of EMA's case against the TUC.

In *UKAPE* the plaintiff association was aggrieved by the failure of ACAS to make a recommendation for its recognition by another company, which belonged to the EEF, on behalf of professional technical staff at one site despite the fact that ACAS's survey of opinions showed that 79 per cent of this group supported it. Both the EEF and the CSEU opposed recognition of *UKAPE* on the ground that the introduction of new organisations into the engineering industry against the background of the national framework of recognition agreements between them would be disruptive. These two cases raised issues of critical importance to the operation of the recognition procedure in EPA ss.11−16 where competing unions were involved and established bargaining arrangements were being challenged.

In *EMA* the Court of Appeal held that ACAS was acting outside its powers by maintaining the suspension of its inquiries until the legal proceedings between EMA and the TUC were resolved. In *UKAPE* the Court of Appeal found ACAS's report void first because it did not contain adequate findings on the appropriateness of bargaining units and arrangements and second because ACAS had misdirected itself in stating that any recommendation for recognition had to be consistent with existing collective bargaining arrangements. However the general tenor of the judgments was more hostile to ACAS's actions in both cases than this bald statement of the decisions suggests. In *UKAPE* Lord Denning even supported the remarkable contention that ACAS's particular duty of 'encouraging the extension of collective bargaining' was not subject to its 'general duty of promoting the improvement of industrial relations' (EPA s.1(2)). While Brandon L.J. disagreed, Lawton L.J. offered no opinion on the point and so in mid-1979 ACAS was left not knowing where it stood on this basic issue.

Repeal and its aftermath

In June 1979 the chairman of ACAS told the Secretary of State that ACAS could no longer 'satisfactorily operate the statutory recognition procedures as they stand'. *Grunwick* had left ACAS with a mandatory duty it could not perform where employers (including for example the well known Michelin company) refused co-operation. *UKAPE* had required ACAS to make detailed findings on a series of matters which ACAS might consider irrelevant or unnecessary and in some cases even harmful to industrial relations. For example, it seemed that ACAS had to make findings on specific bargaining units for small groups of workers whereas the reality of British industrial relations was that 'trade unions organise on the basis of spheres of influence rather than on imposed structural criteria'. *UKAPE* had also prevented ACAS from exercising its industrial relations judgment on matters such as the need to avoid fragmentation and to preserve industrial peace and could have reduced it 'to the role of a balloting agent'. *EMA* had jeopardised ACAS's support for the priority of voluntary procedures. Even the functioning of ACAS's council was 'likely to become impracticable as a result of its being deemed to be acting in a judicial capacity'. All this potentially prejudiced ACAS's voluntary advice and conciliation activities, including conciliation in relation to union recognition. In September 1979 the government issued its Working Paper on Trade Union Recognition which set out the ACAS letter, commented that 'the government sees no grounds in this situation for criticism of the courts' (though the ACAS letter had referred to 'the damaging effect on industrial relations' of judicial decisions) and suggested that the recognition procedure might be either changed or repealed. But by the time the Employment Bill was published the government had decided on repeal.

It is ironic that as the Bill was passing through Parliament the House of Lords reversed the Court of Appeal decisions in *UKAPE* and *EMA*.[16] The priority which ACAS had accorded to the improvement of industrial relations in its interpretation of EPA s.1(2) was vindicated and the grounds for judicial review were confined. What is more Lord Scarman's judgments disclosed a welcome attempt to understand the role that ACAS was intended to fulfil. In *UKAPE* he considered the procedure in EPA ss.11—16 in the context of the post-Donovan developments and concluded that 'the courts have no part to play other than to exercise their function of judicial review. . . . Recognition issues are for ACAS and the CAC. It is their discretion, their judgment which is to determine such issues'.[17] The ambit of judicial review meant that in *UKAPE* the courts could only invalidate ACAS's report if satisfied that no reasonable 'ACAS' with due appreciation of its statutory duties and responsibilities could have reported as it did. Both he and Lord Diplock acknowledged that the complexities of industrial relations might lead

ACAS to conclude that it was unwise to set out certain findings. Its report could not therefore be invalidated on grounds that its findings were inadequate. In *EMA* a majority of the House of Lords held that ACAS had exercised its general power to suspend its inquiries or defer preparation of a report reasonably and consistently with its general duty to improve or prevent the worsening of industrial relations. It was never likely that Lord Scarman's approach to construing the procedure in EPA ss.11–16 by reference to its legislative purpose would affect the government's determination to repeal it. Indeed in the light of its response to the House of Lords' similar approach to the construction of the statutory immunities in TULRA (see chapter nine), it probably viewed the Lords' decisions in *UKAPE* and *EMA* with some disfavour. The restoration of ACAS's proper discretion would hardly have appealed to a government which was committed to weakening the statutory support for collective bargaining and downgrading ACAS's code-making function. Anyway the decisions came too late to dispel the widespread disillusionment with the procedures as a result of the earlier cases. The TUC still less the ACAS council raised little if any resistance to the repeal of EPA ss.11–16.

The repeal has implications for the overall framework of collective labour law. The employer's duties to disclose information and to consult on redundancies, safety and pensions (above p. 15) are owed to the representatives of 'recognised' trade unions. Only officials of independent 'recognised' trade unions have the right to paid time off in respect of industrial relations duties (EPCA s.27). Unions recommended for recognition by ACAS were also entitled to the same rights as recognised unions under these provisions. That principle is no longer applicable (EA Schedule 2), but it was found necessary to re-enact the definition of 'recognition' which was previously in EPA s.11(2) – 'recognition in relation to a trade union, means the recognition of the union by an employer, or two or more associated employers, to any extent, for the purpose of collective bargaining'.[18] But given the crucial importance of recognition to these legal rights, it is hardly satisfactory to leave the tribunals with the exclusive responsibility for determining this complex industrial relations issue as a preliminary to deciding – say – whether or not the employer should have consulted on proposed redundancies.[19] Where so many rights depend on union recognition the logic of the modern legal framework points to the need for a union recognition procedure.

But to what extent did EPA ss.11–16 facilitate union recognition?

By August 1980 (the time of repeal) ACAS had received 1,610 recognition claims under this procedure mainly against small and medium-sized companies. Of those dealt with, over 80 per cent were settled by voluntary means and about two-fifths of these cases resulted in full or partial recognition without the need for a published report. ACAS estimated that these settlements brought some form of collective bargaining to about 48,000 employees. This compared with an estimated total of 16,000 who obtained the benefits of collective bargaining through the 247 references which had gone through the full statutory procedure. Thus over a period of four and a half years collective bargaining had apparently been extended to some 64,000 workers as a direct result of the legislation.[20] This is a modest figure and in fact after the peak year of 1977 there was a decline in the number of references under EPA s.11; after 1976 the number of references to ACAS under EPA s.2 for purely voluntary conciliation on recognition also declined.[21] Yet throughout these years a number of employers were voluntarily conceding recognition to unions either for the first time or in respect of employees hitherto outside collective negotiations. It is likely that management recognition policies were to some extent influenced by the existence of the statutory procedure. The procedure was a concrete expression of the public policy commitment to collective bargaining as the best method of conducting industrial relations. Its repeal at a time when unions are gravely weakened by economic factors signifies a serious modification of that policy.

EPA ss.11–16 could have been strengthened rather than repealed. In order to overcome the weaknesses revealed by *Grunwick*, ACAS's duty to ascertain the opinions of workers might have been limited by some phrase such as 'so far as is reasonably practicable', or ACAS might have been given the kind of powers possessed by the EOC and CRE to demand relevant evidence on pain of criminal sanctions. These powers would have represented the very limit of legal intervention consistent with a voluntarist system. There are moreover some fundamental and unresolved issues in respect of a union recognition procedure in the British context. The job of such a procedure is to specify a trade union if any to negotiate on behalf of defined groups of workers, which ultimately means that there is no escape from some notion of bargaining agents and bargaining units. Again, although Bridlington and voluntary arrangements may be given priority, inter-union disputes are bound to feature in the operation of a recognition procedure as the experience of ACAS under EPA ss.11–16 confirmed. Indeed public policy might legitimately expect a recognition procedure to make a contribution to the resolution of such disputes. Finally, there is the question of judicial review. The provision of statutory criteria for determining recognition issues would be undesirable from an industrial relations point of view and would provide a likely pretext for judicial review. A similar comment might be made in respect of any more direct form of enforcement than arbitration of terms and conditions of employment. But even if such options are eschewed (as they were largely by EPA ss.11–16) it would probably be impossible to keep the judges entirely at arms' length. Certainly Lord Scarman's test of reasonableness left a very wide and uncertain potential for judicial intervention. Needless to say, judicial control of ACAS (or of any successor body with responsibilities under a recognition procedure) would tend towards a legalistic approach on recognition and reinforce the overall trend towards greater legal regulation of industrial relations. Recognition issues could come to be regarded as legal issues, but it is nevertheless arguable that that risk may be worth taking on a question of such fundamental importance as the establishment of collective bargaining.

REPEAL OF SCHEDULE 11

EPA Schedule 11 and the Road Haulage Wages Act 1938 were repealed by EA s.19(c). Schedule 11 brought together two streams of public policy. The first was the series of measures on 'compulsory' arbitration, that is, arbitration which does not depend on the consent of all parties (as is required in voluntary arbitration arranged by ACAS under EPA s.3) and which results in a legally enforceable award. The main antecedents were: Order 1305 of 1940, a wartime provision prohibiting strikes and lockouts and substituting compulsory arbitration; Order 1376 of 1951, which repealed the prohibition on industrial action and narrowed the scope of arbitration; and the Terms and Conditions of Employment Act 1959 s.8, which narrowed the scope still further to claims for 'recognised' terms and conditions of employment. The application of s.8 of the 1959 Act was somewhat broadened however by the IRA which (as recommended by the Donovan Report) made it available in wages council industries in order to encourage the development of collective bargaining and to help resolve the problem of low pay. The second stream of public policy was represented by the House of Commons' Fair Wages Resolution 1946, under which it became a condition of government contracts that employers must pay wages and provide conditions not less favourable than those established for the trade or industry in the district by collective bargaining or, in the absence of such bargaining, not less favourable than the general level. It was thought that a provision combining recognised terms and conditions with the general level would promote the principle of collective bargaining and help to eliminate pockets of low pay. Accordingly Part I of Schedule 11 provided a procedure for arbitration on claims for 'recognised terms and conditions' and, in their absence, for 'the general level of terms and conditions'. Part II was a little used procedure applicable only in wages council industries; all further references to Schedule 11 are to the much more important Part I, which was also available in wages council industries.

A claim for recognised terms and conditions could be initiated by an employers' association or an independent trade union representing a substantial proportion of employers or workers in the trade or industry (or section of it) and party to the agreement or award which settled the recognised terms and conditions. The fact that an employers' association was able to bring a claim reflected the long established public recognition of an employer's interest in preventing competitors from undercutting wage costs. A general level claim could be initiated by an employers' association or a union of which any worker concerned was a member save that where independent trade unions were recognised by *any* employer in the district only such a recognised union could make a claim concerning workers in respect of which it was recognised. A claim under Schedule 11 was reported to ACAS and, if not settled through voluntary conciliation, was referred to the CAC. The CAC decided whether the employer was observing either the recognised terms or the general level and, if not, whether he was observing less favourable terms. If less favourable terms were in force, the CAC made an award which was incorporated into the individual employment contracts of those covered by the claim. In theory they could sue in the County Court for breach of contract if the award was not observed.

Recognised terms and conditions were defined as terms and conditions of workers in comparable employment in a trade or industry (or section of trade or industry) either generally or in the district which were settled by agreement or award where the collective parties were representative employers' associations and trade unions. Furthermore recognised terms expressly included minimum terms. The general level definition was wider and reflected the modern trend towards single employer bargaining: the general level of terms and conditions for comparable workers in the trade or industry in the district observed by employers whose circumstances were similar to those of the employer against whom the claim was made. Where there were recognised terms and conditions of employment a claim could be made to have them extended to a blacksheep employer, whether or not he was federated to the employers' association. But the existence of recognised terms including in particular nationally agreed minima acted as a bar on claims for the normally higher general level. Given that national agreements negotiated with employers' associations tend to stipulate bare minima for large segments of industry, this was a very severe restriction.[22] Another limitation was that a claim was not allowed under Schedule 11 if the terms and conditions were fixed in pursuance of any enactment other than wages council legislation and the Schedule itself. This was held to exclude a claim in respect of the biggest employer in the country, the National Health Service, where remuneration was settled through 'Whitley' machinery and then approved by the Secretary of State for Health and Social Services in accordance with statutory regulations.[23] Generally, however, the CAC's role under Schedule 11 (in contrast to that of ACAS under EPA ss.11–16) was not seriously impeded by judicial review. Indeed in one case the Lord Chief Justice correctly inferred from the absence of a right of appeal from CAC decisions that 'Parliament intended these matters to be dealt with without too much assistance from the lawyers'.[24]

The government's case for the repeal of Schedule 11 was based on three arguments. First the Schedule had not contributed towards the elimination of low pay. Second it had featured in the spiral of inflation especially as awards under it did not count against the limits on increases in the previous government's pay policy. Between January 1977 when Schedule 11 came into operation and August 1980 1,939 references were made to the CAC, about 80 per cent of them under the head of general level and (during the pay policy) many with employer collusion. (For similar reasons there was an upsurge in the number of references to the CAC under the Fair Wages Resolution.) The increase in arbitration, it was argued, was likely to have had a disruptive effect on pay structures and differentials. Moreover the Schedule's emphasis on comparison did not allow full account to be taken of other factors such as market prospects, profitability, labour efficiency and prices. According to a much quoted letter from a director of Courtaulds to the DE: 'the handing down of awards from remote central bodies creates in employees' minds the vision of a bottomless pit of wealth, irrespective of the circumstances of their particular enterprise and totally at variance with the government's philosophy of ability to pay'.[25] Third the Schedule was hindering voluntary industrial relations. In the past it might have been the case that measures such as the Terms and Conditions of Employment Act 1959 s.8 and the Fair Wages Resolution were necessary to support collective bargaining but modern developments in industrial relations rendered them obsolete and unhelpful. In the course of resisting opposition attempts to retain the 'recognised' terms and conditions provision, an important gloss was put on this argument, namely, that Schedule 11 represented 'an unnecessary and unwarranted interference in employers' freedom to negotiate their own settlements'.[26]

These arguments are open to challenge. The Industrial Relations Research Unit at Warwick University found that Schedule 11 did help the relatively low paid and indeed some of the absolutely low paid. Thus in 1977, 1978 and 1979 the vast majority of successful claims under Schedule 11 were made on behalf of groups of manual and non-manual employees whose earnings were below the average indicated by the New Earnings Survey.[27] In the light of such evidence the government's repeal of the Schedule suggests a lack of commitment to the low paid at a time when economic circumstances increasingly favour the undercutting employer. Nor is it easy to sustain the argument that Schedule 11 was inflationary. It provided (as did the Fair Wages Resolution) a means of correcting some of the anomalies generated by the previous government's incomes policy; it was a 'safety valve' without which the policy might have collapsed sooner than it did. In any case the exception for Schedule 11 was hardly a valid reason for its subsequent repeal by a government which set its face against a formal incomes policy. Further although its awards were inevitably based on comparability the CAC was always concerned to take account of labour market and other economic factors. The Schedule itself expressly required it to have regard 'to the whole of the terms and conditions observed by the employer'. In fact the requirements of the Schedule particularly the bar on general level claims where or in so far as there were recognised terms meant that the economic significance of the Schedule was small. In 1979, for example, the CAC made awards in favour of 68,168 workers but made no awards on claims on behalf of 72,294. As the CAC's 1979 Annual Report observed 'the suggestion that the Committee's awards add a twist to the inflationary spiral attributes to the CAC an importance in the national bargaining round which it does not have'.[28] The Schedule also had only a marginal effect on industrial relations, though the evidence suggests that it helped rather than hindered. Another Industrial Relations Research Unit survey of managers who had been involved in cases where the CAC had made an award found that the largest group considered that it had made no difference to industrial relations; the minority who thought that it had caused problems were outnumbered by those who thought that industrial relations had improved after the award. Certainly within the limits of the Schedule the CAC always tried to have regard to the underlying industrial relations problems. Finally, there was the government's insistence on the repeal of the 'recognised' as well as the 'general level' provisions. This was opposed by employers' organisations such as the EEF and, in a remarkable gesture of independence, it was publicly condemned by the CAC's 1979 Annual Report: 'the application of recognised terms and conditions has been a feature of our industrial relations for many decades, serving as it does to protect the worker who may be exploited and the good employer who may be undercut. Support should continue to be given to established negotiating machinery'.[29]

Section 19(c) of the Employment Act also repealed the Road Haulage Wages Act 1938. This Act was part of a small body of what may be called 'fair wages legislation', that is, statutes which embody in some form the principle in clause 1 of the Fair Wages Resolution. The other statutes are the Civil Aviation Act 1949, Films Act 1960, Road Traffic Act 1960 and Independent Broadcasting Authority Act 1973. Part II of the Road Haulage Wages Act provided that in return for the grant of a licence to an employer, the remuneration paid to road haulage workers who drove vehicles used by the employer for his own purposes should be 'fair'. Either a worker or a union could complain to ACAS that the remuneration being paid by an employer was unfair, and these disputes were determined by the CAC. The Act specified certain circumstances in which remuneration was not unfair: if it was in accordance with a collective agreement to which the employer was party, or equivalent to (a) remuneration paid to similar workers in the district under a collective agreement, (b) remuneration in a minimum wage order, (c) the district rate of a joint industrial council or similar body, or (d) a previous CAC award. But failure to meet one of these criteria did not automatically mean that the remuneration paid was unfair: *R* v. *CAC, Ex parte RHM Foods Ltd.* (1979) where it was held that the CAC must have regard to the overall remuneration and not one part such as overtime in isolation. If the CAC found that the remuneration was unfair it was required to fix a new rate. This was enforceable as an implied term in the employment contracts of the workers involved and it was also a criminal offence for the employer not to observe an award. The enforcement procedure was little used after the Second World War, although the number of claims rose significantly in 1978. This was in part attributed by the CAC to the abolition of the Road Haulage Wages Council in that year which meant that the 1938 Act became the only legal protection available for a large group of workers.[30] Unless it is but a step in the progressive dismantling of all the statutory and governmental assistance to collective bargaining, it is difficult to see the point of the repeal of this statute. A not implausible explanation was the government's determination to punish road haulage workers for their strike in 1978–79.

The reasoning behind the repeal of Schedule 11 and the Road Haulage Wages Act does indeed suggest the possibility of further repeals. In fact the Working Paper on Schedule 11 made it clear that the government was contemplating annuling the Fair Wages Resolution, though it acknowledged the embarrassment caused by ILO Convention 94 which requires clauses similar to those in the Resolution to be included in public contracts. But why stop at the Fair Wages Resolution? Why not abolish the tripartite wages councils as well? They might also be categorised as 'an unnecessary and unwarranted interference in employers' freedom to negotiate their own settlements'. It seems that on the government's logic the case for the repeal of what Kahn-Freund called 'auxiliary' labour law is only strengthened to the extent that it assists the low paid, supports the development of collective bargaining and enables the state to stipulate standards of good industrial relations practice.

8

Picketing

The Employment Act restricts the legal freedom to take industrial action. As we explained in chapter one, in Britain this freedom is based on a unique structure of statutory immunities from judge-made liabilities. The 1980 Act both amends and restricts the application of those immunities. It goes a good deal further than the government has been prepared to acknowledge. Although ostensibly aimed at 'secondary' picketing and industrial action, it curtails the legal freedom to engage in 'primary' disputes as well. And although it is supposed to be concerned only with the civil law, s.16 together with the Code of Practice on Picketing may have profound implications for the criminal law. After the Act and the Code the government published its Green Paper *Trade Union Immunities,* which offers the prospect of further restrictive legislation with its attendant legal complexities. We have nevertheless endeavoured to make our exposition as clear as possible. In chapter nine we concentrate on strikes, blacking and other forms of economic sanction; this chapter concerns the more physical manifestation of industrial action, picketing.

The government's argument for amending picketing law was succinctly stated in its Working Paper on Picketing. This claimed that the 1979 Conservative Election Manifesto, on which it was based, reflected 'widespread public concern' over picketing after the industrial unrest in the winter of 1978–79, particularly the tendency 'in the last few years' to picket companies '*not* directly involved in disputes'. Here we have the popular though not legal essence of the very difficult distinction between primary and secondary action: the former is aimed at an employer involved in the dispute and is normally action taken by his own employees; the latter is aimed at employers who are apparently not involved. (We discuss the rather different technical legal definition of 'secondary action' in EA s.17(2) in chapter nine, p. 203.) The Working Paper attributed the growth of secondary picketing to 'easier transport

153

and communication', and 'a greater degree of organisation of picketing
. . . sometimes the work of unofficial groups rather than official union
leaders', and 'the growth and greater formalisation of the closed shop
since 1974. . . . There are indications,' it added ominously, 'of an increasing use of intimidation on picket lines, whether directly through
the threat of physical violence or indirectly through the threat of loss
of union membership, and, as a consequence, of jobs.' The allegation of
intimidation was again raised in connection with the bitter national
steel strike which occurred during the first fourteen weeks of 1980.
After a brief discussion of the government's case, we shall go on to
examine in some detail the scope of the legal freedom to picket as
amended.

PICKETING OLD AND NEW

Picketing has been a feature of industrial disputes in Britain for over a
century. It has frequently been well-organised (whether officially or un-
officially) and almost invariably it has been peaceful. Anyone familiar
with the violence which has often attended picket lines in Canada and
the United States knows just how peaceful the traditional British practice of picketing is. In so far as there have been any exceptional violent
manifestations, they have always been subject to the criminal law. But
is there substance in the government's assertion that intimidatory
picketing has increased in recent years? The evidence for any connection between such picketing and the closed shop is extremely tenuous,
particularly as the recent formalisation of closed shop arrangements has
been associated with a strengthening of the procedures to protect individuals (see chapter four). The more serious allegation is that there has
been a trend towards physical violence. This too is difficult to substan-
tiate, though undoubtedly atypical incidents of a violent character have
occurred during prolonged disputes. There were physical altercations
between the pickets and the police in the Grunwick dispute, but it
raised other questions too including the role of the Special Patrol
Group and the ability of one 'cowboy' employer to frustrate a Court of
Inquiry and an ACAS investigation.[1] In the case of the 'Shrewsbury'
pickets (*R* v. *Jones,* 1974), there was evidence of violent threats against
self-employed blacklegs, but it is questionable whether a display of
force on a building site affords any evidence for a general picture of
mounting violence. What is more likely is that a few isolated incidents

have been dramatised by the media to give the impression that picketing frequently involves violence. The perspective of labour history teaches us that the antecedents of this technique are as old as picketing itself. In the words of George Howell, who was very much a 'moderate' of the Victorian era:

> Hundreds of strikes, with the usual practice of picketing, occur, to which public attention is never drawn; they are not of sufficient importance to attract a crowd of reporters anxious to chronicle every fact which tells against the workmen. Such strikes sometimes result in favour of the men, at other times in favour of the masters; picketing is resorted to in most cases, but the public hear nothing about the alleged evils of the system. Why? Because they seldom take place. But let one single instance of coercion or undue influence be resorted to, and the entire newspaper press will record the fact, not unfrequently colouring it so as to distort its real nature and significance (or rather insignificance); 'leaders' are written in denunciation, not only of the actual perpetrators of the offence, but of the whole class to which they belong, until it becomes a settled conviction in the minds of the majority of the public, that these cases are perpetually recurring; that they form part, an essential part, of the system, and are the absolute and necessary outcome of the practice.[2]

Those words were published in 1890. In 1980 not dissimilar views were expressed by a very authoritative group of persons, namely senior policemen giving evidence to the House of Commons Select Committee on Employment. They confirmed that picketing was normally peaceful, often not requiring any police presence at all, and further that the problems of policing even large numbers of pickets had been exaggerated by the media. The Chief Constable of South Wales said:

> Quite frequently there are occasions when pickets are there in large numbers and all is peaceful and no great difficulties are caused. They are sometimes there for comradeship or solidarity. You must not assume that on every occasion there is a mass picket there is going to be trouble. You sometimes get a very jaundiced picture from the news media who tend to highlight the occasions when things go wrong, but this is by no means the norm because there are many other incidents which pass off day by day without any difficulty whatever.[3]

And even when things do go wrong the media itself may sometimes share the blame. The Chief Constable of South Yorkshire referred to some of the picketing in the 1980 steel dispute in these terms: 'The rapport between my officers and the pickets was very good. Often they

would push for five minutes or however long the television people were
watching and then the whole thing would subside.'[4]

The claim that secondary picketing has assumed a new importance in
the last few years is also debatable. Leading cases at the turn of the century illustrate the point that secondary picketing goes back a very long
way. *Temperton* v. *Russell* (1893) involved the picketing and boycott
of a supplier to the employer in dispute. *Quinn* v. *Leathem* (1901) was
a conspiracy to picket both the employer in dispute and his customer.
In fact the secondary dimension expresses one of the two essential
functions of any form of peaceful picketing.

Picketing is intended first to persuade other workers not to work for
the employer in dispute, and second to persuade third parties, for
example, customers and suppliers not to have dealings with him. This
dual function of picketing was recognised by the Donovan Report:
'Where a strike occurs it is obviously in the interests of the strikers to
dissuade, if they can, other workmen from replacing them *and* customers of the employer from dealing with him while the strike continues. This involves that such other workmen *and* such customers must
know that a strike is taking place and the men's side of the case' (para.
855, our italics). A similar point was made in paragraph 9 of the TUC's
1979 Guide *Conduct of Industrial Disputes*:

> The purposes of picketing are to persuade other employees to
> join in the withdrawal of labour; to dissuade workers recruited by
> the employer during a strike from entering the strikebound prem-
> ises; or to establish checkpoints to ensure that no strikers return
> prematurely. Picketing may also be aimed at deflecting supplies
> or custom from the employer in dispute. The decision to mount a
> picket is for the union in dispute.

In reality it is impossible to separate these two functions because
effective picketing of the employer in dispute must have an adverse
effect on his commercial relationship with his customers and suppliers.
Picketing the customers and suppliers in order to seal off the employer
in dispute is just as fundamental as picketing the employer's premises.
To quote the TUC Guide again: 'Unions should in general, and save in
exceptional circumstances, confine picketing to premises of the parties
in dispute *or* the premises of suppliers and customers of those parties'
(para. 9, our italics). Recognising the facts of industrial life, the Donovan
Report acknowledged the frequency of persuasion of customers (they
might have added suppliers) and found that 'most persons . . . regard it
as legitimate. In our opinion [the law] should be amplified so as to
make such peaceful persuasion lawful' (para. 875).

The need for this protection is underlined by the fact that police-protected blacklegs, as well as customers and suppliers, can today drive past any picket line in lorries or coaches. The TUC has been unsuccessful in its efforts to secure a right for pickets to communicate peacefully but effectively with the occupants of vehicles. But a basic and modern justification for secondary picketing and industrial action is its vital role in maintaining a degree of balance of industrial power at a time when employers operate more and more on a multi-plant, multi-company and multi-national basis. Economic ownership and control in the private sector has since the 1950s become increasingly concentrated in multi-nationals, large financial institutions and groups of companies.[5] At the same time the overall tendency towards centralisation of power and decision-making has been intensified by the growing intervention of the state as employer, law-maker and manager of the economy. In addition it is becoming ever more apparent that employers at large do not necessarily regard themselves as neutral third parties in disputes. In 1980 the CBI which includes nationalised corporations in its membership published a report arguing that employers in conflict with unions represented the collective interest of all employers. It advocated more employer solidarity, including mutual financial support schemes and stiff disciplinary action against workers engaging in secondary or other forms of industrial action, and that employers not in dispute should refrain from taking commercial advantage of employers in dispute.[6]

The Employment Act's restrictions on picketing (and on industrial action at large) are therefore to be seen as a calculated blow against the freedom of unions to attempt to match the organisational strength of employers. Yet the government conveyed the impression that prior to the Employment Act there was a broad right to picket which invited restriction. In order both to give the lie to this impression and to appreciate the real effects of the 1980 Act it is necessary first to understand the previous law.

TULRA s.15 BEFORE THE 1980 ACT

Until 1875 the policy of the law was generally to suppress peaceful picketing along with all other forms of industrial action. The modern law begins with s.7 of the Conspiracy and Protection of Property Act 1875 which is still in force. It provides that any person commits a crime if, wrongfully and without legal authority and with a view to compelling any other person to do or abstain from doing anything lawful, he does any of five specified things: (i) uses violence to or 'intimidates' such other person, his wife or children or injures his property; (ii) persistently follows him; (iii) hides his tools or other property, or deprives him of them, or hinders their use; (iv) 'watches or besets' any house or place where he is or any approach to it; (v) follows him in the street with two or more others in a disorderly manner. These crimes are still applicable to all picketing, irrespective of whether or not there is a trade dispute.

The section sought however to legalise peaceful picketing in a proviso which deemed that attending at or near a place merely in order to obtain or communicate information did not constitute the criminal offence of 'watching or besetting'. The judges moved quickly to emasculate this new freedom. Peaceful picketing which involved persuasion was held to go beyond mere attendance for the purpose of informing, and to be a common law 'nuisance' (unreasonable interference with the use of property). Since the tort of nuisance was clearly wrongful and without legal authority, peaceful picketing could after all constitute the crime of watching or besetting. In addition the tort of nuisance provided the legal basis for civil actions for damages and injunctions against pickets who attempted by purely peaceful means to persuade other workers not to take jobs with an employer in dispute (*Lyons* v. *Wilkins,* 1896, 1899; *Charnock* v. *Court,* 1899). Peaceful picketing was held not to be a nuisance in *Ward Lock* v. *Operative Printers' Assistants' Society* (1906), but there the evidence showed that it was totally ineffectual.

The proviso in the 1875 Act which had sought to legalise peaceful picketing covered only the communication of information and not persuasion, a weakness exposed by *Lyons* v. *Wilkins.* It was remedied in the aftermath of the *Taff Vale* case by s.2 of the Trade Disputes Act 1906. That section declared that it was lawful, in contemplation of furtherance of a trade dispute, to attend at or near a house or place merely for the purpose of peacefully obtaining or communicating information or of peacefully persuading a person to work or to abstain from working. In 1971 this was replaced by s.134 of the Industrial Relations Act, which was substantially similar except that attendance at a place where a person resides was excluded. Finally, on the repeal of the IRA, TULRA s.15 retained this exclusion of attendance at residences but otherwise restored the historic formula of the 1906 Act:

> It shall be lawful for one or more persons in contemplation or furtherance of a trade dispute to attend at or near (a) a place

where another person works or carries on business or (b) any other place where another person happens to be, not being a place where he resides, for the purpose only of peacefully obtaining or communicating information or peacefully persuading any person to work or abstain from working.

The extent of the immunity from common law liabilities provided for pickets by the original TULRA s.15 and its predecessors was very limited. Various aspects of this restrictive ambit remain relevant to the new TULRA s.15 which was substituted by s.16(1) of the 1980 Act. First the opening phrase 'it shall be lawful' gives the form but not the substance of a positive right. Technically speaking there is no legal 'right' to picket just as there is no legal 'right' to strike: the question as ever is one of possible immunity from different kinds of liability. Second like the immunities in TULRA s.13, s.15 is for the benefit of 'a person'. It is not confined to trade union officials and extends even to a person who falls outside the legal definition of a worker. Third it is nonetheless qualified by the golden formula 'in contemplation or furtherance of a trade dispute'. This point must be emphasised. TULRA s.15 gives no protection for persons engaged in picketing unless their actions are in contemplation or furtherance of a trade dispute. For example, it could not provide a defence to members of a tenants' association who were picketing an estate agent in Islington in protest against the 'gentrification' of the area (*Hubbard* v. *Pitt*, 1975). But even in disputes that are clearly industrial the courts may hold that picketing is not covered by the golden formula; pickets and those who organise pickets are thereby exposed to the full rigour of common law liabilities. Thus, in advance of the Employment Act, Lord Denning was of the opinion that secondary picketing could not be in furtherance of a trade dispute: 'when strikers choose to picket, not their employer's premises, but the premises of innocent third parties not parties to the dispute – it is unlawful. "Secondary picketing" it is called. It is unlawful at common law and is so remote from the dispute that there is no immunity in regard to it.'[7] Although such reasoning is inconsistent with the subsequent House of Lords interpretation of the golden formula in *Express Newspapers Ltd.* v. *MacShane* (1980) and *Duport Steels Ltd.* v. *Sirs* (1980), a variant of it has been restored by EA s.17 if there is 'secondary action' within the meaning of that section (see chapter nine). Fourth even if the pickets are acting in contemplation or furtherance of a trade dispute, TULRA s.15 may provide no protection because the behaviour of the pickets goes beyond 'attendance' at or near a place merely for the purpose of obtaining or communicating information or persuading people not to work. Impeding pedestrians or vehicles for example goes beyond mere attendance.

The question must therefore be posed: to what behaviour does TULRA s.15 afford any legal protection? But for the section, mere attendance for the permitted purposes might constitute the torts of nuisance (*Lyons* v. *Wilkins*) or possibly trespass to the highway (see the different opinions of Forbes J. and Lord Denning in *Hubbard* v. *Pitt*). It might also amount to the crimes of 'watching or besetting' under s.7 of the 1875 Act or wilful obstruction of the highway contrary to s.121 of the Highways Act 1959. However even in peaceful picketing a wide range of other civil and criminal liabilities may be committed. The relevant civil liabilities are the economic torts: conspiracy, intimidation, inducing breach of or interference with contract and interference with business by unlawful means. Their scope is discussed in chapter nine. As we shall see, s.16(2) of the Employment Act removes the statutory protection against these liabilities from 'an act done in the course of picketing' outside the new definition of lawful attendance.

CRIMINAL LIABILITIES AND THE ROLE OF THE POLICE

In practice it has been the police and the prosecuting authorities in criminal cases rather than plaintiffs in civil actions who have tested the practical effects of TULRA s.15 and its predecessors. Concentrating for the moment on purely peaceful picketing, and most picketing is peaceful, the following examples illustrate the very narrow scope of the words 'it shall be lawful' in TULRA s.15 as far as the criminal law is concerned, the wide discretion of the police to control picketing and the remarkable fact that peaceful pickets are prone to arrest and conviction for crimes which have the flavour of violence about them.

A police officer decided that two pickets were enough to attend at the back gate of an employer's premises. 'I know my rights' said a third, and, going to join the other pickets, he 'pushed gently passed' the officer and 'was gently arrested'. Although there was no obstruction of the highway and no disorder, he was held to have wilfully obstructed the officer in the course of his duty. The policeman's action was legally justified because he had reasonable grounds for believing that there might have been a breach of the peace unless he thinned out the tiny picket line (*Piddington* v. *Bates* 1960). Forty pickets walked in a continuous circle outside a factory in order to 'seal off the highway' and cause vehicles visiting the factory to stop so as to talk to the drivers. That, the judges found, was not made lawful by the statutory immunity since it went beyond communicating information and peacefully persuading persons to work or not to work. By this literal interpretation of the section the court was able to decide that it did not make it lawful to stop or delay either pedestrians or vehicles. The conviction of the leader of the pickets for obstructing a constable in the execution of his duty by refusing to stop the circling was therefore upheld (*Tynan* v. *Balmer*, 1967).

A full-time officer of UCATT stopped a lorry by stepping out in front of it in order to urge the driver not to enter a building site. He was arrested and convicted for obstruction of the highway, a criminal offence which is committed when 'a person, without lawful authority or excuse, in any way wilfully obstructs the free passage along a highway' (Highways Act 1959 s.121(1)). The House of Lords was adamant that IRA s.134 (operative between 1972–74) gave no right to a picket to stop a vehicle. Lord Reid could 'see no ground for implying any right to require the person whom it is sought to persuade to submit to any kind of constraint or restriction of his personal freedom. One is familiar with persons at the side of a road signalling to a driver requesting him to stop. It is then for the driver to decide whether he will stop or not. That, in my view, a picket is entitled to do. If the driver stops, the picket can talk to him but only for so long as the driver is willing to listen' (*Hunt* v. *Broome*, 1974).[8] In other words, a picket has the same legal rights in this respect as a hitchhiker.

If peaceful picketing by small numbers of pickets often involves criminal liability, peaceful picketing by large numbers is even more at risk. Although mass picketing was no part of the facts of *Hunt* v. *Broome*, Lord Reid took the opportunity to say: 'it would not be difficult to infer as a matter of fact that pickets who assemble in unreasonably large numbers do have the purpose of preventing free passage. If that were the proper inference then their presence on the highway would become unlawful.'[9] On that reasoning mass picketing, however orderly and peaceful, is likely to involve liability for the criminal offence of wilful obstruction of the highway.

Cases such as *Piddington* v. *Bates*, *Tynan* v. *Balmer* and *Hunt* v. *Broome* point to the inescapable conclusion that TULRA s.15 only protects against criminal liability for very minor forms of obstruction and watching or besetting by small numbers of pickets who keep out of everyone's way. In fact the police exercise a wide discretion and often come to some sensible arrangement with pickets. Although pickets have no legal right to stop vehicles, the police sometimes themselves stop lorries so that the pickets may briefly communicate without risk of a road accident. On one occasion in the 1972 miners' strike the police refrained from attempting to arrest thousands of pickets outside the Saltley coke depot, which was eventually shut down on the decision of the police. Clearly TULRA s.15 is not necessarily a guide to what may be common sense in a particular situation. It is also important to emphasise that our police force is still organised on a local basis with roots in the community and still operates, by and large, on the basis of consent.[10] As we shall explain below, all this assumes a new importance in the light of the Secretary of State's Code of Practice on Picketing. The point here is that far from the law giving some wide legal immunity which must be cut down (as the present government implies in its approach to the problem), almost all forms of effective picketing however peaceful tend to be unlawful. Effective peaceful picketing, so far as the criminal law goes, is possible only at the discretion of the police.

Criminal liabilities for physical and verbal force

It goes without saying that the use of force in picketing is criminal. Indeed, in the most extreme circumstances envisaged by the Riot Damages Act 1886, if the police fail to take steps to restrain pickets or others who behave 'riotously and tumultuously' they may themselves be liable to pay compensation to the owners of property. The Grunwick affair provides an example of strict enforcement of the criminal law.[11] In that dispute there were 503 arrests between June 1977 and January 1978. Over 80 per cent of those prosecuted were convicted, mostly for the offences of obstructing a police officer in the course of his duty, threatening behaviour, obstructing the highway or assaulting a police officer.

There are however many varieties of physical force. The over-vociferous picket, for example, may easily commit the offence of threatening words or behaviour, which arises if a person in a public place 'uses threatening, abusive or insulting words or behaviour ... with intent to provoke a breach of the peace or whereby a breach of the peace is likely to be occasioned'.[12] Nor on the evidence of the Grunwick dispute is it too difficult to commit a technical 'assault', or even the offence under s.51 of the Police Act 1964 of obstructing a police constable in the course of his duty.

Serious violence may involve the commission of several crimes, including intimidation under the Conspiracy and Protection of Property Act 1875 s.7. The criminal offence of intimidation (which must not be confused with the quite different tort of intimidation, see chapter nine) is not defined in the 1875 statute, but, according to the Court of Appeal in the 'Shrewsbury' picketing case (*R* v. *Jones*), it 'includes putting persons in fear by the exhibition of force or violence, and there is no limitation restricting the meaning to cases of violence or threats of violence to the person'.[13] Thus displays of force and violence against buildings and equipment are sufficient for intimidation, though it is not clear what else might be included; for example, is offensive language which does not threaten violence enough? Threatening a non-striker with withdrawal of his union card is almost certainly not the criminal offence of intimidation. Intimidation should perhaps be considered with two other crimes which also featured in the Shrewsbury case: unlawful assembly, which some of the accused were found to have committed, and affray, of which they were acquitted. These are not defined by statute and are judge-made common law crimes. Unlawful assembly consists of (a) the assembly (usually stated as being of three or more persons) and (b) the intention of fulfilling a common purpose in such a manner as to endanger the public peace. Affray consists of unlawful fighting by one or more persons in a public place or a display of force by one or more persons without actual violence in such a manner that a bystander of reasonably firm character might reasonably be expected to be terrified.

The national strike in the construction industry in 1972, which gave rise to both *Hunt* v. *Broome* and the Shrewsbury case, posed the difficult problem for the unions of how to make the industrial action effective on the hundreds of building sites manned by self-employed, non-unionised 'lump' labour. The solution was the organised flying picket. This development together with the mass picketing in the miners' dispute of 1972 formed the background to the House of Lords' decision in *Hunt* v. *Broome* on 20 December 1973, by which time another miners' dispute, which was to be the pretext for calling the election of February 1974, was already under way. Then, in February and March 1974, the Court of Appeal heard and decided the appeal of the convicted Shrewsbury pickets (*R* v. *Jones*). Flying and mass picketing evinced a predictably hostile response from the 'establishment' and this factor may help to explain some of the unusual features in the Shrewsbury affair: the delay of five months between the alleged incidents and the charges, the massive police operation involving the interviewing of hundreds of witnesses, the suspicion that the police were acting under some kind of centralised government directive, the trial which lasted for over two and a half months, and the extraordinary deterrent sentences imposed on two of the accused of two years and three years of imprisonment which were served in full.[14] The charges moreover involved not only substantive criminal offences but also conspiracy.

Criminal conspiracy

The seriousness of a crime may be enhanced if there is a conspiracy to commit it. As we mentioned in chapter one, the nineteenth-century judges considered that combining for trade union purposes was a criminal conspiracy (*R* v. *Bunn*), a liability which received protection in trade disputes under s.3 of the Conspiracy and Protection of Property Act 1875. This section was repealed and replaced by the Criminal Law Act 1977, which provides that a conspiracy is a crime only when the act to be done is itself criminal. Section 1(3) of the 1977 Act gives an immunity for combinations, in contemplation or furtherance of a trade dispute, to commit summary offences not punishable with imprisonment. That however gives no immunity for conspiracy to commit other crimes which are punishable by imprisonment, for example, conspiracy to 'intimidate', which was one of the charges against the Shrewsbury pickets. The sentences in that case were possible because the usual statutory limits on sentence lengths for statutory offences (three months for intimidation under s.7 of the 1875 Act) were inapplicable to the common law judge-made crime of conspiracy.

After the Criminal Law Act 1977 pickets may still be charged with criminal conspiracy, but s.3(3) provides that the maximum penalty for conspiracy is the maximum for the substantive offence. Unfortunately this does not eliminate the possibility of severe sentences against trade unionists because not all substantive offences are tied by statute to a maximum sentence length. Some are judge-made creations for which there is no maximum, for example, unlawful assembly and affray. These crimes were singled out for special mention in the Attorney-General's Statement on Picketing Law to the House of Commons at the height of the steel strike in February 1980: 'Are large numbers really necessary in the name of lawful, peaceful persuasion? They are more likely to lead to unlawful assembly, or even an affray.'[15] Where there is flying or mass picketing these possibilities will be known to the prosecuting authorities.

Workplace occupations

The Criminal Law Act 1977 also creates new criminal offences which are ostensibly aimed at squatters but which could equally be used against workers taking part in a sit-in or work-in. The relevant offences are of uncertain ambit: using or threatening violence to secure entry to premises (s.6); trespassing with a weapon of offence — an elastic concept (s.8); and resisting or obstructing a court officer who is enforcing a court order for repossession of the premises (s.10). Workers who take part in any form of workplace occupation have never qualified for the protection of TULRA s.15 or its predecessors. The words in the section are 'at or near' a place, not in or on it. Apart from possible criminal liability under the 1977 Act the workers concerned are potentially subject to civil liability for the tort of trespass. If they unlawfully detain goods which are not theirs, as they almost certainly will in a work-in, they may also incur civil liability under the Torts (Interference with Goods) Act 1977. In any event they are subject to the rapid repossession procedure in Order 113 of the Rules of the Supreme Court, under which persons need not be individually identified.

TULRA s.15 AFTER THE EMPLOYMENT ACT

From the analysis so far it is clear that acts of violence on the picket line are in all circumstances illegal, and that even purely peaceful picketing is subject to police control. Even before the Employment Act TULRA s.15 provided only a very narrow immunity from civil and criminal liabilities. Section 16(1) of the 1980 Act reduces the scope of this immunity still further by substituting the following as the new TULRA s.15:

15. (1) It shall be lawful for a person in contemplation or furtherance of a trade dispute to attend
  (a) at or near his own place of work, or
  (b) if he is an official of a trade union, at or near the place of work of a member of that union whom he is accompanying and whom he represents,
for the purpose only of peacefully obtaining or communicating information, or peacefully persuading any person to work or abstain from working.
(2) If a person works or normally works
  (a) otherwise than at any one place, or
  (b) at a place the location of which is such that attendance

there for a purpose mentioned in subsection (1) above
is impracticable,
his place of work for the purposes of that subsection shall be any
premises of his employer from which he works or from which his
work is administered.

(3) In the case of a worker who is not in employment and
whose last employment was terminated in connection with a
trade dispute, subsection (1) above shall in relation to that dispute have effect as if any reference to his place of work were a
reference to his former place of work.

(4) A person who is an official of a trade union by virtue only
of having been elected or appointed to be a representative of
some of the members of the union shall be regarded for the purposes of subsection (1) above as representing only those members; but otherwise an official of a trade union shall be regarded
for those purposes as representing all its members.

Own place of work

The new basic principle is that, subject to a qualification for trade
union officials, the immunity is confined to a person who attends at or
near his 'own place of work'. The Act makes a special provision for the
application of this concept to certain specific groups. If a person works
at more than one place (e.g. a lorry driver), or if it is impracticable for
him to picket lawfully at his own place of work because of its location
(an off-shore oil rig worker perhaps) his place of work for this purpose
is 'any premises of his employer from which he works or from which
his work is administered'. The government intends that this provision
should be narrowly interpreted. In the case of lorry drivers, for example,
it 'will usually mean in practice those premises of their employer from
which their vehicles operate' (Picketing Code, para. 13). Special provision is also made for one category of persons who no longer have their
own place of work. A 'worker who is not in employment and whose
last employment was terminated in connection with a trade dispute'
may 'in relation to that dispute' picket his former place of work. This
too is very limited. The ex-employer may be picketed only if the
worker has lost his job 'in connection with' a trade dispute. Whether or
not this requirement is satisfied could be a matter for argument in
many cases. It would appear to cover a worker who was dismissed while
he was on strike or locked out providing that the picketing is in relation
to that dispute. Furthermore, though the employment may have been
terminated in connection with a trade dispute, because of the phrase
'not in employment' the worker loses the statutory protection for

picketing his former employer if he finds new employment elsewhere. Even taking a part-time job would probably have the effect of removing the immunity.

Whether or not a worker is covered by one of these special provisions, the lawfulness of his picketing turns on whether he is attending at or near his 'own place of work'. This basic concept is not defined by the Employment Act. Why? According to the government's own Notes on the Employment Bill 'for most workers the term has an obvious meaning'. The Secretary of State acknowledged that 'it would be impossible to define it in such a way as to cover all the varieties of work place'. But perhaps the Attorney-General with his greater legal experience came nearest to the truth of the matter when he declared that to attempt to define it would lead to 'disaster', to a 'dog's breakfast' and to 'the most awful mess'.[16] The courts will therefore determine its meaning, but with the assistance of one brief but important piece of guidance which the government was willing to offer in paragraph 12 of the Picketing Code:

> In general . . . lawful picketing normally involves attendance at an entrance to or exit from the factory, site or office at which the picket works. It does not enable a picket to attend lawfully at an entrance to or exit from any place of work which is not his own, even if those who work there are employed by the same employer or covered by the same collective bargaining arrangements.

The restrictive implications of that formulation will pose enormous difficulties for all pickets, including those who wish to picket their own employer ('primary' pickets). For example, is an employee at one Ford plant at Dagenham entitled to regard Ford's entire Dagenham estate as his place of work? An affirmative answer to that very question was given by the National Insurance Commissioner in a decision on the meaning of 'place of employment' for the purposes of the trade dispute disqualification from unemployment benefit (R(U)1/70). This broad interpretation had the effect of disqualifying from unemployment benefit large numbers of workers who were laid off because of a strike in one segment of the production process. In picketing the principle would work in reverse; the narrower the concept of place of work the greater the likelihood of unlawful picketing, a perspective that would no doubt be appreciated by the courts even without the prompting of paragraph 12 of the Picketing Code. Different Ford plants at Dagenham therefore might be designated as different workplaces, and the Ford plant at Halewood would certainly not fall within the place of work of a picket from Dagenham. Many similar examples could be cited from British Leyland, British Steel Corporation, Imperial Chemical Industries and other major multi-plant employers in the private and public sectors. There is no statutory protection for the worker who ventures away from his own place of work, as narrowly understood, in order to picket at the employer's head office or at another plant belonging to his employer, even if production is being transferred from one plant to another as part of the dispute. Again, if the employer is involved in national collective bargaining through an employers' association, pickets must remain at their own place of work if they are to retain their immunity under TULRA s.15; they must not join picket lines mounted at other employers who may also be federated to the employers' association and thereby in dispute with their union. That is the case even if the other employers are giving material support to the pickets' employer.

The impact of the concept of 'own place of work' is increased by the trend towards operating single business enterprises through a number of different companies. If each plant on a multi-plant site is owned by a different company, even if the companies are associated employers, every plant will be a different place of work and a no-go area for pickets from any other plant on the site. (This may be contrasted with the extension of permitted secondary action in EA s.17(4) to action against an associated employer of an employer in dispute, albeit in very restricted circumstances — see chapter nine.) Any picket who mistakenly confuses industrial reality with the legal fiction of separate corporate identity is legally at risk. Nor is it totally inconceivable that some employers will consider forming separate companies to convert their own employees at one plant owned by one company into 'unlicensed' pickets at another plant owned by a different company. Finally, employers who refuse to recognise trade unions are assisted by the Act's discouragement of sympathetic picketing on behalf of those who may have little negotiating power, for example, the low-paid predominantly immigrant workers at Grunwick and at Garners Steak Houses.

Trade union officials

If picketing is to take place it is good industrial relations practice for a trade union official to be present and in charge. On that point at least there is agreement between the TUC Guide (*Conduct of Industrial Dis-*

putes, para. 13), the government (Picketing Code, para. 32) and the Chief Constables in their evidence to the House of Commons Select Committee on Employment. The new TULRA s.15 however gives an immunity to the trade union official only if he accompanies a member of his own union at the member's place of work and he personally represents that member.

'Official' in relation to a trade union means a full-time officer or a branch officer or a person elected or appointed in accordance with the rules of the union to be a representative, including a shop steward (TULRA s.30). Although this definition has a wide ambit, for the purposes of TULRA s.15 the only licensed official is one who personally represents the member he is accompanying: a person who is an official 'by virtue only of having been elected or appointed to be a representative of some of the members of the union shall be regarded ... as representing only those members' (TULRA s.15(4)). An official, according to paragraph 16 of the Picketing Code, 'cannot, therefore, claim that he represents a group of members simply because they belong to his trade union'. Thus a shop steward may attend only with members whom he represents at a particular place of work, a branch official only with members of his branch, a district or regional official only with members of his district or region and a national official responsible for a trade group or section only with members of that group or section.

The Code goes further and categorically states that the official 'must represent and be responsible for [the picketing members] in the normal course of his trade union duties' (para. 16). But this statement may be misleading. The terms of appointment or election of a union official may give him a wide representative role, including the conduct of disputes for members in addition to those for whom he has a day-to-day responsibility. In practice it may be difficult to discern the scope of representation. For the quite different purpose of the EPA's duty on employers to consult with representatives of recognised trade unions over redundancy, a 'trade union representative' means a person 'authorised' by the union to undertake negotiations with the employer in question (EPA s.99(2)). The notion of authorisation in a trade union context is fraught with technicalities, some of which were raised in one of the leading cases under the Industrial Relations Act (*Heaton's Transport* v. *TGWU,* 1972). Once the courts enter the murky waters of express and implied authorisation the law of picketing will become even more complicated.

There are many other limitations on the activities of the trade union official. He must be 'accompanying' a member. What if the member is absent for a few moments — does the official temporarily forfeit his immunity? Although multi-unionism is common throughout British industry, the member must belong to the same union as the official. This restrictive principle affects full-time officers and shop stewards, especially senior shop stewards and 'convenors'. Suppose the convenor in an engineering firm is a patternmaker (or a sheet metal worker or a metal mechanic) from a small craft or occupational union but that the large majority of union members and of stewards are from the AUEW and the TGWU. The office of the convenor is probably not even within the statutory definition of a union 'official' because a convenor as such is not 'a person elected or appointed in accordance with the rules of the union to be a representative of its members or of some of them' (TULRA s.30). The shop steward may come within that definition but not the convenor qua convenor, who is elected or appointed by the other shop stewards from a variety of unions to be their spokesmen for the entire plant, factory or company. The convenor who happens to be a pattern-maker ought not to join any picket line unless it includes one of his own patternmaking members. But the situation is only marginally different if the convenor is from the AUEW or the TGWU. If the pickets do not include a member from the particular small section which originally elected him as a steward, which in a large plant would be the exception rather than the rule, the convenor's presence with the pickets would be legally perilous both for himself and for them.

One may view these restrictions as a justified legal deterrent against picketing. But in reality they are more likely to damage the cause of industrial peace. The paradox of collective bargaining is that it is both the expression of industrial conflict and the means for its resolution. The union official's functions of organising and settling disputes are inseparable. If fear of legal liability leads full-time officers and lay officials to steer clear of picket lines, their authority and credibility in negotiations will be weakened. This argument may seem strange to those who have been conditioned to regard the shop steward as a dangerous militant. It should be remembered however that the Donovan Report found that the steward was 'more of a lubricant than an irritant' (para. 110), and the constructive and responsible leadership role of the senior shop steward has been confirmed by subsequent research.[17]

THE EMPLOYMENT ACT AND THE CRIMINAL LAW

Pickets whose actions fall outside the scope of the new TULRA s.15 are deprived of the immunities against civil liabilities provided by TULRA s.13 (EA s.16(2), see below), but there is no express reference in the Act to criminal liabilities. What then are the implications if any for the criminal law? Is the picket who is not at or near his own place of work more likely now to be subject to criminal liabilities than he was before the enactment of s.16 of the 1980 Act? According to the Secretary of State for Employment, s.16 has no implication whatsoever for the criminal law: it 'does not create any additional burden on the police because it does not create any new criminal offence', and it 'has absolutely nothing to do with the police. It has nothing to do with criminal law. It is entirely a matter for the person who believes that his contracts are in some way being broken to take action through the civil court. The police are in no way involved in this.'[18] His assumption is that TULRA s.15 is concerned exclusively with civil liability and cannot provide immunity against criminal liability. This is also the assumption of the Green Paper *Trade Union Immunities* (para. 169) and of the Picketing Code, which states that if 'a picket commits a criminal offence he is just as liable to be prosecuted as any other member of the public who breaks the law. The immunity provided under the civil law does not protect him in any way' (para. 22, and similarly para. 3). It is of course true that s.15 of TULRA as substituted by s.16 of the 1980 Act creates no new criminal offence. There is nevertheless a disagreement over whether the new TULRA s.15 expands the application of existing criminal liabilities and the role of the police.

It is arguable that TULRA s.15 does provide an immunity from liability for certain criminal offences, including minor forms of wilful obstruction of the highway and watching or besetting. Naturally there can be no immunity for crimes arising from any kind of force, including the physical obstruction of pedestrians and vehicles. That is not in contention. Here we are concerned solely with the picket who may have technically committed some minor degree of watching or besetting or of obstruction of the highway but still ends up in a magistrates' court and who wishes to plead that TULRA s.15 gives him a defence. The proposition that this immunity exists is supported by the legislative history. As we have seen, s.7 of the Conspiracy and Protection of Property Act 1875 as originally drafted provided that attendance merely to communicate information was not to be deemed the criminal offence of watching or besetting. Later s.2 of the Trade Disputes Act 1906 enacted the phrase 'it shall be lawful', words which still introduce TULRA s.15 and are wide enough to give an immunity for criminal as well as civil liability. Section 134 of the IRA was the most explicit of all: for the phrase 'it shall be lawful' it substituted the formulation that attendance for the permitted purposes would not of itself constitute a criminal offence under s.7 of the 1875 Act 'or under any other enactment or rule of law'. 'But for [s.134],' said Lord Salmon in *Hunt* v. *Broome*, 'the mere attendance of pickets might constitute an offence under section 7(2) and (4) of the Act of 1875 [persistent following and watching or besetting] or under the Highways Act 1959 [wilful obstruction of the highway] or constitute a tort, for example, nuisance. The section, therefore, gives a narrow but nevertheless real immunity to pickets.'[19]

The Employment Act reduces that immunity as the new TULRA s.15 no longer protects pickets at a place other than their own place of work. The Attorney-General (in contrast to the Secretary of State) made it clear that he was perfectly well aware of the arguable existence of the immunity in respect of minor obstructions and that s.16 of the Employment Act inevitably had the effect of curtailing it.[20] The fact that the government resisted every attempt to confine EA s.16 to the civil law by expressly excluding the criminal law from its reach may be indicative of an underlying intention to widen the application of existing criminal liabilities. The Working Paper on Secondary Industrial Action perhaps envisaged this aspect when it sought to justify s.16 by reference to 'public order'. Public order is maintained through criminal not civil law. Ultimately the police have to enforce the criminal law, and the Picketing Code provides further encouragement to them to prosecute for even minor crimes committed by persons outside the statutory immunity.

STATUTORY CODE ON PICKETING

The legal effect of a Secretary of State's Code (as explained in chapter seven) is that it is admissible in evidence in proceedings before a court, industrial tribunal and the CAC and, if relevant to any question, must be taken into account in determining that question (EA s.3(8)). The Picketing Code applies as much to proceedings in criminal as in civil courts. Indeed we would argue that it is analogous in function to a centralised directive to the police. The Picketing Working Paper of July 1979 stated that the Code would be designed to bring about 'a more consistent interpretation of the law by police and magistrates', which was probably intended to mean a more consistently stringent enforcement of the criminal law against pickets. This possibility alarmed the police as well as the TUC. The chief constables, who have their own operational guidelines on handling picketing, told the House of Commons Select Committee on Employment that they did not want the Code to apply to them as it might have the effect of limiting their discretion, and, in the light of that evidence, a majority of the all-party Committee recommended that the Code ought not to specify a maximum number of pickets.[21] In response government spokesmen sought to shift the emphasis of the Working Paper and to play down the impact of the Picketing Code on the administration of criminal justice. The Code itself purports to give advice only to pickets, other workers, employers and members of the public (para. 1), a list which significantly omits to mention the police. Nevertheless the police may well amend their own operational guidelines to make them consistent with the Secretary of State's Code.

While the Code specifically disclaims the intention of narrowing police discretion 'to limit the number of people on a particular picket line' (para. 28), it requires 'pickets and their organisers' to 'ensure that in general the number of pickets does not exceed six at any entrance to a workplace; frequently a smaller number will be appropriate' (para. 31). This limitation is relevant to prosecutions for such criminal offences as wilful obstruction, watching or besetting, threatening words and behaviour and intimidation. If, for example, the 'seventh' picket is charged with obstruction, the argument in the magistrates' court may turn as much on the Code's stipulation as on the substantive offence. Moreover mass picketing is categorised by the Code as 'obstruction, if not intimidation' (para. 30).

It is again the police who have to liaise with an important individual known as the 'picket organiser', depicted by the Code as an 'experienced person, preferably a trade union official' (para. 32). But he is, as McCarthy has pointed out, an official with a difference: 'halfway between a scoutmaster and a friendly regimental sergeant-major'.[22] Armed with a 'letter of authority' from his union, he must get his 'directions' from the police on both the number and placement of pickets (para. 33). According to paragraph 34 he must ensure that the pickets understand the law and the Code and that their conduct is lawful and peaceful; the maintenance of 'essential' supplies; the clear identification of the pickets; and that any unlicensed pickets from other places of work are kept at bay. Failure to consult with the police and to take their advice on the disposition of the pickets is likely to be relevant to charges of obstructing the police. It is difficult to see how the police are to avoid asking the question 'do you work here?', at which point the principle of the new TULRA s.15 as well as the Picketing Code filter down into the administration of the criminal law. Certainly they will feature in the argument in criminal trials which are defended.

On the other hand, the impression must not be given that the Picketing Code is concerned only with potentially criminal activity: it has many implications for civil liabilities as well. A union ought not to discipline a member because he has crossed a picket line 'which it had not authorised or which was not at the member's place of work' (para. 36, and Closed Shop Code para. 55). As we explained in chapter five, evidence of breach of this rule could be decisive in legal actions both in the High Court for breach of the union rule book and in the industrial tribunals under ss.4 and 5 of the 1980 Act. The Code warns pickets to 'take very great care to ensure that their activities do not cause distress, hardship or inconvenience to members of the public who are not involved in the dispute' and to 'take particular care' to maintain 'essential supplies' (para. 37), as illustrated by a voluminous but non-exhaustive list including pharmaceutical products, goods and services for the maintenance of plant and machinery, heating fuels and meals on wheels (para. 38). This list is actually wider than both the concept of 'emergency' in s.1 of the Emergency Powers Act 1920 and the grounds on which criminal liability may still attach to breaches of the individual contract of employment under s.5 of the Conspiracy and Protection of Property Act 1875 (below p. 222). Since both these measures remain in force, what is the intended legal effect of the Code's provisions on essential supplies? Perhaps the judges will use breach of the Code as the basis for a new heading of 'unlawful means' for the purposes of civil liability; they may also regard it as relevant to the exercise of their residual discretion to grant interlocutory injunctions (see chapter nine).

Whether the liability is criminal or civil, it seems that the picket organiser is to be at the sharp end. The Green Paper *Trade Union Immunities* makes this abundantly clear in respect of civil liability. The fact that there may be difficulty in ascertaining the names and addresses of pickets 'should not', according to the Green Paper, 'normally be a problem for the employer because an injunction can be sought against the picket organiser (who is normally readily identifiable) even if, as may be the case with a trade union official, he is not himself present on the picket line' (para. 172). In addition, the picket organiser and/or the trade union official may be party to an agreement with the pickets and thus potentially liable for civil conspiracy. It seems unlikely that anyone would wish to assume the picket organiser's onerous responsibilities as set out in the Code when the consequences may be an injunction or damages or a criminal conviction. This whole legal initiative may yet prove to be counter-productive, assuming that management and union officials take notice of it.

CIVIL LIABILITY OF PICKETS

Picketing beyond the narrow scope of the new TULRA s.15 involves loss of the statutory protection against liability for nuisance and trespass. In addition, EA s.16(2) provides: 'Nothing in section 13 of the 1974 Act shall prevent an act done in the course of picketing from being actionable in tort unless it is done in the course of attendance declared lawful by section 15 of the Act.' TULRA s.13 provides defences to liability for some of the economic torts. As a result of s.16(2) therefore there are no immunities for unlicensed pickets, that is, workers or union officials whose picketing is not covered by TULRA s.15.

The use of the word 'picketing' in EA s.16(2) is new. Though it appears in the marginal note to TULRA s.15, it is not mentioned in the body of the section and it has not hitherto been a legal term of art. Section 15 of the 1974 Act (like its predecessors in 1906 and 1971) refers not to acts done in the course of picketing but to attendance by persons at or near a place for the purpose only of peaceful communication or persuasion. Does 'picketing' have a different meaning from 'attendance'? Suppose a placard is left against a factory wall saying 'TGWU Official Picket: This Factory is Black', and that on reading the message lorry drivers turn away without delivering their loads to the factory in question. Is such 'ghost' picketing an act done in the course of picketing and therefore covered by EA s.16(2)? If so, it would seem that the use of the word 'picketing' has extended the notion of attendance from a physical to an implied presence. An implied presence might conceivably cover all sorts of oral and written communications between workers in dispute and others.

Section 16(2) also appears to withdraw the protection of the defences to economic tort liability from acts done in the course of picketing by workers (and union officials) picketing their own place of work if they go beyond the prescribed purposes of peacefully obtaining or communicating information or persuading people to work or not to work. Such acts are not 'done in the course of attendance declared lawful' by the new TULRA s.15. As already noted, only picketing by a very small number of workers who keep out of everyone's way can be sure of remaining within the scope of lawful attendance. Section 16(2) could thus expose to the labour injunction all action in the course of picketing which is not both at the right place and only for the permitted purposes.

The government's assumption is that persons engaged in trade disputes are legally privileged, and that s.16(2) of the Employment Act restores 'to employers and others, who are harmfully affected by the consequences of people acting as pickets inducing breaches of contract, their common law rights that statute has taken away'.[23] But, as we explained in chapter one, if all the common law rights that statute has taken away were restored trade unionism and any form of direct industrial action would become completely unlawful. It is therefore of the greatest significance that EA s.16(2) deprives the unlicensed picket of all the protection from tort liabilities which TULRA s.13 gives to those whose actions are in contemplation or furtherance of a trade dispute. The nature of this protection and of the corresponding liabilities are more fully discussed in chapter nine. What follows is an outline in order to explain their impact on picketing.

TULRA s.13(1) provides protection against liability for inducing breach of or interfering with contract and threatening to break, induce breach of or interfere with contract. The removal of this immunity means that unlicensed pickets, including pickets at their own place of work who go behond the permitted purposes, may now be sued for inducing breach of or interfering with employment contracts or threatening to do so. Almost any kind of industrial action, whether primary or secondary, involves inducing breach of employment contracts. Picketing certainly does so because in persuading people not to work pickets are, in legal terms, inducing them to break their contracts of employment. All persons engaged in trade disputes have been statutorily protected from this most basic of liabilities since the Trade Disputes Act 1906. It is remarkable that a statute of 1980 should take away this immunity from a person who happens to picket at the wrong place or who goes beyond the permitted purposes. Removal of the immunity for inducing breach of or interfering with commercial contracts, or threatening to do so, is hardly less sweeping in its effect, since even primary picketing also normally involves interference with commercial contracts made with other enterprises.

TULRA s.13(4) provides that persons who act in combination in contemplation or furtherance of a trade dispute cannot be liable for the tort of conspiracy unless the acts which they agree to commit are themselves tortious. The removal of this protection by EA s.16(2) means that those who agree to do acts in the course of picketing outside the scope of attendance declared lawful by the new TULRA s.15 can be liable for conspiracy even if those acts are not themselves tortious. If those acts are in no sense unlawful they could still be liable for simple conspiracy or conspiracy to injure, but only if their predominant purpose is to injure someone rather than to further their own legitimate interests (which is unlikely, see chapter nine). However, after the repeal of TULRA s.13(3) by EA s.17(8), it is much more likely that they could be liable for conspiracy to commit unlawful acts. TULRA s.13(3) provided that an act which was not actionable by virtue of s.13(1) or (2) and a breach of contract in contemplation or furtherance of a trade dispute were not to be regarded as unlawful acts for the purposes of liability in tort. Workers on the picket line who go beyond the bounds of the new TULRA s.15 could therefore be liable for conspiracy to break their own contracts of employment.

Union officials or picket organisers may also be liable for this conspiracy whether or not they actually join the picket line and even if they have no contracts of employment to break. This possibility follows from *Rookes* v. *Barnard* (1964) where one of the defendants was a full-time union officer. Even though he had no relevant contract of employment which he could threaten to break, he (together with the other two defendants who were employees of BOAC) was held liable for conspiracy to threaten a strike in breach of employment contracts. According to Lord Devlin, once the tort was proved against one defendant the plaintiff could sue 'the doer of the act and the conspirators, if any, as well'.[24] In addition pickets and picket organisers are clearly vulnerable to liability for conspiracy to induce breach of or interfere with contracts after the repeal of TULRA s.13(3) (whether or not they also lose the protection of s.13(4) by virtue of EA s.16(2)).

Even pickets at their own place of work whose behaviour falls within the permitted purposes of TULRA s.15 may be liable for conspiracy if they act in combination with unlicensed pickets who are either not at their own place of work or who go beyond the permitted purposes. It is of course possible that the licensed pickets and their organisers may have taken the precaution of going out of their way to dissociate themselves from the unlicensed pickets. In the real world however that is a little unlikely. Pickets more often than not welcome the support and solidarity of fellow workers. They may then be held liable with them for conspiracy to break, induce breach of or interfere with contracts.

In depriving unlicensed pickets of the entire range of TULRA s.13 immunities, s.16(2) goes further than the 1980 Act's other provisions which are designed to restrict industrial action. Section 17 on secondary action and s.18 on acts to compel trade union membership effectively remove the immunities contained in TULRA s.13(1), but leave intact the immunity in TULRA s.13(4). The width of EA s.16(2) is perhaps an example of overkill.

Pickets and picket organisers who are deprived of the protection of TULRA s.13 — and indeed all pickets and organisers who are vulnerable to economic tort liability because of the general repeal of TULRA s.13(3) — may be subject to legal action by a wide variety of plaintiffs. The most obvious are the employer in dispute and his customers or suppliers. Another possible plaintiff is a worker who suffers loss because of a picket line, for example if he is sent home without pay because there is no work for him to do, assuming that the employer has power to do this under the contract of employment. Whether other persons such as retail traders can sue if they can show that they have suffered loss because of the unlawful acts is doubtful but arguable.

LABOUR RELATIONS AND THE LABOUR INJUNCTION

The main civil remedies obtainable in the High Court against unlicensed pickets are damages and injunctions. Since the defendants are individuals (trade unions as such are still immune from liability in tort under TULRA s.14) and since the objective is normally to get a quick legal remedy to stop the industrial action in its tracks, the favoured remedy is the injunction which is known in this context as the 'labour injunction'. In the words of the Under-Secretary of State for Employment, 'immediate injunctions not damages are the name of the game'.[25] An injunction is an order to a person either to cease doing something, or in its mandatory form, to do something. Breach of the terms of an injunction may lead to punishment including imprisonment for contempt of court, a possibility which blurs the line between civil and criminal sanctions. The nature of 'interlocutory' injunction proceedings and the principles by which a court exercises its discretion to grant an injunction are discussed in chapter nine. Here our concern is with the aspect which is most relevant to the industrial relations implications of the labour injunction: the identification of defendant pickets.

In proceedings for an injunction the plaintiff must be able to identify the individuals he wishes the court to enjoin. With this prospect in mind picket organisers may decide to keep a very low profile and the picket who is not at his own place of work may be equally elusive. Indeed one of the first cases after EA s.16 came into force led to a new phenomenum in British labour law: the 'organised disappearance' of those named as defendants.[26]

Who then is to carry out the invidious task of identification? It will not be the police. As the Picketing Code categorically states: 'An employer cannot require the police to help in identifying the pickets against whom he wishes to seek an order from the civil court' (para. 27). One naturally assumes that employers do not receive information from the Special Branch who are said to keep a watch on active trade unionists, particularly in outbreaks of mass and flying picketing.[27] The employment of private detectives may provide an effective solution. In *Midland Cold Storage* v. *Turner* (1972), a case brought against picketing dockers under the Industrial Relations Act, the plaintiff employed a firm of inquiry agents – 'Eurotec' – to keep watch on the pickets and the agents' evidence established an overwhelming prima facie case against each of the individual dockers. If the terms of a court order are not obeyed, a plaintiff seeking to initiate contempt proceedings also has to show that there is sufficient evidence against the named defendants. In one of the famous cases under the IRA the Court of Appeal, at the request of the Official Solicitor, cancelled orders issued by the NIRC to commit defendants to prison on the ground of inadequate evidence (*Churchman* v. *Joint Shop Stewards Committee of the Workers of the Port of London*, 1972). In this instance the private detectives had failed in their task.

In the light of such practical difficulties of enforcement, it is perhaps not surprising that the Picketing Code (para. 21) gives the impression of a very wide scope of liability in respect of pickets not named as defendants. The true position of pickets under injunction and the question of contempt has been succinctly summarised as follows: 'An injunction against named persons restraining them from engaging in illegal picketing can be evaded if the named workers withdraw from the picket lines and from organising the illegal picketing and their place as participants and organisers is taken by other workers. It is, of course, the law that a person who aids a party enjoined to break an injunction is himself guilty of contempt, but where the enjoined pickets withdraw from participation in, or organisation of, the picket line, there would appear to be no breach by the enjoined parties for the third parties to aid and abet'.[28] But if the named defendants under injunction fail to withdraw from the organisation of the action, then the other participants may be aiding and abetting and may consequently run into liability for contempt. Bearing that important qualification in mind, then as Lord Diplock put it: 'Civil actions cannot be brought against trade unions, but against individual defendants only; and only those individuals are bound to observe the injunction. Everyone else involved in the industrial action can carry on with impunity doing that from which the individual defendants have been restrained.'[29]

In view of these sometimes severe problems of identification and enforcement, is the Employment Act (as opposed to the economic recession) likely to have any restrictive effect on the incidence of picketing, whether primary or secondary? If it is, there has to be litigation. In theory s.16 of the Act ushers in a new era of labour injunctions against unlicensed pickets. But will this lawyers' paradise really materialise? As in the case of the Industrial Relations Act when the legal resources of employers and others were augmented by an armoury of 'unfair industrial practices', there may be some hesitation in the front line. British employers are often as reluctant as trade unionists to become reliant on the legal profession. Many of them see the dangers of souring industrial relations by the use of legal tactics. Identifying and suing workers is not necessarily the best method of securing their co-operation after a dispute. Perhaps for this reason the employer in dispute will be less likely to issue a writ than his customers or suppliers. It is likely that the large majority of employers will turn aside from this offer of new legal sticks with which to beat off unwelcome pickets. But there will always be a few who may be tempted to leap into the fray upon the backs of their QCs and, on the experience of the Industrial Relations Act, to run the risk of turning some quite ordinary dispute into a national *cause célèbre*.

9

The Right to Strike

Industrial action may take many forms. On the employer's side the best known is the lock-out or closure of the workplace. There are however other forms of action which may be open to employers although they receive little publicity. They include withdrawal of recognition or facilities from unions and shop stewards, unilaterally altering working arrangements, transfering workers to less pleasant jobs, withdrawal of bonuses and reduction of overtime. Such action may be in breach of agreed procedures or legal obligations. But the law has a far greater impact on industrial action taken by workers. The strike receives most attention but go-slows, working to rule, overtime bans, working without enthusiasm, non-cooperation and workplace occupations may be equally effective in particular circumstances.

The law seeks to regulate industrial conflict first by imposing limits on the lawful nature of the conduct of disputes, that is, picketing and allied matters. Second where industrial action occurs it affects the legal rights and obligations of employer and employee in the context of the individual labour relationship. Third those who organise and take part in industrial action may be made liable for or restrained from committing certain torts or civil wrongs in some circumstances. Finally there are special provisions in respect of emergencies and particular groups of workers. Apart from the law concerning picketing which has already been discussed in chapter eight, this chapter analyses the changes made by the Employment Act and the further modifications mooted in the Green Paper *Trade Union Immunities* within these broad categories. The possibility raised by the Green Paper of completely reformulating the law by replacing the negative immunities with positive rights is discussed in chapter ten.

INDUSTRIAL ACTION AND THE INDIVIDUAL
LABOUR RELATIONSHIP

The crucial legal question in this area is how and when workers can take industrial action without acting in breach of their contracts. Some action appears to be clearly in breach of contract in all circumstances, for example, a strike not preceded by any notice. Is there any form of industrial action which does not involve workers breaking contracts? In the *ASLEF* case in 1972 the Court of Appeal found that the railwaymen's work to rule and ban on rostered overtime were in breach of contract. The three members of the Court expressed themselves differently but the case is generally taken to establish that there is an implied term in the individual employer-employee contract based on their mutual interest in the employer's business. Action by the employee defeating the commercial intention of the parties (Buckley L.J.), disrupting the system the efficient running of which he is employed to ensure (Roskill L.J.) or wilfully disrupting the employer's undertaking in order to produce chaos (Lord Denning) was therefore in breach of contract. On this approach even a ban on completely voluntary overtime could be held to be in breach of contract. However in the *ASLEF* case itself it was conceded that the bans on Sunday and rest day working were not in breach of contract. Similarly in *Seaboard World Airlines Inc.* v. *TGWU* (1973), the NIRC exempted the withdrawal of voluntary overtime and a decision not to perform work which there was no contractual obligation to perform from its opinion that any form of action short of a strike after due notice always involved workers in breaking their contracts.

If a strike takes place without any prior notice it seems clear that it must almost always be in breach of the worker's contract since it involves his disregarding one of his essential obligations under it: to do the work he is employed to do. In *Simmons* v. *Hoover* (1977) after an extensive review of the previous case law the EAT rejected an argument that the individual contract of employment was suspended during a strike. Does the giving of prior notice of a strike make any difference to the position? In the words of the Donovan Report 'Every employee has, however, the right to withdraw his labour upon giving to his employer the notice called for in that event by his contract of employment. He may then lawfully leave when the notice expires. The same is true of several employees acting in combination' (para. 931). But in practice where strike notices are given they rarely if ever take the form of notice to terminate as such. It therefore appears to be more accurate to regard a strike notice as what lawyers call an 'anticipatory breach' of contract, that is, notice to the employer that the workers are going to break their contracts by going on strike. This was the view expressed by Donovan L.J. and Lord Devlin in *Rookes* v. *Barnard* (1964). Lord Denning in *Morgan* v. *Fry* (1968) and Parliament in s.147 of the IRA attempted to create a middle position by regarding a strike notice as notice to suspend the contract, at least where the notice given was as long as or longer than that required to terminate the contract. However in *Simmons* v. *Hoover* the EAT concluded not only that a strike did not suspend the individual contract but also that a strike notice could not be regarded as notice to suspend which somehow avoided the strike constituting a breach of contract by the individual workers involved. This is now generally accepted to be the law.

Where industrial action is in breach of the employees' contracts, the employer can if he wishes sue each of them for damages. This rarely if ever happens nowadays. It would neither make for good industrial relations nor provide the employer with significant compensation since the measure of damages is the loss attributable to each individual employee: *NCB* v. *Galley* (1958). If it is a serious enough breach to be in legal terminology a 'repudiation' of the contract, as in the opinion of the EAT in *Simmons* v. *Hoover* a 'real strike' always is, the employer is entitled to treat the contract as at an end. This means that he may dismiss the worker 'summarily', that is, without giving him any notice. It is less certain whether he can treat the worker as having terminated his own employment so avoiding the impact of any of the potential rights available to dismissed employees against their employers. In any event employees dismissed during a strike or other industrial action cannot complain of unfair dismissal unless one or more of those taking part in the action was not dismissed or was offered re-engagement (EPCA s.62).

This outline analysis is sufficient to demonstrate that it is impossible to establish satisfactory legal boundaries for legitimate industrial action by reference to the common law rights and duties of employer and employee under the contract of employment. The fact that almost all industrial action inevitably involves breaches of contract may not be widely appreciated. In *Express Newspapers Ltd.* v. *Keys* (1980) Griffiths J. pointed out that whether or not union circulars calling on their members to support the TUC's 'Day of Action' against government policies in May 1980 were unlawful, any workers who took part would be breaking their contracts by not turning up for work. It was evident from the way in which this part of his judgment was reported that this

was a matter of surprise to some people. It is an issue of crucial importance to union officials and others who organise industrial action that
the workers concerned are breaking their contracts. Section 13(3) of
TULRA made it clear that a 'breach of contract in contemplation or
furtherance of a trade dispute' was not to be regarded as unlawful
means or an unlawful act for the purposes of liability in tort. In repealing this provision, EA s.17(8) has, as will be seen, left strike organisers
unprotected against actions for labour injunctions in a wide and uncertain range of circumstances.

THE GOLDEN FORMULA

Workers who take part in industrial action are almost invariably breaking their contracts of employment. Similarly industrial action almost
always involves the commission of one of the civil wrongs known as
economic torts. It may possibly also amount to a criminal conspiracy
at common law. Workers taking part in the action might be made liable
for these wrongs but those who organise industrial action are the ones
most at risk. In order to provide any degree of legal recognition for a
right to strike it is essential to prevent these liabilities from applying at
least in some circumstances. The principal function of the phrase 'in
contemplation or furtherance of a trade dispute' is to delimit the area
of industrial conflict in which they, or at least some of them, will not
apply. As we explained in chapter one this 'golden formula' was first
used in s.3 of the Conspiracy and Protection of Property Act 1875,
which provided that those party to an agreement or combination to do
or procure to be done an act in contemplation or furtherance of a trade
dispute could not be made liable for criminal conspiracy unless the act
in question was itself a crime. This protection is now provided by s.1 of
the Criminal Law Act 1977. Defences to certain economic tort actions
against *individuals* where they acted in contemplation or furtherance of
a trade dispute were provided by ss.1—3 of the Trade Disputes Act
1906 later supplemented by the Trade Disputes Act 1965, and the term
trade dispute was defined in s.5(3) of the 1906 Act. Trade unions were
provided with a defence to *any* action in tort by s.4 of the 1906 Act.

    In 1971 the Industrial Relations Act repealed this framework of
immunities against civil liabilities. By this time it had become clear that
restrictive interpretation of the golden formula and judicial development of the tort liabilities had considerably weakened the extent of

the statutory protection. When it was restored by the Trade Union and Labour Relations Act in 1974 and 1976 it was in a revised form intended, as Lord Scarman put it in 1979 'to sweep away ... the restraints of judicial review which the courts have been fashioning one way and another since the enactment of the Trade Disputes Act 1906'.[1] Nevertheless in a series of decisions from 1977–79 the Court of Appeal fashioned new restraints. These were removed by the House of Lords in three key cases in 1979–80 on the grounds that they were inconsistent with the intention behind the legislation. The Employment Act reflects a completely different legislative intention from that of TULRA. Although it has not amended the golden formula as such, s.17 has effected some backdoor amendments and the Green Paper indicated that the government was contemplating further restrictions.

Interpretation of the definition of a trade dispute and of the limiting words 'in contemplation or furtherance' is clearly a vital factor in determining the nature and degree of legal restraints that may be imposed on resort to industrial action. Before examining the detail of the immunities and the limitations imposed on them by the Employment Act it is necessary first to provide an outline analysis of the golden formula, noting in particular the developments in the late 1970s.[2] The basic definition of a trade dispute in TULRA s.29(1) is as follows:

a dispute between employers and workers, or between workers and workers, which is connected with one or more of the following, that is to say —

(a) terms and conditions of employment, or the physical conditions in which any workers are required to work;

(b) engagement or non-engagement, or termination or suspension of employment or the duties of employment, of one or more workers;

(c) allocation of work or the duties of employment as between workers or groups of workers;

(d) matters of discipline;

(e) the membership or non-membership of a trade union on the part of a worker;

(f) facilities for officials of trade unions; and

(g) machinery for negotiation or consultation, and other procedures, relating to any of the foregoing matters, including the recognition by employers or employers' associations of the right of a trade union to represent workers in any such negotiations or consultation or in the carrying out of such procedures.

This definition is expanded in certain respects in the remaining sub-sections, some of which are referred to below.

Subject matter of a trade dispute

A dispute may qualify as a trade dispute if it is connected with any of the matters set out in paragraphs (a)–(g) of s.29(1). The action in *BBC* v. *Hearn* (1977) arose out of the decision of the Association of Broad-casting Staff, in conformity with its policies on racialism, to take action to prevent the BBC from transmitting television coverage of the Cup Final to South Africa. The Court of Appeal reversed the decision of Pain J. and held that on the evidence before the court there was no trade dispute between the parties. But in confirming that 'terms and conditions of employment' in s.29(1)(a) had to be given a very wide meaning it arguably supported his view that the phrase extended beyond contractual terms of employment to include conventions or understandings between employer and employee.[3]

Paragraphs (d)–(g) spell out various issues which were impliedly covered by the more general 1906 definition although it referred only to 'employment, non-employment, terms of employment or conditions of labour of any person'. As the Green Paper conceded, the scope of the 1974 definition is not significantly different from that of its pre-decessors (para. 186). The current definition does however clarify one important issue. Section 29(3) states that there is a trade dispute even though it relates to matters occurring outside Britain. Thus for example it was arguable that the one week boycott of postal and telecommuni-cations between Britain and South Africa proposed by the UPW and POEU in 1977 was in furtherance of a dispute between the South African government in its capacity as an employer and other employers on the one hand and trade unions in South Africa on the other (*Gouriet* v. *UPW* 1977, below p. 222).

There has been little concern expressed over the areas covered in paragraphs (a)–(g) of the definition in s.29(1) either on the grounds that they are too wide or that they are too limited. The crucial factor which determines whether or not a dispute is a trade dispute is the phrase 'connected with'. The absence of any qualifying words suggests that any connection is sufficient. Nevertheless some limitations have been read into it. The invalidity of such limitations is clear beyond doubt after the House of Lords decision in *NWL Ltd.* v. *Woods* (1979). This case was one of a series in recent years arising out of action taken by the ITF against ships flying flags of convenience, that is, the flag of a country other than that where the beneficial owner is domiciled. When the 'Nawala' arrived at Redcar in June 1979 an ITF official told her agent that appropriate action would be taken if the owners did not enter into the ITF collective agreement. This provided terms and conditions of employment for the crews of such ships based on an average of ten West European countries. The House of Lords had no doubt that there was a dispute connected with terms and conditions of employment and therefore a trade dispute within paragraph (a) of the definition. They emphatically rejected the owners' argument that the existence of another object or motive could make any difference to the position, even if it was an extraneous – e.g. personal or political – motive and even if it was predominant. The decision is of particular importance to the ITF as it is often argued that their acts in disputes such as this one are predominantly motivated by a political campaign against flags of convenience. It was for this reason that the Court of Appeal in an earlier case, *Star Sea Transport Corporation* v. *Slater* (1979), had held either that there was no trade dispute or that the defendant ITF officials were not acting in furtherance of a trade dispute. This decision was overruled by the House of Lords in *NWL Ltd.* v. *Woods.* In the subsequent case of *Universe Tankships Inc. of Monrovia* v. *ITF* (1981) the question was raised whether a dispute as to whether or not the employer should make a payment to the ITF welfare fund was a trade dispute. The Court of Appeal held that since seamen might derive fringe benefits from this fund, a sufficient, albeit tenuous, connection with paragraph (a) of the trade dispute definition was established.

It was however pointed out in the *NWL* case that the requisite connection must be genuine and not a sham. Thus while it may no longer be appropriate or correct to construe the words 'connected with' to import a limitation into the definition of a trade dispute based on the parties' motives, the problems of distinguishing genuine from sham connections remains. The exclusion of disputes with only a sham connection could thus replace the test of predominant motive to achieve a not too dissimilar limitation to that which has led to the exclusion of disputes on the ground that they were concerned with inter-union rivalry (*Stratford* v. *Lindley,* 1965), spite and malice (*Conway* v. *Wade,* 1909) and personal prestige (*Huntley* v. *Thornton,* 1957). All these cases were referred to in the House of Lords' judgments in *NWL Ltd.* v. *Woods* without any suggestion that they were wrong.

The remarkable decision of the Court of Appeal in *Hadmor Produc-*

tions Ltd. v. *Hamilton* in early 1981 may possibly be rationalised on this basis. The case arose because of a decision taken at an ACTT meeting to black a series of programmes which the plaintiffs, a 'facility company' which produced programmes for sale to television companies, had made and were in the process of selling to Thames Television for transmission. At first instance Dillon J. could see 'no other possible explanation of the union's conduct' than that the relevant acts were done in contemplation of a trade dispute, inter alia, as to whether technicians employed by Thames should show programmes made by facility companies. But the Court of Appeal disagreed for reasons which are neither consistent nor wholly clear. According to Lord Denning the dispute was not a trade dispute but an attempt to dictate to Thames the way in which they should conduct their business. The fact that it succeeded did not make it a trade dispute any more than the attempt which failed in *BBC* v. *Hearn*. Watkins L.J. found that there was no trade dispute 'in connection with' any of the matters set out in TULRA s.29(1). 'What is involved here has all the appearance of a kind of restrictive practice dignified by the word "policy".... Recognition of it for what it is is ... important since by its very nature it clearly signifies that it has nothing to do with a trade dispute.'[4] For O'Connor L.J. the issue turned on the absence of any substance in the submission that there was a dispute connected with either the termination of employment within TULRA s.29(1)(b) (because of fears of redundancies at Thames if it bought programmes from facility companies rather than producing them itself) or machinery for consultation within s.29(1)(g). There could be no dispute within s.29(1)(b) because there had been no mention of redundancies and no dispute within s.29(1)(g) because the relevant agreement on prior consultation before employing the services of facility companies did not in his view cover buying a ready made programme.

What this aspect of the Court of Appeal decision reveals is a continued determination on the part of some of the judges to reach a conclusion on the existence of a trade dispute — and thus on the availability of the golden formula defences, now severely limited by the Employment Act — based on their view of the merits of a dispute and without regard to the clear direction of the House of Lords in *NWL Ltd.* v. *Woods* as to the wide ambit of the definition. That decision was not even referred to in any of the judgments.

In any event the status of disputes where one of the parties has a political motive remains uncertain. In the 'Day of Action' case referred to above (p. 183) the defendant union officials did not even argue that there was a trade dispute. The decision in *BBC* v. *Hearn* was expressly endorsed by the House of Lords in the *NWL* case, although it was pointed out that it would have been easy to turn the dispute into a trade dispute by rephrasing the union's objections to transmission of the Cup Final to South Africa in the form of a demand for amendments to terms and conditions of employment. The Green Paper is therefore correct in stating that so long as there is a genuine connection with any of the subject matter in s.29(1), a dispute is a trade dispute however political it may seem. It is not however enthusiastic about the idea of expressly excluding political disputes in view of the problems of definition involved. The Green Paper also raises the possibility of reverting to the formulation of the industrial dispute definition in the IRA. This required disputes to 'relate wholly or mainly to' the listed subject matter rather than merely be connected with it. This is proposed not only as a means of excluding political disputes but also to limit the effects of the *NWL* decision generally. To this latter end requiring one or more of the subjects listed to be predominant or a substantial or significant element in the dispute is also suggested. This would in effect restore the decision in the *Star Sea* case which *NWL* overruled. While none of these changes (which are discussed in paras. 187–200) would leave the law clear, they would make it impossible to predict in a wide range of circumstances whether or not the dispute came within the definition. For this reason it might be thought that they would appeal to a government which supported s.17 of the 1980 Act partly on the grounds that the similar uncertainty it creates would operate as a deterrent to industrial action.

Persons concerned with a trade dispute

The persons concerned in a labour dispute fall into two categories: the parties to the dispute and the persons whose position, rights or obligations form the subject matter of the dispute. The latter are also frequently parties to the dispute. But this is not necessarily so nor is it required before a dispute can qualify as a trade dispute. TULRA s.29(1) provides that 'trade dispute means a dispute between employers and workers or between workers and workers'. While the subject matter of a qualifying dispute set out in paragraphs (a)–(g) of s.29(1) is mostly concerned with aspects of the employment rights of workers, paras. (f) and (g) allow the persons whose rights or obligations are the subject of a trade dispute to extend to anyone who may be concerned with the matters they refer to.

The IRA excluded disputes between workers and workers from its definition of an industrial dispute. This inevitably gave rise to the problem of deciding whether employers were parties to disputes between unions over recognition, demarcation and membership recruitment. The answer given was very much a question of impression as *Cory Lighterage Ltd.* v. *TGWU* (1973) demonstrated. There the dispute arose when a lighterman employed by the plaintiffs was suspended on full pay because the other lightermen who were all union members refused to work with him after he had allowed his union membership to lapse. While the court at first instance found that the employers were party to this dispute the Court of Appeal held that they were not. The Green Paper raises the question whether the current trade dispute definition should be similarly confined to disputes between employers and workers. It is disarmingly frank in admitting that the exclusion of worker-worker disputes has already in effect been achieved by s.17 of the Employment Act, concluding that formal amendment might be justified on the grounds that the reference to them in the definition has now been made redundant (paras. 203–5). Section 17 effectively withdraws the protection against civil liability from the organisers of secondary action. As defined in s.17(2) all action which induces breach of or interferes with a contract of employment or threatens to do so is secondary action 'if the employer under the contract of employment is not a party to the trade dispute'. The government's justification for withdrawing the immunity from all worker-worker disputes was that in the normal run of such disputes the employer was inevitably involved. In disputes which were strictly between different groups of workers, employers were innocent bystanders and therefore it was consistent with the policy behind s.17 to remove the protection of TULRA where action was taken against them. In the words of Lord Gowrie this was 'just the kind of thing we are here to try to correct'.[5]

This reasoning overlooks the realities of litigation in these cases. Employers may be normally 'involved' in worker-worker disputes but that does not mean that the courts will hold that they are parties to them as the *Cory Lighterage* case demonstrates. Similarly in *Stratford* v. *Lindley* (1965) the employer, who had accorded recognition to the TGWU, was clearly involved in the dispute over non-recognition of the rival Watermen's Union but the House of Lords held that it was merely a case of inter-union rivalry (and even then not a dispute sufficiently connected with the subject matter in the 1906 trade dispute definition). Indeed employers are now well-advised to do everything to maintain an appearance of neutrality in inter-union recognition disputes so that if they subsequently wish to obtain a labour injunction to restrain industrial action which is affecting their commercial contracts or threatens to do so, there will be no possibility of the statutory defences applying. This introduction of such a fundamental amendment to the law by the backdoor without even acknowledging that it was happening until challenged on the point in Parliament is but the first of several instances of how the effects of s.17 extend beyond its ostensible purpose.

Section 29(4) of TULRA expressly provides that a dispute to which a trade union is party is treated as a dispute to which workers are parties. Although there was no such provision in the definition in the 1906 Act, judicial interpretation made it clear that unions could be parties in their capacity as representatives of workers. In that capacity they could initiate disputes without referring back to their members. Section 29(4) is thus essentially a provision which merely makes this clear. However in *NWL Ltd.* v. *Woods* Lord Diplock, compounding errors in earlier judgments in the Court of Appeal, stated that the 1974 definition was wider than that of 1906 in particular in that a trade union could not be party to a trade dispute under the 1906 Act. On this basis he asserted that a union could now intermeddle with impunity and initiate a dispute with an employer even though perfect peace prevailed at the workplace. This was but one emotively charged illustration he gave of a situation where the golden formula protection could apply, although he quite clearly felt that it would be better if it did not. Paragraphs 206—13 of the Green Paper take up this thinly disguised invitation to the government to consider changes in the law. They raise the possibility either of reversing the express provision in s.29(6), which states that there can be a trade dispute between an employer and workers who are not employed by him, or providing that a union can be party to a trade dispute only if some of the employees in dispute are members of the union or want to join. It is admitted that this would provide a strong incentive to anti-union employers to make it clear that anyone who joined a union would be sacked.

As for changes designed specifically to exclude international shipping disputes like that in the *NWL* case, the Green Paper noted that even Lord Denning has recognised that blacking is 'the only weapon . . . at the disposal of the ITF (which they can use to ensure fair play for seaman and the like)'. The cases arising out of action taken by the

ITF in pursuit of its policy against flags of convenience demonstrate how extensive the effect would be of restricting trade disputes to disputes between employers and their own workers, with trade unions permitted to be parties only where they had members among those workers. Since there could be no trade dispute involving the owners of ships flying flags of convenience, no effective action could be lawfully taken against them. If it was taken in contemplation or furtherance of a trade dispute between another employer and his workers it would be secondary action within s.17 of the Employment Act and therefore certainly unprotected against legal restraint.

Contemplation or furtherance

The statutory protection provided for individuals is only available where they act 'in contemplation or furtherance' of a trade dispute. The limitation imposed by this phrase is twofold. First it requires acts to be related to a dispute in point of time. Furtherance relates to an existing dispute, contemplation to a dispute that is imminent.[6] In *Conway* v. *Wade* (1909), the leading case on the meaning of the golden formula in the 1906 Act, Lord Loreburn said that action also had to be taken 'in expectation of or with a view to the dispute or in support of one side to it'. What this required can be illustrated by the reasoning of the majority of the Court of Appeal in *Beaverbrook Newspapers Ltd.* v. *Keys* (1978). A pay dispute between the *Daily Mirror* and its journalists resulted in non-publication of the *Mirror*. The plaintiff owners of the *Daily Express* therefore decided to print extra copies. The defendant general secretary of SOGAT then ordered SOGAT members not to handle or distribute these extra copies. The Court of Appeal granted an injunction against the defendant to restrain him from inducing *Express* employees who belonged to SOGAT from thereby breaking their contracts. The court found that there was no dispute between the *Express* and its employees. Nor was the defendant acting in furtherance of the admitted trade dispute between the *Mirror* and its employees. Goff and Cumming-Bruce L.JJ. based their decision on this point on the ground that this was not what the defendant thought he was doing when he gave the instructions in question to his members, a conclusion supported by his own affidavit evidence. Cumming-Bruce L.J. thought that this indicated that he had the alleged — but non-existent — trade dispute between the *Express* and its employees in mind.

Lord Denning adopted a different approach, holding that in order to be within the golden formula an act had to be directly in furtherance of a trade dispute. In the *MacShane* case in the Court of Appeal he added that for an act to be in contemplation or furtherance of a trade dispute it had to help one side to the dispute in a practical way by giving support to the one or bringing pressure on the other. The majority of the Court of Appeal, Lawton and Brandon L.J., agreed that the requirement of furtherance included an objective element but they expressed it rather differently saying that the acts must be reasonably capable of furthering the dispute. In the one reported case arising out of the much publicised picketing during the 1978–9 'winter of discontent' disputes, Ackner J. in *United Biscuits Ltd.* v. *Fall* (1979) added to these limits the opinion that acts contrary to union policy or instructions could not be in contemplation or furtherance of a trade dispute. In *Associated Newspapers Group Ltd.* v. *Wade* (1979) Lord Denning summed up this rapid development of the law by saying that it was all a question of remoteness, so that where unions chose to cause loss to innocent third persons this might be so remote from the dispute that it could not be regarded as in furtherance of it.

This spate of judicial creativity was abruptly halted by the House of Lords in *Express Newspapers Ltd.* v. *MacShane* (1980). The NUJ was involved in a trade dispute with the proprietors of provincial newspapers over pay. It called on its members employed by the Press Association which supplies copy to both the national and provincial press to strike in order to reduce the copy available to provincial papers. Because its members at the Press Association were divided over whether or not to strike, the NUJ went further and instructed its members on national newspapers to black Press Association copy in order to encourage its members there to strike and to fortify the morale of those who did so. The defendant officials of the NUJ argued that they were protected against liability for inducing members employed by the plaintiff owners of the *Daily Express* to break their contracts because they were acting in furtherance of the dispute between provincial newspapers and their journalists. The House of Lords reversed the Court of Appeal and upheld this claim. In the opinion of the majority a person acts in furtherance of a trade dispute if he honestly and genuinely believes that his acts will further the interests of one of the parties to the dispute.[7]

The Law Lords were given an opportunity to reaffirm this opinion less than two months later in *Duport Steels Ltd.* v. *Sirs*, a case arising out of the steel dispute in 1980. The Court of Appeal appeared to flagrantly disregard the House of Lords' decision in *MacShane* in granting an injunction against ISTC officials restraining them from calling on their members employed by private steel companies to come out on strike in support of the union's pay dispute with the British Steel Corporation. The House of Lords reversed the Court of Appeal decision on the grounds that, applying the subjective test of furtherance as they had explained it in *MacShane,* the defendant's action was in furtherance of the trade dispute between British Steel and ISTC. This purely subjective test of furtherance nevertheless envisages that there is some limitation in contemplation or furtherance based on the actor's honesty of purpose. Notwithstanding the reservations expressed by the House of Lords in both the *NWL* and *MacShane* cases about the authority of the decision in *Conway* v. *Wade* today, it may be that Lord Loreburn's dictum referred to above is still a correct formulation of one of the requirements embodied in the formula.

The government's reaction to the House of Lords' decision in *MacShane* was to produce its Working Paper on Secondary Industrial Action in February 1980. This stated that the decision had dashed hopes that the limitations on the golden formula developed by the Court of Appeal could form the basis of a consensus on the extent of the immunities by limiting the protection for secondary action so that it did not go far beyond action taken against the first customer or supplier of the employer in dispute. It therefore proposed that to qualify for the statutory immunities all action would have to satisfy two general tests. It would have to be first reasonably capable of furthering the trade dispute and second predominantly in pursuit of the trade dispute and not principally for an extraneous motive. The first of these is clearly taken from the majority of the Court of Appeal in *MacShane*, with whom Lord Wilberforce in the House of Lords agreed, though he found that it produced a different result on the facts of the case. The second appeared to be intended to reinstate the Court of Appeal decision in *Star Sea Transport Corporation* v. *Slater* which was overruled by the House of Lords in the *NWL* case. As has been noted the predominant purpose test could be used either to find that there was no trade dispute or that while there was a trade dispute the action was not in furtherance of it because it was predominantly motivated by an extraneous object such as a political campaign against flags of convenience.

In the event s.17 of the 1980 Act did not give effect to this proposal because, in the words of the Secretary of State for Employment 'it left the judges so much in the driving seat'.[8] Instead the concept of secondary action which still attracts the immunities includes three tests which are taken from the 1977–79 era of judicial creativity in the Court of Appeal: principal purpose (*Star Sea Transport* v. *Slater*), directness (Lord Denning in *Beaverbrook Newspapers* v. *Keys*), and likelihood of achieving the purpose (objective test of the majority of the Court of Appeal in *MacShane*). The aim according to Lord Gowrie was 'to get at what I would, in shorthand, call the "Denning doctrine of remoteness" '[9] (as fully expounded in *Associated Newspapers Group* v. *Wade*). Of course it is the judges who decide whether or not these tests are satisfied and the government were clearly quite happy that the law should be left in a state where a trade union official could not be certain in advance whether or not he could negotiate these hurdles in court. The Lord Advocate said that if an official was in any doubt that the action would achieve the specified purpose, he should not embark on secondary action at all.[10]

After the House of Lords' decisions in *NWL, MacShane* and *Sirs* one view was that the golden formula and its trade dispute protections could remain as a reasonable basis for trade union liberties. While they restrained some of the excesses to which several judges were prepared to go to avoid the application of the immunities, they still left ample scope for judicial discretion. This lay in the exclusion of disputes with a no more than ostensible connection with the subject matter of a trade dispute and the recognition of some limitation in the words 'contemplation or furtherance' based on the actor's honesty of purpose. (Indeed as already noted, in *Hadmor Productions Ltd.* v. *Hamilton* (1981) the Court of Appeal appeared to be determined to maintain an even wider discretion to find that action is outside the golden formula.) To this has now been added the effective exclusion of worker-worker disputes from the trade dispute definition by the EA's concept of secondary action and the reinstatement of three of the Court of Appeal's restrictive tests for potentially lawful secondary action. In the light of this emasculation of the golden formula it is hardly surprising that one item absent from the Green Paper's deliberation is any express limitation on the words 'in contemplation or furtherance' themselves.

TRADE UNIONS' IMMUNITY FROM LIABILITY IN TORT

The immunity from liability in tort established for trade unions as such by s.4 of the Trade Disputes Act 1906 was restored on the repeal of the IRA by TULRA s.14(1). It is in fact not a total immunity because s.14(2) enables trade unions to be sued for negligence, nuisance or breach of duty resulting in personal injury, or breach of duty in connection with property in respect of acts not in contemplation or furtherance of a trade dispute. But it is generally accepted that this reservation does not concern liabilities which may arise in strikes.[11] In *Gouriet* v. *UPW* (1977) the House of Lords confirmed that the immunity in respect of such liabilities was, contrary to what Lord Denning in the Court of Appeal appeared to think, not confined to acts threatened or done in contemplation or furtherance of a trade dispute.[12] The Donovan Commission did in fact recommend that the immunity should be generally confined to acts within the golden formula (para. 909). While the Employment Act has not formally altered the position it has paved the way for a more radical proposal which is mooted in the Green Paper. This is the repeal of s.14 so that trade unions as such could only rely on the protection of TULRA s.13 as reduced by the 1980 Act. Paragraph 136 of the Green Paper asserts that since 'industrial relations have undergone great changes since the present immunity was introduced in 1906 . . . it must now be considered whether the extent of the immunity then thought necessary to safeguard the existence and operation of trade unions is still appropriate seventy-five years later'. It has already been noted that the provisions in EA ss.10 and 15(4), which enable trade unions (and other persons) to be joined to certain complaints of unfair dismissal and action short of dismissal for the purpose of contribution to compensation awards, perhaps anticipate the removal of the tort immunity. What effect this would have in practice is difficult to predict. The different experience of the two periods when trade unions could be made liable to employers for the consequences of unlawful industrial action, 1901–06 and 1972–74, indicates that one important factor would be the circumstances in which unions were held to be vicariously liable for the acts of their officials and members. Sections 10 and 15(4) of the 1980 Act have already revived this as an issue. The Green Paper concluded that if TULRA s.14 were simply to be repealed, the courts would have a wide and uncertain discretion as to when trade unions could be made responsible for unofficial action (paras. 116–22).

Given the efficacy of the labour injunction against union officials, it seems probable that employers would gain a significant advantage from being able to sue trade unions in tort only if they wished to pursue claims for damages. The experience of the IRA suggests that there will always be some employers willing to do this: in *General Aviation Services Ltd.* v. *TGWU* the plaintiff claimed £2 million as compensation for a fairly minor dispute. Awards of this magnitude would soon bankrupt the trade union movement. This possibility could be reduced by the imposition of a limit on the damages which could be claimed, as was made by IRA s.117 in respect of unions which registered under the Act. Even so it is hardly likely that new *Taff Vales* would enhance the climate of relations between employers and unions. Protagonists of removal of the immunity argue that it would lead to unions exercising greater control and discipline over their members and officials at all levels. While accepting that this would be desirable even the Green Paper acknowledged that it might indeed have the opposite effect given that there would be some unofficial action for which unions could not be made responsible (paras. 123–9).

As a result of the joinder provisions of the 1980 Act, trade unions can now be made to pay if they use industrial action in pursuit of the right to organise. In view of the restrictions already made by this Act on the protection for individuals who organise industrial action the removal of trade unions' complete protection against liability in tort would mean that they could be made to pay for exercising the right to strike in a wide range of circumstances, the precise extent of which would be within the discretion of the courts. For this reason alone trade union resistance to the repeal of a provision which is admitted to have immense symbolic and psychological significance is understandable.

ECONOMIC TORT LIABILITIES

Organising and taking part in industrial action almost always involves someone committing one of the civil wrongs known as economic torts. The detail of these torts is complex and their extent uncertain.[13] What follows is a broad outline of the liabilities and the defences provided to them by TULRA s.13. The effect of the Employment Act in extending the range of the liabilities and reducing the availability of the defences is then analysed.

Conspiracy

The tort liability for conspiracy has two forms. In the form in which it originally developed, the essence of the liability lay in the economic loss caused by otherwise lawful action taken by two or more people acting in combination. This is known as simple conspiracy or conspiracy to injure. If the combiners can establish that they were acting with the predominant purpose of furthering their own legitimate interests they cannot be made liable for this form of the tort. In the *Crofter* case (1942) the House of Lords clearly established that the interests of labour are legitimate interests in this context (above p. 9). This decision represented judicial recognition at the highest level of the right of workers to combine to pursue their own legitimate interests by lawful means. As a result liability for conspiracy to injure is unlikely to arise very often in labour disputes.

The second form of the tort arises where two or more people combine and cause loss to another by use of means in themselves unlawful – conspiracy to commit unlawful acts. In this form the liability is attracted by the unlawful means used to inflict harm. Doubts as to whether these include breaches of contract as well as torts and crimes were raised by *Rookes* v. *Barnard* (1964), where it was held that a breach of contract was an unlawful act for the purposes of the tort of intimidation.

The defence originally provided by s.1 of the Trade Disputes Act 1906 was re-enacted in an amended form in TULRA s.13(4):

> An agreement or combination by two or more persons to do or procure the doing of any act in contemplation or furtherance of a trade dispute shall not be actionable in tort if the act is one which, if done without any such agreement or combination, would not be actionable in tort.

So far as liability for conspiracy to injure is concerned this means that even if the predominant purpose of the defendants is not to further the legitimate interests of workers and trade unions, so long as it has a more than ostensible connection with the subject matter of a trade dispute set out in TULRA s.29(1), they will not be liable. Nor can they be liable for conspiracy to commit an unlawful act unless their actions are in themselves tortious. Whereas s.1 of the 1906 Act only required the defendant's acts to be 'actionable' for the defence to be lost, TULRA s.13(4) requires them to be 'actionable in tort'. Since a breach of contract is not actionable in tort, the protection does now apply in any proceedings against workers for conspiracy to break their contracts of employment by taking industrial action. Conspiracies to commit torts remain actionable and are not protected by TULRA s.13(4).

Even where the unlawful means are in themselves tortious the element of conspiracy may be material. This is clearly so if the tortious means are intimidation, the essence of which is a *coercive* threat of an unlawful act. Since very few, if any, individual threats of strike action can be coercive, an allegation of conspiracy is an almost essential pre-requisite for establishing the necessary element of coercion.

Intimidation

The essence of intimidation is an unlawful threat against another to compel him to act in a way which causes damage either to himself or to a third party. Where compliance with the threatener's wishes causes damage to the person threatened himself, this is known as two-party intimidation; where the damage is caused to a third party it is known as three-party intimidation. The chief difficulty is in distinguishing lawful threats from unlawful threats. It seems clear that a threat can only be unlawful if an unlawful act is threatened. The scope of unlawful acts includes crimes, torts and, after the House of Lords' decision in *Rookes* v. *Barnard* (1964), breaches of contract. In that case it was held that a threat by two shop stewards and a full time union officer that draughts-men employed by BOAC would go on strike, admittedly in breach of their contracts of employment, unless Rookes, a non-unionist, was dis-missed amounted to the tort of intimidation for which they were liable to Rookes once BOAC complied with their wishes and dismissed him. The decision called in question the legality of the strike threat in general since, as has been explained, most strike action involves workers in breaking their contracts of employment. A strike threat is therefore a threat of an unlawful act which becomes the tort of intimidation if it is effective in securing compliance with the wishes of those who make it.

The Trade Disputes Act 1965 was passed to provide protection against liability for intimidation for acts in contemplation or further-ance of a trade dispute in respect of threats of breach, or to induce breach, of contract of employment. It was re-enacted in TULRA s.13(1)(b). As amended in 1976 it extends to threats of breach of or inter-ference with — or to induce breach of or interfere with — *any* contract.

Inducing breach of and interference with contract

In the middle of the nineteenth century the courts established that it is a tort to induce or procure another person to break a contract to which he is party. We have already seen that almost all industrial action by workers involves them breaking their contracts of employment. Trade union officials and others who call on workers to take industrial action are therefore committing the tort of inducing these workers to break their contracts.

Even before its considerable extension in the 1960s and 1970s this tort liability was very complex in its application in labour disputes. The leading case was *Thomson* v. *Deakin* (1952), where the action taken by officials of several trade unions against Thomsons, an employer in the printing industry who operated the 'yellow dog' contract of employment (see p. 6), was held not to amount to procuring breaches of the commercial contract between Thomsons and their suppliers, Bowaters. The Court of Appeal held that in order to succeed, the plaintiff would have to establish that the defendant had sufficient knowledge of the contract and intended to cause breach of it, that it was broken and that he had suffered damage in consequence. Where the relevant contracts were contracts of employment these requirements were fairly easy to establish against a defendant who had called on workers to break their contracts by taking strike action. Where as in *Thomson* v. *Deakin* the contracts were commercial the situation was different. Defendant union officials or unofficial strike leaders might not have sufficient knowledge of these contracts or might intend that they should be lawfully terminated rather than broken.

If he can establish these fundamental requirements the plaintiff must then show that the defendant induced or procured the breach. There are essentially two ways relevant to labour disputes in which this can be done. The first is *directly* inducing breach by persuading one of the parties to the contract to break it, for example, persuading workers to come out on strike. In *Thomson* v. *Deakin* it was argued that the defendants had directly persuaded Bowaters not to deliver supplies to Thomsons, but the court found no evidence of this. The second way is *indirectly* procuring breach by doing an unlawful act or using unlawful means which renders performance of the contract by one of the parties impossible. This is the form usually alleged where the contracts are commercial ones between employers and their customers or suppliers. Thus in *Thomson* v. *Deakin* one argument was that the defendants procured breach of the commercial contract between Thomsons and Bowaters by the unlawful means of inducing Bowaters' employees to break their contracts of employment by refusing to deliver supplies to Thomsons. This argument failed because there was no evidence that Bowaters' lorry drivers had been asked to make such deliveries once it was known that Thomsons were being blacked.

In the 1960s a series of decisions starting with *Stratford* v. *Lindley* (1965) developed the liability so as to make it virtually impossible to argue that those responsible for organising industrial action were not committing this tort. Thus it now no longer has to be shown that the defendant had any knowledge of the contracts in question if the plaintiff can show that the defendant's acts were undertaken with the attitude 'whether it is a breach of contract or not I care not' (Lord Denning in *Daily Mirror* v. *Gardner* (1968)). More fundamentally, the requirement of breach of contract was removed by the Court of Appeal's decision in *Torquay Hotel Co. Ltd.* v. *Cousins* (1969). In that case the defendants' embargo on deliveries of oil to the plaintiffs' hotel arguably did not cause a breach of the contract between the plaintiffs and Esso because it contained a 'force majeure' clause which provided that Esso would be under no liability for failure to deliver in the event of labour disputes. This led Lord Denning to express the opinion that 'the time has come when the principle should be further extended to cover deliberate and direct interference with the contract without causing any breach'.

In the post-TULRA cases attention has focused on the defence provided for acts in contemplation or furtherance of a trade dispute by TULRA s.13(1)(a). Section 3 of the 1906 Act provided a defence only in respect of inducing breach of contracts *of employment*. While this is the most obvious effect of calling or organising industrial action, after *Thomson* v. *Deakin* and particularly by the late 1960s it was clear that disruption of commercial contracts was an almost equally inevitable consequence. While it may not always be possible to hold that inducement to break these occurs by means of direct persuasion, it is easy to establish liability for indirectly procuring breach of or interfering with them by the unlawful means of persuading workers to break their contracts of employment. Although the Donovan Commission was of the opinion in 1968 that 'the law on the subject is far from clear' (para. 889), it recommended that the protection should be extended to inducing breach of any contract. As amended in 1976, TULRA s.13(1)(a) has done this. It has also extended the protection to cover interference with the performance of contracts in order to meet the extension of the liability in *Torquay* v. *Cousins*.

It may be, particularly as a result of that case, that the liability extends to interference with future contracts or even that inducing breach of or interference with contract is but one illustration of liability for 'interference with business by unlawful means'. Before turning to this wider and uncertain liability it is necessary to consider the intended effect of ss.17 and 18 of the Employment Act, which limit the circumstances in which the protections in TULRA s.13(1) are available.

EMPLOYMENT ACT s.17

Section 17 removes the protection provided by TULRA s.13(1) against liability for interfering with commercial contracts by secondary action unless it satisfies conditions which enable it to pass through one of three 'gateways'. In introducing this provision the Secretary of State for Employment made it clear that the government had identified secondary action as the evil which had to be eradicated because it was secondary action which was used to spread the disruptive effects of disputes to industry and the community at large. The pre-Employment Act law after the House of Lords' decision in *MacShane* was seen as a licence to spread industrial action far and wide beyond the original dispute. However s.17 was designed to preserve the immunity for action affecting current business between the employer in dispute and his immediate customers and suppliers.[14]

The actual effects of the provision are nothing like so simple. It applies where one of the facts relied on for the purpose of establishing liability is that there has been secondary action as defined in s.17(2). Unless that action can pass through one of the three gateways in subsections (3)–(5), s.17(1) restricts the protection provided by TULRA s.13(1) for acts done in contemplation or furtherance of a trade dispute to liability for inducing breach or interfering with performance of a contract *of employment* and intimidation by threatening breach or to induce breach or to interfere with the performance of such a contract. Before turning to the definition of secondary action and the gateways it should be noted that the protection in relation to contracts of employment which is retained is effectively worthless. Breaches of contracts of employment are almost inevitably causally linked to consequential interference with or breach of commercial contracts. Paragraph 157 of the Green Paper states that a general restriction of the immunity to inducing breach of contract of employment would place most industrial action at risk if it was nevertheless unlawful means for the purpose of liability for interference with commercial contracts. After the repeal of TULRA s.13(3) by EA s.17(8) the Court of Appeal has already held, as the opposition in Parliament predicted, that even though not actionable as such, inducing breach of contract of employment remains unlawful means for the purposes of other liabilities (*Hadmor Productions Ltd.* v. *Hamilton,* 1981). The general point is discussed further below. In this context suffice it to say that any suggestion that s.17 preserves the legitimacy of some secondary action (apart from that which passes through one of the three gateways) is false for reasons which were made clear in the Green Paper, which was published before there was any case law on the Act.

Section 17(2) provides that there is secondary action in relation to a trade dispute when a person

(a) induces another to break a contract of employment or inter-feres or induces another to interfere with its performance, or

(b) threatens that a contract of employment under which he or another is employed will be broken or its performance inter-fered with, or that he will induce another to break a contract of employment or to interfere with its performance,

if the employer under the contract of employment is not a party to the trade dispute.

It has already been noted that the final words effectively exclude dis-putes between workers and workers from the trade dispute definition (p. 190). A technical point concerning the definition of a trade dispute for the purpose of s.17 is that s.17(7) provides that an employer who is a member of an employers' association which is party to a trade dispute (which it may be according to TULRA s.29(4)), is only to be himself regarded as a party to the dispute by virtue of his membership if he is 'represented' by the employers' association in it. It is by no means clear when an employers' association represents an employer.

Subsection (2) contains a much more fundamental difficulty. It defines secondary action 'in relation to' a trade dispute. This is presum-ably intended to be of unqualified width so as to cover all industrial action where one of the torts in (a) or (b) is committed and the em-ployer is not party to the trade dispute in contemplation or furtherance of which the action was taken. However this could well turn a lot of primary action into secondary action within the definition where there are separate trade disputes involving different employers. Inducing breaches of contracts of employment by workers of the employer in the first trade dispute is clearly secondary action in relation to the second trade dispute and vice versa. If there is any sort of link between the normal course of business for both these two employers which is disrupted by the disputes in which they are involved, each may be able to rely on the action in the other's dispute – which is secondary action in relation to his dispute — as one of the facts for the purposes of establishing liability to bring the case within EA s.17(1). The organisers of the industrial action in both disputes will then be denied protection against liability for interfering with commercial contracts. For example, suppose that A, a haulage firm, is involved in a trade dispute with his workers over pay and that there is a trade dispute between B and his workers over the recognition of the X trade union to which workers employed by both A and B belong. There is a link between the normal course of business of A and B because C, a wholesaler who takes supplies from B, normally engages A to deliver orders made by retailers for B's products. If A and B decide to take legal proceedings to restrain the industrial action, each may be able to rely on the secondary action in the other's dispute as one of the facts for the purposes of establishing liability. The fact that the workers of A and B belong to the same trade union would strengthen the argument that the action against the one employer was sympathetic action in support of the workers in dispute with the other employer. There would then be no protection for the organisers of the action in either dispute against liability for interfering with commercial contracts.

On the other hand it appears to be the case that a direct approach to an employer to treat another employer who is party to a primary dispute as 'black' is not secondary action. Although it might amount to inducing breach of or an interference with commercial contracts, it does not involve one of the torts in paragraphs (a) and (b) of s.17(2), and so falls outside the definition of secondary action. These points of interpretation are but one demonstration of the impossibility of establishing any realistic division of industrial action into 'primary' and 'secondary' categories.

The main gateway for secondary action to pass through in order to retain the full protection of TULRA s.13(1) is in EA s.17(3). This requires the principal purpose of the action to be to directly prevent or disrupt, during the dispute, the supply (under a contract subsisting at the time of the secondary action) of goods or services between an employer party to the dispute and the employer party to the contracts of employment to which the secondary action relates. In more intelligible language this means that secondary action against the first or immediate customers and suppliers of an employer party to a trade dispute may retain the full protection of TULRA s.13(1). There are, however, a number of conditions which have to be satisfied the ambit of which is far from clear.

First the purpose of the action must be to prevent or disrupt supplies 'during the dispute'. If the prevention or disruption must necessarily continue after the dispute ends, can a defendant say that his purpose was limited to preventing or disrupting supplies only during the dispute? In any event it may be difficult to determine when a dispute ends. Second the purpose must be to cause this prevention or disruption 'directly'. As explained in s.17(6)(b) this means other than by means of preventing or disrupting the supply of goods or services by or to any other person. In other words preventing a first supplier, for example, from delivering supplies to the employer in dispute by cutting off the supplier's source of raw materials does not qualify. But what is the position where action aimed directly at the commercial contracts of an employer party to the primary dispute and his first customers and suppliers necessarily affects other parties, as in most cases it will? For example, if the employer's first customer, a wholesaler, does not receive goods from an employer party to the primary dispute, he will be unable to fulfil his contracts to supply retailers. Whether such action can pass through the gateway in subsection (3) appears to depend on its principal purpose. If it cannot, virtually all secondary action will be unlawful, a possibility recognised in paragraph 161 of the Green Paper.

Third, it was apparently the government's intention that it should be impossible to pass through this gateway unless the supply of goods or services in question is under subsisting contracts. It was originally intended by the Working Paper to make the criterion whether the customer or supplier regularly conducted a substantial part of his business with the employer, but this would have unfairly discriminated against small firms. The Act's requirement of a subsisting contract is however rather more unfair to the organisers of industrial action because in many cases they will not know whether or not there is a contract. Where business is conducted under a course of dealing under which individual contracts are made for each delivery, there might well be no subsisting contract at the time when the secondary action is taken. Further it would be possible to draft commercial contracts in terms such that they ceased to subsist, possibly at the option of either party, during industrial disputes. It is arguable that the absence of any subsisting contracts does not preclude a defendant from negotiating this gateway since he could nevertheless maintain that his principal purpose was to disrupt such contracts which he believed to exist as that is the normal way for business to be conducted.[15] However those who organise secondary action would be unwise to rely on the courts accepting that that was his purpose where no contract existed. That apart, no account is taken of the fact that such commercial contracts will often necessarily involve a number of other subsidiary contracts, performance of which will inevitably be disrupted or prevented along with the main contract for supply or delivery. Contracts for carriage of goods from the suppliers to the employer or from the employer to his customer are examples. It is not clear whether secondary action can pass through the gateway in s.17(3) if it also causes disruption of these incidental contracts. It may be that the action would be protected as against the supplier or customer but not as against the carrier.

The final and general uncertainty in every case is that even if all the difficulties about prevention or disruption during the dispute, directness, subsisting contracts and other incidental contracts are resolved, or in particular cases do not exist, there remain the problems of whether the 'principal purpose' of the action is within the subsection and whether the action is 'likely' to achieve that purpose. As we have seen, both these criteria were rejected by the Law Lords as limits on the golden formula. In *NWL* v. *Woods* they rejected predominant purpose as the test of whether or not a dispute was sufficiently connected with the subject matter of a trade dispute set out in TULRA s.29(1), and in *MacShane* they rejected the existence of any objective element in the words 'in furtherance of' a trade dispute. What these criteria do of course is give maximum scope for the judges to have the final say on whether or not the requirements of the gateway are satisfied. Anyone contemplating organising secondary action could never be certain in advance that he could satisfy s.17(3). Indeed this uncertainty is apparently one of the intended effects of s.17. In the words of Lord Gowrie it requires

> anyone contemplating sympathetic action at least to exercise the greatest care before doing so, to consider carefully the effects the action may have, what it is designed to achieve and against whom it is directed. If he does not pause and weigh all these matters carefully, he may well find that he is acting outside the immunity conferred by this clause and that the law does not protect him.[16]

The gateway in s.17(4) is an extension of s.17(3) in one respect. It legitimises secondary action against an associated employer of an employer party to a trade dispute, and the first customers and suppliers of the associated employer, where he is providing goods or services in substitution for those which would otherwise be provided by the employer in dispute. The potential width of this gateway is very limited. The definition of associated employer in TULRA s.30(5), which is applied for this purpose by EA s.17(7), provides that 'any two employers are to be regarded as associated if one is a company over which the other (directly or indirectly) has control or if both are companies of which a third person (directly or indirectly) has control'. Thus employers who are not companies — e.g. most employers in the public sector — can never be associated (above p. 28). Even where employers are associated because for example they belong to the same group of companies, it will be necessary for two companies to be in the same line of business so that the one can substitute for the other. But where this is so, it will be virtually impossible to prove that the commercial contracts of the employer not in dispute were for the supply of goods or services in substitution for those of the company in dispute. This difficulty is admitted by the Green Paper in considering a proposal for legitimising secondary action only against a firm providing goods to an employer in dispute in substitution for those which the employees on strike would normally make (paras. 151–53).

Section 17(5) is the licensed pickets' gateway. Secondary action passes through it if it is done in the course of attendance declared lawful by the substituted TULRA s.15 either by a worker employed (or if not in employment, last employed) by a party to the dispute, or by a union official whose attendance is lawful under TULRA s.15, that is, he is accompanying a member whom he represents at or near the member's place of work. Section 17(5) was barely discussed in Parliament, as it was common ground apparently that it was necessary simply to ensure that licensed pickets who remain within the new TULRA s.15 retain the full range of the remaining protections in TULRA s.13. Since licensed pickets are by definition attending at or near their own place of work only for the prescribed purposes of peacefully obtaining or communicating information or peacefully persuading people to work or not to work, it might be asked how such behaviour could amount to secondary action. The answer is that even a worker picketing his own place of work by holding up a placard may succeed in persuading a lorry driver to turn back and not to deliver the goods he is carrying. The picket will then have induced the lorry driver to break his contract of employment and, unless the lorry driver's employer is a party to the trade dispute in contemplation of furtherance of which the picketing was taking place, that will be secondary action as defined in s.17(2).

Not all persons who peacefully picket their own place of work will be able to negotiate the gateway in s.17(5). TULRA s.15(1) protects a *person* picketing his own place of work in contemplation or furtherance of *a* trade dispute. Section 17(5) is only open to a *worker* picketing his own place of work if he is employed (or was last employed) by a party to *the* dispute. Limiting the gateway to workers employed by a party to the dispute is an essential part of its narrow ambit. TULRA s.15 protects pickets who peacefully picket their own employer in furtherance of a trade dispute even though neither the pickets nor the employer are party to that dispute. For example white collar workers who belong to the A trade union and are employed by X, a supplier of raw materials, might picket X in order to try to persuade manual workers employed there not to load and deliver supplies destined for Y until Y agrees to recognise the A trade union to which his white collar workers also belong. Such picketing could not satisfy s.17(5) because X is not a party to the dispute, assuming that to mean the trade dispute in relation to which the action of the pickets is secondary action according to the definition in s.17(2). Of course since X is the first supplier of Y, the action might pass through the gateway in s.17(3). But if the white collar workers at Y went to picket X, it would be irrelevant whether their action could pass through s.17(3), since they would be unlicensed pickets deprived of all the protection of TULRA s.13 by EA s.16(2) in any event. Union officials who accompany members picketing their own place of work may have more scope for passing though this gateway since s.17(5)(b) only requires their attendance to be lawful by virtue of the new TULRA s.15(1)(b). It does not require the members they are accompanying to be employed by a party to *the* dispute. Thus in the example given above, if an official of the A trade union who represented the white collar workers employed by X, accompanied them in picketing X, he could apparently pass through the gateway in s.17(5) even though the workers could not.

Most of the debate about s.17 has focused on the policy of restricting the extent of protection against civil liability for secondary action. Although the Green Paper does not really advance the argument beyond that which took place on the provisions of s.17 itself, it does raise the possibility of varying them so as, for example, to provide protection only where the second employer provided material support or assistance to an employer party to the dispute or where primary action was not possible. The government's case against a complete removal of protection for all secondary action was that it could be portrayed as a fundamental attack on trade union rights and that to provide trade unions with such a rallying call would be out of line with the 'step by step' approach to reform of labour law. This argument in fact overlooks the point that the exclusion of all purely sympathetic action from the protection which has already occurred constitutes just such an attack on the fundamental trade union principle of solidarity. The premise on which s.17 and the discussion in the Green Paper is based is that industrial action which can be described as secondary is inherently less justified and more damaging than primary action and should therefore be subject to greater legal restraint. However, as McCarthy pointed out, whether or not secondary action is taken has nothing whatever to do with the justice of the cause and very little to do with the long term consequences for society as a whole. Some workers have no need to rely on secondary action because there is no alternative labour force, or they work for a monopoly employer or the consequences of their taking industrial action are immediate and devastating.[17] The whole basis of s.17 is unsound in that it makes an unrealistic distinction between primary and secondary action. Its attempts to make exceptions to that distinction compound the 'legal mysteries' in the section that 'remain to be probed'.[18] The greatest uncertainty it creates without doubt arises through its repeal of TULRA s.13(3). To this we shall return below.

EMPLOYMENT ACT s.18

Section 18 was enacted in order to ensure that the law provided a means of redress for an employer whose workforce was the target of certain trade union recruitment practices which were described in the Leggatt Report.[19] This one-man inquiry, which was boycotted by the unions, was principally concerned with the tactics used by SLADE to recruit workers in the artwork, advertising and associated industries. The issue arose because of the impact of new technology on work traditionally performed by members of craft unions in the printing industry. In order to protect its position SLADE decided to recruit members in art studios, photographic laboratories and advertising agencies into a new section established in 1975, the Slade Art Union. The Report found that where attempts to recruit workers in these industries by persuasion failed, the union informed the management of individual businesses that SLADE members employed by printing firms would black all work from them unless their employees joined the union. By this means they succeeded in recruiting a significant number of reluctant members. The Report concluded that, although there might be some doubt about whether or not freelancers in the relevant industries were workers within TULRA's definition, SLADE's recruitment activities were within the law in the sense that s.13 of TULRA as amended in 1976 would provide a good defence to any tort action by an employer who was blacked or threatened with blacking. In the Working Paper which immediately followed publication of the Leggatt Report the government announced that this was unacceptable. It considered that the law might be amended to provide the necessary 'protection' for employers in a number of ways, including an unspecified amendment to the definition of 'trade dispute'.

In the event s.18, like s.17, operates by excluding certain action from the protection given by TULRA s.13(1) in respect of liability for inducing breach of or interfering with contracts and intimidation. Although it is a short section the meaning of s.18 would not be readily apparent to anyone uninitiated in the intricacies of the law of industrial conflict. It removes the protection of TULRA s.13(1) where action is taken to compel workers to belong to a particular trade union or one of two or more unions if that action induces breach of or interferes with contracts of employment, or interferes with commercial contracts by means of inducing breach of or interfering with contracts of employment, or threatens to do either of these things, *and* none of the workers 'compelled' works either for the same employer or at the same place as employees working under the contracts of employment referred to. The activities of SLADE as described in the Leggatt Report would fall within the section because they sought to compel workers in an artwork company, for example, to belong to SLADE by calling on their members employed in printing firms to break their contracts of employment by blacking work from the artwork company, given that the employees who would be doing the blacking and the workers in the artwork company had different employers and worked at different places.

The problems caused by s.18 concern rather the uncertainty as to whether it catches other practices so that they lose the protection of TULRA s.13(1). If, as *Torquay* v. *Cousins* suggests, the tort liability for interference with contracts extends to future contracts, s.18 could cover action taken against an employer who announces that he intends to take supplies from a business employing non-union labour. It could also apply where workers refused to work on materials from a supplier unless he allowed his workers to belong to TUC-affiliated unions, since it covers action to compel membership of 'one of two or more particular trade unions'. Of course in all cases the factor which determines the applicability of s.18 is whether the purpose of the action was to compel workers to belong to particular trade unions. (The same problem arises under EPCA s.23(1)(c) as amended by EA s.15(1), see p. 68). Interpreted literally even in the cases described in the Leggatt Report no one was compelled to join SLADE in an absolute sense. However the Solicitor-General advised the House of Commons Standing Committee on the Bill that 'compel' was not an absolute concept. His suggested definition was: '[to] compel somebody to do something is to try to make him do it by putting him in a position where he has no practical alternative'. In the context of trade union recruitment it meant action that went beyond persuading, encouraging or inducing workers to join.[20] Wedderburn's rather more specific explanation of what it really means in this context was the use of industrial or economic pressure via one employer to the other such that the other employer compelled his workers to be unionised.[21] That being so how is the 'purpose' of action determined when it is taken in pursuit of a policy of not handling work from a non-union source? This practice is sometimes embodied in a 'fair list' of businesses from which supplies will be accepted. While the Secretary of State for Employment said that s.18 would not interfere with this practice because its purpose is not to compel union membership,[22] the Green Paper said more guardedly that it 'might' not do so (para. 289). Similar doubts must exist about the practice of refusing to work with non-union labour where, for example, a worker from a firm to which work is sub-contracted might have to work with employees of the main contractor.

The government's response to pressure to legislate against the more formal practice of 'union labour only' clauses imposed on sub-contractors was to include in s.10 of the 1980 Act provisions enabling a sub-contractor, who is forced to dismiss non-union employees because of such a requirement, to join the main contractor to a consequent complaint of unfair dismissal for the purpose of requiring him to make a contribution to any compensation award. The main contractor can then in turn join a union or other person who puts pressure on him to insist on the union labour only stipulation by taking or threatening industrial action (see above p. 71). In considering the possibility of further amendments to the law in respect of these practices the Green Paper makes it clear that the main constraint is concern about the 'practical limitations on the extent to which such longstanding practices can be eradicated by law' and 'uncertainty as to what would be the effects of trying to do so' (para. 304). Indeed it is arguable that s.18 will anyway have no impact where an employer and a trade union *agree* that work will not be accepted from a particular source unless the workers there belong to trade unions. Moreover since s.18 speaks of compulsion it assumes that the non-unionists whose recruitment into membership the action is designed to achieve do not want to join. But what if some of them do? The only safeguard against s.18 becoming a weapon in the hands of an anti-union employer concerned to frustrate the right to organise is a restricted construction of the phrase 'purpose of compelling', which is not something which the judges can be relied on to provide. Despite the government's protestations to the contrary, it would be entirely consistent with other parts of the Employment Act for s.18 to become a legal obstacle to organisational rights.

INTERFERENCE WITH BUSINESS BY UNLAWFUL MEANS

Section 13(3) of TULRA provided:

> For the avoidance of doubt it is hereby declared that —
> (a) an act which by reason of [s.13(1) or (2)] is itself not actionable;
> (b) a breach of contract in contemplation or furtherance of a trade dispute;
> shall not be regarded as the doing of an unlawful act or as the use of unlawful means for the purpose of establishing liability in tort.

It was repealed by EA s.17(8) because it was thought that it would have provided grounds for arguing that despite s.17 there was still no redress for secondary action which only indirectly interfered with commercial contracts. That is tortious only where unlawful means are used; inducing breaches of contract of employment or threatening to do so normally supply the unlawful means for this form of the tort liability. It would have been arguable that they could not have done so if s.13(3) had been left unamended because they were not themselves actionable by reason of s.13(1). But since EA s.17(1) begins with the words 'nothing in s.13 of the 1974 Act shall prevent an act from being actionable in tort' it may be doubted whether this would have been the case. The reference to s.13 includes s.13(3) and therefore s.13(3) arguably could not have prevented secondary action from being actionable as s.17 intended.

Nevertheless EA s.17(8) repeals TULRA s.13(3) for all purposes and not just for the purposes of the application of EA s.17. It has thereby opened up the possibility of outflanking the defences in TULRA s.13 in respect of any action whether primary or secondary. This is so for two reasons. First TULRA s.13(1) and (2), like their predecessors in s.3 of the Trade Disputes Act 1906 and s.1 of the Trade Disputes Act 1965, provide that an act done in contemplation or furtherance of a trade dispute shall not be actionable on the ground *only* that it induces breaches of contract etc. After the repeal of TULRA s.13(3) inducing breach of or interference with contract, intimidation by a threat to break, to induce breach of or to interfere with contract and perhaps a breach of contract itself remain potentially unlawful means for the purposes of other tort liabilities. (On the possible liability of unlicensed pickets for conspiracy to commit unlawful acts, see above p. 177.) It is even arguable that although action is taken in contemplation or furtherance of a trade dispute, if it indirectly interferes with commercial contracts by the means of inducing workers to break their contracts of employment, s.13(1) provides no defence because it is not actionable on the ground only that it interferes with commercial contracts or only that it induces breaches of contracts of employment but on the ground that it does the former indirectly by the unlawful means of the latter.

The second reason why the repeal of s.13(3) may outflank the s.13 defences is that the liabilities referred to in s.13(1) can now constitute unlawful means for the tort of 'interference with business by unlawful means'. While s.13(3) was in force that was not possible. It might be thought that s.13(2) would provide a defence to this tort. This re-enactment of the second limb of s.3 of the 1906 Act provides that an act done in contemplation or furtherance of a trade dispute is not actionable in tort on the ground only that it is an interference with the trade, business or employment of another person, or with the right of another person to dispose of his capital or his labour as he wills. However in *Rookes* v. *Barnard* (1964) the House of Lords decided that it was originally passed to provide a defence to a form of liability which might have developed but which had not done so. In any event where the interference is by unlawful means it is not actionable on the ground only that it is an interference with trade, business or employment and therefore not covered by s.13(2) anyway.

The government denied that the repeal of s.13(3) could effectively remove the protection of s.13 from all industrial action for either of these reasons. On the first reason it argued that after the 1976 amendments s.13(3) became unnecessary because s.13(1) provided substantive immunity for both direct and indirect forms of the torts. On the second it denied that there was any such tort as interference with business by unlawful means. This second argument was not tenable because by 1980 there was a clear body of case law establishing that the tort existed and it was recognised in leading textbooks. The doubts concerned — and still concern — not its existence but its boundaries. In *Stratford* v. *Lindley* (1965) Lords Reid and Radcliffe stated the nature of the defendant's liability as interference with business by unlawful means. The Court of Appeal in *Daily Mirror* v. *Gardner* (1968) upheld an injunction against officials of the retail newsagents' federation on the grounds that their action — distributing 'stop' notices to their members for them to send to wholesalers discontinuing their orders for the *Daily Mirror* for one week — amounted to interference with the plaintiff's business by the unlawful means of operating a restrictive trading agreement, which would be condemned under the Restrictive Trade Practices Act 1956. As Lord Denning put it 'if one person interferes with the trade or business of another and does so by unlawful means then he is acting unlawfully even though he does not procure or induce breach of any contract. Interference by unlawful means is enough'. In *Torquay* v. *Cousins* (1969) he explained both *Rookes* v. *Barnard* and *Stratford* v. *Lindley* on this basis and added that unlawful means meant an act which the actor was not at liberty to commit.

There were stronger grounds for arguing that once an act was not actionable it could not be unlawful means. It is however difficult to accept that the government believed in that argument since its own Working Paper on Secondary Industrial Action stated that s.13(3) had enlarged the immunities. The case law before 1974 was divided on the point. But after the repeal of a provision passed 'for the avoidance of doubt', Lord Denning, with whom Watkins L.J. expressly agreed, unequivocally asserted that acts which before were not to be regarded as unlawful were now to be regarded as unlawful. They were not actionable by the employer, but were unlawful so as to be available as unlawful means in tort: *Hadmor Productions Ltd.* v. *Hamilton* (1981).[23] Further the tort liability imposed in *Hadmor* was interference with business by unlawful means, the existence of which, according to Lord Denning, was well established by a line of cases going back to *Allen* v. *Flood* (1898). Watkins and O'Connor L.JJ. agreed that the tort existed and that the defendants had committed it. As noted in connection with the other point raised in the judgments, the existence of a trade dispute (above p. 187), the case arose because of a decision taken at an ACTT meeting to black a series of programmes which the plaintiffs had made and were in the process of selling to Thames Television for transmission. Four programmes had been shown out of an intended thirteen which, though there was no formal binding contract, there was every expectation as a matter of business practice that Thames would take. The defendant ACTT officials were held to be liable for interference with the business of Hadmor by the unlawful means of inducing technicians employed by Thames to break their contracts of employment or threatening to do so by blacking the programmes.

Even before the Employment Act the extent of unlawful means was of vital importance to the legality of industrial action because the tort of interference with business by unlawful means could outflank the defences of TULRA s.13. In *Camellia Tanker Ltd.* v. *ITF* (1976) the attempt to find unlawful means unprotected by TULRA s.13 in breaches of local byelaws made under the Harbours, Docks and Piers Clauses Act 1847 failed not only because no such breaches were proved but also because the plaintiffs did not establish that they had any right to bring an action in respect of breach of the byelaws. However in 1979 Lord Denning stated that interference with freedom of the press and interference with a public authority's statutory duty were both unlawful means for the purposes of the liability for interference with business by unlawful means: *Associated Newspapers Group Ltd.* v. *Wade.* The case was brought by various publishers and advertisers against the general secretaries of the NGA and SLADE. It arose out of action taken by these unions in a longstanding dispute with the owners of the Nottingham Evening Post, who permitted their employees to belong to trade unions but refused to recognise the NGA for collective bargaining. The unions had succeeded in persuading most of the concerns which advertised regularly in the Post to cease to do so. To bring pressure on the remaining sixteen they instructed members in newspaper offices and printing houses not to handle their advertisements for newspapers and certain other publications. Lord Denning found that the defendants were liable for interference with the plaintiffs' business not only by inducing breaches of contract but also by interference with press freedom. Such interference was so contrary to the public interest that it was to be regarded as the employment of unlawful means.

Further, because of the defendants' actions two of the plaintiffs, the Severn Trent Water Authority and the Nottingham Area Health Authority, were unable to publish notices and advertise job vacancies in newspapers and journals (other than the Nottingham Evening Post) as they were required to do by statute. Lord Denning's opinion that the defendants had no immunity when a public authority was disabled from performing its statutory duties was based on *Meade* v. *Haringey London Borough Council* (1979). That action arose out of the defendant local education authority's decision to keep schools closed during a strike by ancillary workers including school caretakers whose normal duties included opening schools. Both Lord Denning and Eveleigh L.J. asserted that in calling on the defendant to break its statutory duty, unions and their officers would be acting unlawfully and that TULRA s.13 gave no immunity against inducing a local authority to do this. Eveleigh L.J. added that an agreement between a public authority and unions for the former to act in breach of its statutory duty to assist the latter's pay claim could well be a civil conspiracy to which s.13 would not provide any defence.

With respect to breach of statutory duty as unlawful means the Employment Act has extended the area of potential liability for organising industrial action. It is easy to see that industrial action could contravene at least the spirit and in some cases the letter of many of the provisions in the Act. It could, for example, take place without prior approval by ballot even though the union's rules provided for a ballot to be held and state finance under s.1 or the employer's premises under s.2 were available. It could easily contravene the guidance in the Closed Shop and Picketing Codes issued under s.3. Industrial action might be taken in order to put pressure on a union not to admit or re-admit a person whose right under s.4(2) not to be unreasonably excluded or expelled had been infringed. A strike might be called because of the employer's refusal to dismiss a non-union employee in accordance with a closed shop practice where to do so would be unfair and unlawful after s.7. Industrial action might be taken to put pressure on the employer to take action short of dismissal against a non-unionist to compel him to join a union, thus infringing his right in EPCA s.23(1)(c) as amended by EA s.15(1). Some of these provisions provide a remedy for those adversely affected by such action: ss.4 and 5 for the person unreasonably excluded from a union; s.7 for the unfairly dismissed employee, with s.10 providing a remedy for the employer in respect of the unfair dismissal compensation which he has to pay that employee (plus the parallel provisions in respect of employees subjected to action short of dismissal). However, on the authority of the *Daily Mirror, Associated Newspapers Group* and *Meade* cases in particular, it is at least arguable that such 'infringements' of the Act may be breaches of statutory duty sufficient to constitute unlawful means for the purpose of the tort of interference with business by unlawful means. Indeed some breaches of statutory duty might arise without any industrial action, for example, a refusal to admit an applicant held to have been unreasonably excluded from a trade union contrary to EA s.4(2).

The government countered amendments moved to try to remove the possibility of the Act containing this hidden minefield of liabilities first by doubting whether any of the situations referred to could give rise to liability; the authorities cited were said to be distinguishable or unsatisfactory. Second it was suggested that no liability could be incurred via any such unlawful means to a person for whom the Act itself provided a remedy. If this is so it may be asked why it was thought necessary to include subsection (8) in s.2 of the 1980 Act. This states that the only remedy for a trade union against an employer who unreasonably refuses to permit it to hold a ballot on his premises is that provided by s.2, whereas there are no equivalent limitations in respect of the other legal rights under the Act. That apart, even if the government were correct, it would still be open to third parties to seek labour injunctions for interference with business by the unlawful means of breaches of the Employment Act. Finally, as has already been noted with reference to s.4 (p. 121), the government acknowledged that if tortious liability based on infringements of the Act were to be developed then it was inclined to support it.[24]

It must be conceded that this particular problem is at the outside edge of the penumbra of uncertainty which has always surrounded the economic tort liabilities. There seems to be no doubt that breach of statutory duty can constitute unlawful means in tort – unless and until the House of Lords rules otherwise. While the specific limitations imposed on the extent of the statutory protection for organising and taking part in industrial action by the Employment Act may be supported or opposed as a matter of policy, the half concealed and half denied extension of the range of liabilities which restrict the right to strike is difficult to justify on any grounds.

THE LABOUR INJUNCTION

As essential characteristic of tort liability is that it gives the injured party a right to claim damages to compensate him for his loss. But legal actions arising out of labour disputes only rarely proceed beyond the stage of an application for an 'interlocutory' injunction. This is a court order to the defendants to call off the strike or other industrial action until the case is heard at a full trial. It would be months or even years before a full trial could be held and, whether or not an interim injunction is obtained, the dispute would almost certainly have been resolved long before the trial would take place. It is therefore easy to see why claims are rarely pursued to this stage.

It may be a matter of surprise to many people that it is possible to obtain an injunction on an application made ex parte, that is, without the person against whom it is made being given an opportunity to be heard in his defence. In order to prevent the seeking of snap labour injunctions, s.17(1) of TULRA provides that where in the opinion of the court the party against whom an ex parte injunction is sought would be likely to claim that he acted in contemplation or furtherance of a trade dispute, it must not grant an injunction unless satisfied that all steps which were reasonable in the circumstances were taken with a view to seeing that he had notice of the application and an opportunity to be heard. One of the unsatisfactory aspects of the Court of Appeal's decision in *Gouriet* v. *UPW* (1977), which was reversed by the House of Lords, was that it granted an injunction against the POEU, which was not at the time a party to the proceedings, on the strength of a report in *The Times* that it had said that it would instruct its members not to provide or maintain telecommunication circuits to South Africa as part of a proposed one week international boycott. A majority of the Law Lords agreed that this injunction should not have been granted.

Even where applications for interlocutory injunctions were heard inter parties so that the defendants had some opportunity to present their case (although it usually has to be on the basis of hurriedly prepared affidavits), the protection provided against the tort liabilities by TULRA appeared to be of little use in preventing a labour injunction from being granted after the House of Lords decision in *American Cyanamid Co.* v. *Ethicon Ltd.* (1975). This established that if the plaintiff could show that there was a serious question to be tried, the grant or refusal of an injunction should depend on the 'balance of convenience'. In labour disputes this will always weigh heavily in favour of the plaintiff employers who can point to mounting economic loss if the industrial action continues.[25] Against this the defendant union officials or workers can only place the loss of a bargaining tactic, a loss which in legal terms is only temporary if the subsequent trial of the case should be resolved in their favour. For this reason s.17(2) was added to TULRA by the EPA 'for the avoidance of doubt'. It provides that where a party against whom an interlocutory injunction is sought claims that he acted in contemplation or furtherance of a trade dispute, the court shall have regard to the likelihood of that party's succeeding in establishing a golden formula defence under TULRA ss.13–15.

The combined effects of the decision in *Cyanamid* and TULRA s.17(2) were considered by the House of Lords for the first time in *NWL Ltd.* v. *Woods.* One of the most remarkable aspects of the judgments is the recognition they afford to what Lord Diplock called the 'practical realities' which lie behind such applications: that the interlocutory proceedings almost invariably dispose of the case because industrial action can only be pursued effectively by 'striking while the iron is hot'. The Law Lords therefore considered that s.17(2) had been passed to restore the pre-*Cyanamid* law. Thus in addition to seeing whether there was a serious question to be tried and where the balance of convenience lay, a court must also consider the 'likelihood' of a golden formula defence being established either as part of the balance of convenience or as a separate factor. However it is clear from their decisions in *NWL*, *MacShane* and *Sirs* that the courts retain a residual discretion to grant an injunction sometimes even where it is virtually certain that a golden formula defence will succeed. When this discretion could properly be exercised is not clear. In *NWL* Lord Diplock said that there might be cases where the consequences of industrial action to the employer, third parties, the public or the nation were so great that an injunction ought not to be refused unless there was a high degree of probability that the golden formula defence would succeed. While in *NWL* Lord Scarman said that such cases would be rare, in *MacShane* he said that the discretion might be properly exercised where industrial action endangered the nation or put at risk such fundamental rights as the right of the public to be informed and the freedom of the press.

This residual discretion was one of the issues in the case arising out of the steel dispute in 1980, *Duport Steels Ltd.* v. *Sirs.* Although the Law Lords were impressed by the serious consequences of that industrial action, they did not consider that it created the exceptional circumstances sufficient to warrant exercising the residual discretion to grant an injunction notwithstanding the likelihood of the golden formula defence succeeding. Lord Fraser gave as examples of matters which might support the proper exercise of the discretion action having an immediate and devastating effect on the plaintiff's person or prop-

erty, for example, ruining plant that could not be replaced without
large expenditure and long delay, and action causing immediate and
serious danger to public health and safety where no other means
seemed to be available for averting the danger in time. As Lord Scarman
recognised, other means were available to deal with the wider consequences of the steel dispute since there was time for the government to
act by taking emergency powers (see below). In his words 'when
disaster strikes it is ordinarily for the government not the courts to act
to avert it'.[26] Wedderburn referred to this view when moving an amendment to the Employment Bill which might have had the effect of
removing this discretion.[27] It would have replaced the obligation on a
court to have regard to the likelihood of a golden formula defence
succeeding by a direction not to grant an injunction where the defendant established a likelihood that the case fell within the restricted circumstances where the statutory immunities still applied. Not surprisingly
the government supported the existence of the residual discretion
which could not, it argued, be represented as a serious threat to the
ability of trade unions to take industrial action. As circumscribed by
the House of Lords in the three 1979/80 decisions this is true. However, like the need for a 'more than ostensible connection' with the
subject matter of a trade dispute and the limitation on contemplation
or furtherance based on the defendants' honesty of purpose, the residual discretion remains a potential means for limiting the right to strike
quite apart from the restrictions already imposed by the Employment
Act and those suggested in the Green Paper.

EMERGENCIES AND SPECIAL GROUPS OF WORKERS

The 1980 Act contains no provisions on 'national emergencies', but
Section G of the Picketing Code ('Essential Supplies and Services')
advises pickets to ensure that 'the provision of services essential to the
life of the community are not impeded, still less prevented', and then
gives a voluminous list of illustrations of essential supplies and services.
As we suggested in chapter eight, breach of this part of the Code could
conceivably provide a basis for unlawful means for tortious liability and
may be relevant to the judges' discretionary power to grant interlocutory injunctions. However public policy has always distinguished
between the legal liabilities of strikers and the measures which the
government may take to safeguard the community in national emergencies.

Under the Emergency Powers Acts 1920 and 1964 the government may declare a 'state of emergency' and take emergency powers where 'essential supplies' are threatened, that is, the supply and distribution of food, water, fuel, light and means of locomotion. Regulations may be made to secure 'the essentials of life to the community'. Though the armed forces may be used to this end and criminal offences created, the introduction of any form of industrial conscription is expressly proscribed. Nor may it be made an offence to take part in a strike or peacefully persuade others to do so. Further the exercise of these powers is subject to close Parliamentary control. In addition s.2 of the 1964 Act, which gives permanent effect to one of the wartime regulations, enables the government to use the armed forces on 'urgent work of national importance'. This is a more extensive power not subject to any Parliamentary controls and it has been used in a number of disputes over the last decade. There have also been important developments in the government's general contingency planning for dealing with emergencies.[28]

In a section headed 'Protecting the Community' the Green Paper asked 'whether there comes a point at which the interests of the nation must override the freedom to take industrial action in order to protect the community and the national interest' (para. 307). It considered whether new powers were needed to enable the government to deal not only with the consequences of an emergency but also the industrial action itself. Not surprisingly after the experience of the emergency procedures in the Industrial Relations Act,[29] it was not enthusiastic about the reintroduction of any provisions for imposing a statutory cooling off period. Removal of the restriction in the Emergency Powers Act 1920 on the government's power to make a strike or peaceful picketing illegal and a separate power to enable it to obtain a court order banning a strike were also considered. But the technical problems of drafting a satisfactory definition of an emergency and devising effective sanctions were raised as major difficulties, apart from the possibility that such powers would undermine basic liberties in a way that many would find objectionable (paras. 309–29).

However the basic liberties of certain groups of workers are already undermined to the extent that their freedom to take industrial action is circumscribed by the criminal law. The legislation regulating the obligations of the armed forces, police and merchant seamen contains provisions which effectively make industrial action by them an offence, although in the case of merchant seamen this is subject to the right established by the Merchant Shipping Act 1970 to give forty-eight hours notice of such action after their ship is moored at a safe berth in the United Kingdom. Further s.5 of the Conspiracy and Protection of Property Act 1875 makes it a criminal offence to wilfully and maliciously break a contract of employment where there is reasonable cause to believe that human life will be endangered, serious bodily injury caused or property exposed to destruction or serious injury. Although it could apply to industrial action by a wide variety of workers — drivers, signalmen, pilots, surgeons, hospital staff, sewage workers, haulage contractors, firemen, gas, water and electricity workers, and seamen — it appears that no one has ever been prosecuted for this offence.

Nor has there been any prosecution of workers in the Post Office (and now British Telecommunications) for committing offences under the Post Office Acts or the Telegraph Act by taking part in or organising industrial action. However it is clear from *Gouriet* v. *UPW* (1977) that the offences of wilfully detaining the mail under s.58 of the Post Office Act 1953 and wilfully omitting to transmit or deliver any message under s.45 of the Telegraph Act 1863 or procuring others to do so apply to industrial action. The proposed one week boycott of post and telecommunications to South Africa would therefore have involved criminal offences.[30] If criminal offences are committed they could provide unlawful means for the purposes of liability in tort.

Postal and telecommunications workers were not mentioned in the section of the Green Paper which considered the question of restrictions on workers in essential industries. This concluded that such restrictions have been little used and that there would be a great difficulty in deciding the criteria for extending them and the sanctions to be imposed (paras. 330–6). The suggestion in paragraph 337 that possibly the most effective way of making progress would be through voluntary no strike provisions in collective agreements in those sectors of industry where strikes might threaten the national interest is a curious final thought from a government which has demonstrated in the Employment Act its belief in legal sanctions as a means of regulating industrial conflict and restricting the right to strike.

10

Conflict and Controversy:
The Employment Act and Beyond

The government's 'step-by-step. approach to labour law reform has the strategic aim of reducing trade union power. It believes that this is an indispensable condition for securing industrial peace, curbing inflation, raising profits and eventually creating more jobs. Our review and analysis of employment law after the 1980 Act suggests however that the legal restriction of unions may conflict with other public policy goals and that the costs may outweigh the imagined benefits.

The first casualty of the government's strategy is the weakening of public support for the principle of joint regulation of employment through collective bargaining. To the limited extent that the procedure in EPA ss.11–16 facilitated union recognition, its repeal must be seen as a blow against the ability of trade unions to engage in collective bargaining and as an encouragement to 'Grunwick style' employers. The repeal of EPA Schedule 11 and the Road Haulage Wages Act removes two of the statutory props for collective bargaining. The autonomy of ACAS as the public agency with responsibility for promoting the improvement of industrial relations and the extension and reform of collective bargaining is threatened by the Secretary of State's new power to issue codes of practice. The erosion of employment protection at a time of mounting unemployment is also part of the strategy of reducing union power, in this instance by lowering the minimum starting point for collective negotiations and restoring some of the traditional prerogative of management to hire and fire at will. It is significant that the IPM neither pressed for nor welcomed these changes, which patently undermine the public policy of encouraging good personnel management practice. They also diminish the rights of the individual employee notwithstanding the government's identification with the cause of individual liberty. Individual rights are extended only in so far as they are exercised at the expense of trade unions.

The Employment Act and the Closed Shop Code embody a massive onslaught on the organisational strength of trade unions. The Act gives the individual the right not to be subjected to action by his employer short of dismissal in order to compel membership of a union. It gives automatic redress for unfair dismissal to an individual dismissed for non-membership of a specified union in a closed shop if he comes within one of three broad categories: if he objects to union membership on grounds of conscience or deeply held personal conviction, if he is employed and not a member at the time when the closed shop is introduced, or if he has remained a non-member in a post-Act closed shop. Post-Act closed shops have to be approved by at least 80 per cent of those eligible to vote before employers can rely on them to avoid unfair dismissal liability to employees dismissed for non-membership who do not fall into one of these categories. Under the Act's joinder provisions a trade union or other person who puts pressure on an employer by industrial action may be ordered to indemnify the employer for any compensation paid to the individual dismissed for non-membership, whether in a closed shop or not. Further the Closed Shop Code provides guidance for the confinement and progressive elimination of the practice. The individual is also (in addition to his common law rights) given the right enforceable against the union not to be unreasonably excluded or expelled from membership. This has major implications for the ability of unions to maintain discipline in industrial disputes. Whether this formidable battery of measures offers the individual any real protection is debatable, but it is likely to have some damaging side effects. It may undermine the TUC's voluntary arrangements for containing inter-union competition as well as the stability of collective bargaining arrangements between employers and recognised unions. The main bequest of the Industrial Relations Act's attempt to subvert the closed shop was not the enhancement of individual liberty but the exacerbation of the problems of multi-unionism; there is no reason to suppose that the Employment Act will have any other effect. Moreover the legislation's many technical uncertainties — such as the meaning of 'deeply-held personal conviction' — will provide lawyers with a lucrative field day. Finally there is grave risk to the acceptability of the tribunals who are thrown into the thick of collective industrial conflicts.

The establishment of a scheme for providing state finance for postal ballots held by unions and the creation of a legal right to hold workplace ballots on certain issues may appear to be uncontroversial. But the former in particular poses a threat to trade union autonomy and freedom from state control. The Employment Act's most controversial provisions restrict the legal freedom to strike by removing the TULRA immunities from those engaged in most secondary action and picketing away from their own place of work or outside the permitted purposes. Union officials, 'picket organisers' and workers engage in these forms of action only at the risk of incurring legal liabilities. But ss.16–18 of the 1980 Act and the Secretary of State's Codes have wider ramifications. The criminal as well as the civil law is affected by the provisions on picketing and much primary as well as secondary action is rendered unlawful. Moreover the Act's expansion of the doctrine of 'unlawful means' may have dealt a mortal blow to any legal freedom to take industrial action. Our conclusion on this point cannot be firm because one of the effects of the Act is to turn what was always a very difficult area of law into a morass of technical complexity. The shadow employment minister was surely right in arguing that: 'Whoever loses out when the Conservatives introduce industrial relations legislation, the lawyers always win.'[1] Once again however the standing of the judicial system may be in jeopardy, especially if there are problems of identifying defendants and enforcing court orders. But mindful of the experience of the Industrial Relations Act, wise employers will think very seriously before using the law as a tactic in an industrial dispute. An injunction may sometimes stop a strike but it may also serve to alienate employees and their unions. The use of the law is a symptom of industrial conflict not a solution for it.

The government's Green Paper *Trade Union Immunities* was issued in January 1981 when the Employment Act was in force but untested. Its theme was how further to strengthen the laws against strikes, closed shops and trade union power in general. To that end it considered a wide range of possible options but made no commitment to any specific legislative programme. Apart from the idea of replacing the immunities with positive rights, all the options in the Green Paper had been canvassed at one time or another since the publication of the Donovan Report in 1968 and some were in fact embodied in the Industrial Relations Act. In the light of the experience of that Act, the Green Paper itself convincingly knocked down the case for the legal enforceability of collective agreements, compulsory strike ballots, narrowing the definition of trade dispute and withdrawing the TULRA s.14 immunity from trade unions as such. It persuasively argued against the involvement of the police in the direct enforcement of the civil law against off-site picketing basically because that might destroy what remained of police neutrality in industrial disputes. Despite its strong moral condemnation of the practices, it set out some of the pragmatic objections to further legal restrictions on the closed shop and secondary industrial action. All these topics have been discussed in earlier chapters. We shall however conclude with a consideration of the Green Paper's most radical idea: the replacement of the immunities with positive rights.

A POSITIVE RIGHT TO STRIKE

In chapters one and nine we explained how the legal freedom to organise industrial action in Britain rests on not a positive right to strike but a structure of negatively expressed statutory immunities from judge-made common law liabilities. These immunities do not give trade unions privileges which put them above the law. Rather they are the British equivalent of what in other countries takes the form of a positive right to strike guaranteed by legislation or by the constitution. The Green Paper itself acknowledged that without the immunities, at the mercy of the common law, trade unions simply could not exist or function lawfully (paras. 34, 93, 342 and 384). On the other hand, a positive right would not automatically resolve the issue of the scope of trade union illegalities for, as the Green Paper said, 'decisions still have to be made about where the limits of lawful industrial action should be drawn' (para. 384). The positive right then would be accompanied by a positive duty to refrain from redefined and specified forms of unlawful industrial action. Certainly a positive rights system could be at least as restrictive as the immunities, and possibly more so.

This is perhaps what the CBI had in mind in 1980 when it stated:

> thought must be given to the unsatisfactory nature of the immunities. A better balance is necessary between accountability at law of unions and their members and their freedom to bring reasonable pressure to bear in the furtherance of their legitimate aims — even perhaps by a positive right to strike, subject to reasonable limitations, being created.[2]

What might these 'reasonable' limitations consist of? Where would the positive right end and the positive duty to refrain from unlawful industrial action begin? It seems unlikely that a positive right to strike would protect or permit unofficial industrial action or official action in breach of agreed procedures. According to the Green Paper the limitations might cover secondary action, picketing, political strikes, strikes in breach of contract and industrial action short of strikes (paras. 355—

9). It was also envisaged (para. 351) that unions might be placed under a duty to refrain from taking disciplinary action against members who refused to participate in unlawful industrial action, a rule which may already have been indirectly 'enacted' through paragraph 54 of the Closed Shop Code (above p. 120). Furthermore, if the move away from immunities was linked to the introduction of a Bill of Rights, and the Green Paper asserted that this whole issue 'cannot, logically, be isolated from the question whether there should be some general form of Bill of Rights' (para. 345), the ambit of the limitations could be still wider. A Bill of Rights might include, for example, a right *not* to belong to a union.

A system of positive rights is likely to be no less complex than the present position. As the Green Paper suggested there would have to be a new set of liabilities, remedies and perhaps courts, and some attempt would have to be made at dealing with the overlap between the new system and the existing common law liabilities (paras. 365–76). The document tended to emphasise the idea of a positive right for trade unions and organisers, but if also there were to be a right exercisable by individual employees it would entail further technical difficulties relating to the contract of employment, unfair dismissal and social security. We have seen how the state seeks to maintain a semblance of 'neutrality' when strikers complain of unfair dismissal (p. 13) and how, in contrast, the present government has stacked the cards of the social security system against the striker and his family (p. 40). Under a regime of positive rights such issues should arguably be determined by reference to the legality of and even justification for the industrial action. A fundamental problem would be how to reconcile an individual positive right with the fact that industrial action almost invariably involves (as we explained in chapter nine) breach of the contract of employment. Should those who take part in a strike be free to do so without fear of being sued for breach of contract or having their contracts summarily terminated? French law, which gives individuals a positive right, regards the strike as suspending not breaking the employment contract. But the common law rejects the doctrine of suspension of the contract during industrial action. The introduction of suspension into our law would involve overcoming all the difficulties which were raised in paragraph 943 of the Donovan Report. For example, would suspension apply to unofficial and unconstitutional strikes, industrial action short of strikes, 'lightening' strikes or strikes in contravention of s.5 of the Conspiracy and Protection of Property Act? Or what of situations where the employee commits misconduct during a strike or takes another job during the suspension period?

The Green Paper suggested (para. 379) that a positive right would enable the law to

> relate more directly to industrial experience . . . to the reality of industrial disputes. To the extent that a positive rights system succeeded in moving the language and concepts of the law on industrial conflict away from immunities against tortious liability, it might be easier to understand and more straightforward to apply, not just for unions and management but for the courts as well. Indeed, it is possible that a system of positive rights would help remove the unions' traditional suspicion of the courts.

This is perhaps the Green Paper's most naive statement. It appears to envisage a positive rights system in which the state would in effect be specifying in industrial relations terms what industrial action it considered to be legitimate and illegitimate and therefore lawful and unlawful. Of course in every case involving legal proceedings the courts would have to interpret such a right and the concomitant limitations. This would make the judges the arbiters of the moral as well as the legal rights and wrongs of industrial disputes. To a degree this development was foreshadowed by the role of the NIRC under the Industrial Relations Act. Sir John Donaldson, President of the NIRC, in looking back at the court's brief but exciting history emphasised the need for 'guidelines' on all aspects of industrial relations and argued:

> With such guidelines the courts could be given their traditional role of investigating the merits of disputes and helping the party who is right. . . . The public suffers from every industrial dispute. Ought they not to know who is right? Adopting this new approach they *would* know, for the court which investigated the dispute would tell them. Those who suffered injustice would then be supported by the courts.[3]

But should the judges be entrusted with the task of determining the merits of collective industrial conflicts? British judges have traditionally shown a marked inability to appreciate the needs of trade unions to take industrial action or indeed of collective as opposed to individual interests. It may be asked how far this consistent tendency reflects their narrow experience, training and conceptual framework with its emphasis on individual, contractual and property rights; or their middle-class backgrounds; or their overall view of the world which, according to Professor Griffith, strongly favours the preservation of private property and the existing social order.[4] Whatever the explanation, the fact of the generally (there were some exceptions) uncomprehending and unsympathetic attitude of the judges towards trade unions led to the development of the unique structure of statutory immunities from judge-made liabilities. One of the relative virtues of this structure is that it allows judicial decisions to be based in form at least on the application of technical legal rules, though of course there is still considerable scope for judicial creativity in the interpretation of the rules. But a system of positive rights which left the judges to interpret 'pure' industrial relations criteria would thrust them even further into the centre of political controversy. Most judges would prefer not to be taken down that road, and already there is some evidence that the government itself has lost any enthusiasm it might have had for replacing the immunities with positive rights.[5]

However the extent to which the Employment Act has already cast the judges in an overtly political role should not be underestimated. The Act's restriction of the immunities together with the dubious industrial relations guidance of the Picketing Code go some way towards the state of affairs which the President of the NIRC apparently wanted but which Lord Scarman warned against (above p. 6), namely, making the judges backseat drivers in industrial disputes. And with the aid of the equally dubious guidance of the Closed Shop Code, the tribunals and the appellate courts must provide their own interpretations of, for example, the reasonableness of a trade union's actions and rule book. Those who do not share our own critical view of the judiciary should nevertheless appreciate the danger which legislation such as the 1980 Act poses to the standing of judicial institutions. Seventy years ago Winston Churchill formulated it in words which are still apposite:

> It is not good for trade unions that they should be brought in contact with the courts, and it is not good for the courts. The courts hold justly a high and I think, unequalled pre-eminence in the respect of the world in criminal cases, and in civil cases between man and man, no doubt, they deserve and command the respect and admiration of all classes of the community, but where class issues are involved, and where party issues are involved, it is impossible to pretend that the courts command the same degree of general confidence. On the contrary, they do not, and a very large number of our population have been led to the opinion that they are, unconsciously, no doubt, biased.[6]

STRIKING A BALANCE?

The stated aim of the Green Paper was 'to prompt a wide and informed debate' not only 'on the law concerning industrial action' but also 'on the role in modern life of trade unions and employers and their duties and obligations' (para. 33). It criticised employers for their reluctance 'to enter into precise or legal commitments' and 'to involve employees and their representatives in policies and decisions which affect their working lives', and also for their readiness to recognise 'unofficial elements', that is, their own shop stewards (paras. 22–4). Apart from these broad and debatable generalisations and the normal exhortation to management 'to be firm and to give a lead' (para. 27), the role of employers was glossed over. The Green Paper's real concern was with trade unions; the debate it was intended to inform arose from 'a widespread public feeling' that unions 'have too few obligations and too much power' (para. 12). The Green Paper in short reinforced the syndrome we described in chapter one, namely, the widespread belief that industrial relations and ultimately Britain's economic decline are rooted in what the document described as the unions' 'enormous disruptive power' (para. 15).[7]

Throughout the last decade and a half the need to be seen to be doing something about 'trade union power' has been at the top of the political agenda. What is meant by the term has varied according to the prevailing pattern and incidence of industrial conflict and sometimes according to the latest big strike. The focus has shifted from the spontaneity of the shop floor, to the tactics of trade union leaders, to any manifestation of industrial struggle at a time of inflation and severe economic competition, to the more intangible notion of union 'political' influence. At different times the strategy of the state has emphasised 'reform' – harnessing official trade union organisation to the joint regulation of a more orderly system of industrial relations – and 'restriction' – the legal coercion of trade unions and their members. The Employment Act is part of the restrictive strategy. It assumes that the mischief is trade union power. It is as though employers never provoke or prolong strikes. The preoccupation with unions so assiduously cultivated by a large segment of the media no doubt provides a convenient diversion from the government's performance in managing the economy. It also diverts attention away from the fact that a handful of financial institutions and multi-national corporations control large areas of the British economy, including much of its rapidly diminishing manufacturing base. Their power to switch production from one plant or country to another or to invest or not cannot be matched by trade unions. An invisible strike of capital has a more devastating effect on economic performance and job opportunities than a highly visible strike of labour.

But whatever the economic circumstances or the party label of the government the relationship between labour, capital and the state will remain controversial. The elements of consensus and equilibrium which were apparent in the 1940s and 1950s have all but disappeared along with much of the characteristically non-interventionist framework of labour law. That hallowed tradition grew out of a specific balance of forces under which abstention of the law from industrial relations accorded with the interests of capital and was compatible with the ideology and limited objectives of labour. In more recent times the role of the law and other forms of state intervention in industrial relations have become ever more extensive. The statutory floor of individual rights, the main legacy of the state's reform strategy, will remain a permanent feature. This is so despite the Employment Act's mean and petty erosions and the fact that mass unemployment restricts the application of the statutory protection to the elite of workers who have jobs. The appropriate role of the law in the regulation of collective industrial conflict is still however an open question. Will the Employment Act achieve its objective? Can the law, or rather a combination of law and monetarist economics, induce enough caution or fear in the trade union movement to force new patterns of behaviour and attitudes? The experience of the Industrial Relations Act is not a good augury. Moreover the attainment of the 'new balance' envisaged by the 1980 Act may itself generate social and political costs of an unpredictable nature.

Notes

CHAPTER 1

1 *Conservative Manifesto 1979* Conservative Party, 1979, pp. 6–9.
2 R. Lewis 'The Historical Development of Labour Law' (1976) 14 *British Journal of Industrial Relations* 1.
3 D. Barnes and E. Reid *Government and Trade Unions: The British Experience 1964–79* Heinemann, 1980, p. x.
4 F. A. Hayek *1980s Unemployment and the Unions* Institute of Economic Affairs, 1980, p. 55, Other publications of this Institute (IEA) arguing the 'legal privileges' case include J. A. Lincoln *Journey to Coercion* 1964 and C. Hanson *Trade Unions: A Century of Legal Privilege* 1973. The Prime Minister confirmed that she was a 'great admirer' of Hayek's 'absolutely supreme' works immediately before the budget statement of 10 March 1981: House of Commons Debates, Vol. 1000, col. 756.
5 K. W. Wedderburn *The Worker and the Law* Penguin, 2nd edn, 1971, p. 317. For Wedderburn's analysis of the immunities in the context of the overall development of labour law, see his 'The New Structure of Labour Law in Britain' (1978) 13 *Israel Law Review* 435 and 'Industrial Relations and the Courts' (1980) 9 *Industrial Law Journal* 65.
6 *NWL Ltd.* v. *Woods* [1979] I.C.R. 867, 886.
7 *Duport Steels Ltd.* v. *Sirs* [1980] I.C.R. 161, 189.
8 *Express Newspapers Ltd.* v. *MacShane* [1980] I.C.R. 43, 65.
9 *Duport Steels Ltd.* v. *Sirs* [1980] I.C.R. 161, 177 and 184 respectively.
10 Ibid. p. 188.
11 O. Kahn-Freund *Labour and the Law* Stevens, 2nd edn, 1977, p. 2.
12 O. Kahn-Freund 'Labour Law' in M. Ginsberg (ed.) *Law and Opinion in England in the Twentieth Century* Stevens, 1959, p. 244. See further his 'Legal Framework' in A. Flanders and H. A. Clegg (eds) *The System of Industrial Relations in Great Britain* Blackwell, 1954. Cf. R. Lewis 'Kahn-Freund and Labour Law: An Outline Critique' (1979) 8 *Industrial Law Journal* 202.

13 *Trade Union Immunities* Cmnd. 8128, HMSO, 1981, para. 10.

14 Our characterisation of the voluntarist system draws on Kahn-Freund *Labour and the Law*; A. Flanders *Management and Unions* Faber, 1970; and A. Flanders 'The Tradition of Voluntarism' (1974) 12 *British Journal of Industrial Relations* 352.

15 For contrasting analyses of the strategies of the state in industrial relations, see W. E. J. McCarthy and N. P. Ellis *Management by Agreement: An Alternative to the Industrial Relations Act* Hutchinson, 1973; R. Hyman *Industrial Relations: A Marxist Introduction* Macmillan, 1975; L. Panitch *Social Democracy and Industrial Militancy: The Labour Party, the Trade Unions and Incomes Policy 1945–74* Cambridge University Press, 1976; C. Crouch *Class Conflict and the Industrial Relations Crisis: Compromise and Corporatism in the Policies of the British State* Heinemann, 1977; H. A. Clegg *The Changing System of Industrial Relations in Great Britain* Blackwell, 1979.

16 *Royal Commission on Trade Unions and Employers' Associations 1965–68, Report,* Cmnd. 3623, HMSO, 1968.

17 These contracting-out provisions are in respect of guarantee pay (EPCA s.18(4)(b)); unfair dismissal (EPCA s.65); redundancy pay EPCA s.96(2)(3); redundancy procedure agreements (EPA s.107(2)(b)). The only contracting-out provision which has been extensively used is that for guarantee pay. Contracted-out agreements tend to be drafted by lawyers and are exceedingly legalistic. See further C. Bourn 'Statutory Exemptions for Collective Agreements' (1979) 8 *Industrial Law Journal* 85.

18 See K. W. Wedderburn 'Industrial Action, the State and the Public Interest' in B. Aaron and K. W. Wedderburn (eds) *Industrial Conflict: A Comparative Legal Survey* Longman, 1972.

19 *In Place of Strife: A Policy for Industrial Relations* Cmnd. 3888, HMSO, 1969.

20 See W. W. Daniel and E. Stilgoe *The Impact of Employment Protection Laws* PSI, 1978, ch. 4.

21 Except for contravention of a recognised safety representative's right to paid time off, which is enforceable by a claim to the industrial tribunal: Safety Representatives and Safety Committees Regulations S.I., 1977 No. 500, regulation 4.

22 *Report of the Committee of Inquiry on Industrial Democracy* Cmnd. 6706, HMSO, 1977.

23 *Industrial Democracy,* Cmnd 7231, HMSO, 1978.

24 Kahn-Freund *Labour and the Law* 2nd edn, p. 112.

25 EEC Council Directive on the Approximation of the Laws of the Member States Relating to Collective Redundancies, Council Direc-

tive No. 75/129, (O.J.) 1975 L.48/29. See M. Freedland 'Employment Protection: Redundancy Procedures and the EEC' (1976) 5
Industrial Law Journal 24.

26   *The Economy, The Government and Trade Union Responsibilities:
      Joint Statement by the TUC and the Government* HMSO, 1979.

27   A. Fox and A. Flanders 'The Reform of Collective Bargaining:
      From Donovan to Durkheim' (1969) 7 *British Journal of Industrial
      Relations* 151, 180 (reprinted in Flanders *Management and
      Unions.*)

28   O. Kahn-Freund *Labour Relations: Heritage and Adjustment* Ox-
      ford University Press, 1979, p. 81.

29   K. W. Wedderburn 'Labour Law and Labour Relations in Britain'
      (1972) 10 *British Journal of Industrial Relations* 270, 282. For
      further analysis of the Industrial Relations Act from the perspec-
      tives of law, politics and industrial relations, see O. Kahn-Freund
      Labour and the Law Stevens, 1st edn, 1972; R. Simpson and J.
      Wood *Industrial Relations and the 1971 Act* Pitman, 1973; B.
      Weekes, M. Mellish, L. Dickens and J. Lloyd *Industrial Relations
      and the Limits of Law* Blackwell, 1975; A. Thomson and S. Engle-
      man *The Industrial Relations Act: A Review and Analysis* Martin
      Robertson, 1975; M. Moran *The Politics of Industrial Relations*
      Macmillan, 1977.

30   The Department of Employment's eight consultative Working
      Papers were on: 'Picketing', 'Closed Shop' and 'Public Funds for
      Union Ballots' (July 1979); 'Employment Protection', 'Trade
      Union Recognition' and 'Schedule 11' (September 1979); 'Trade
      Union Recruitment Activities' (October 1979); and 'Secondary
      Industrial Action' (February 1980). On the July Working Papers,
      see R. Lewis, P. Davies and K. W. Wedderburn *Industrial Relations
      Law and the Conservative Government* Fabian Society, 1979; on
      the September Working Papers, see L. Dickens, M. Hart, M. Jones
      and B. Weekes *A Response to the Government Working Papers on
      Amendments to Employment Protection Legislation* Discussion
      Paper, SSRC Industrial Relations Research Unit, University of War-
      wick, 1979.

31   At the time of writing, the main legal literature on the Employ-
      ment Act comprised P. Elias 'Closing in on the Closed Shop', B.
      Bercusson 'Picketing, Secondary Picketing and Secondary Action'
      and G. Pitt 'Individual Rights under the New Legislation', in
      (1980) 9 *Industrial Law Journal* 201, 215 and 233; and R. Simpson
      'Employment Act 1980' and R. Lewis 'Codes of Practice on
      Picketing and Closed Shop Agreements and Arrangements', in
      (1981) 44 *Modern Law Review* 188 and 198. See too P. Davies and

M. Freedland *Supplement* (1980) to *Labour Law: Text and Materials* Weidenfeld and Nicolson, 1979 and J. McMullen *Employment Law under the Tories* Pluto Press, 1981.

CHAPTER 2

1 The employment protection laws are authoritatively analysed in B. A. Hepple and P. O'Higgins *Employment Law* Sweet and Maxwell, 1979, 3rd edn. For further reference: P. Davies and M. Freedland *Labour Law: Text and Materials* Weidenfeld and Nicolson, 1979, chs. 4—6, 10.

2 House of Lords Debates Vol. 401, cols. 1942—3, 25 July 1979.

3 W. W. Daniel and E. Stilgoe *The Impact of Employment Protection Laws* PSI, 1978; also W. W. Daniel 'The Effects of Employment Protection Laws in Manufacturing Industry' (1978) 86 *DE Gazette* 658.

4 R. Clifton and C. Tatton-Brown *Impact of Employment Legislation on Small Firms* DE Research Paper No. 6, 1979.

5 A. Westrip *An Investigation into the Impact of Employment Protection Laws on the Small Firm* Small Business Research Unit, Central London Polytechnic, 1979.

6 House of Commons Standing Committee A, col. 929, 4 March 1980.

7 See further Westrip op. cit; *Employment Bill Briefing No. 3* Low Pay Unit, 1979; L. Dickens, M. Hart, M. Jones and B. Weekes *A Response to the Government Working Papers on Amendments to Employment Protection Legislation* Discussion Paper, SSRC Industrial Relations Research Unit, University of Warwick, 1979; J. Curran and J. Stanworth 'Worker Involvement and Social Relations in the Small Firm' (1979) 27 *Sociological Review* 317.

8 Unfair Dismissal (Variation of Qualifying Period) Order, S.I. 1979 No. 959.

9 *MANWEB* v. *Taylor* [1975] I.C.R. 185, 189 (O'Connor J. interpreting the Industrial Relations Act 1971 s.24(6)). See also M. Freedland 'The Burden of Proof in Claims of Unfair Dismissal' (1972) 1 *Industrial Law Journal* 20.

10 Dickens *et al.* p. 7.

11 Median figures estimated from grouped data published in (1981) 89 *DE Gazette* 82.

12 The Court of Appeal gave an authoritative explanation of the principles of contributory fault for the purposes of both compen-

satory and basic awards in *Nelson* v. *B.B.C. (No. 2)* [1980] I.C.R. 110.

13 House of Commons Standing Committee A, col. 1015, 6 March 1980.

14 L. Dickens 'Unfair Dismissal Applications and the Industrial Tribunal System' (1978/9) 9 *Industrial Relations Journal* 4, 18 and see too (1979) 87 *DE Gazette* 233.

15 *Income During Initial Sickness: A New Strategy* Cmnd. 7864, HMSO, 1980. After a generally hostile reception, these proposals have been deferred for further refinement: *The Guardian* 14 February 1981.

16 See M. Partington 'Unemployment, Industrial Conflict and Social Security' (1980) 9 *Industrial Law Journal* 243. On the limited impact of the previous law on the behaviour of strikers, see J. Gennard *Financing Strikers* Macmillan, 1977.

17 Employment Protection (Handling of Redundancies) Variation Order, S.I. 1979 No. 958.

18 See chapter 1, n. 25.

19 Reported in *The Guardian*, 6 November 1979, as a quotation from the BBC Television programme *Man Alive*.

20 EPCA s.31A(2)(3). Contrast EPCA s.31 (time off to look for work or training while under notice of dismissal for redundancy) in respect of which no evidence of any appointment or interview is required: *Dutton* v. *Hawker Siddeley Aviation Ltd.* [1978] I.C.R. 1057.

21 *A Fresh Look at Maternity Benefits: A Consultative Document* DHSS, October 1980.

22 House of Commons Debates Vol. 997, Written Answers, col. 519, 29 January 1981.

23 *I Want to Have a Baby . . . But What About My Job?* EOC, 1979.

24 This qualification was given a restricted interpretation in *Nu-Swift International Ltd.* v. *Mallinson* [1979] I.C.R. 157.

25 For the Under Secretary of State's speculation on possible liability for negligent misrepresentation in these circumstances, see House of Commons Standing Committee A, col. 1176, 13 March 1980. If established, this would be a remarkable extension of such liability.

26 Cf. the extensive case law on the similar aspect of the redundancy payments provisions, EPCA s.82(5); see C. Grunfeld *The Law of Redundancy* Sweet and Maxwell, 2nd edn, 1980, ch. 7.

27 EPCA s.61(1) provides that the dismissal of an employee informed in writing on engagement that he or she is only being employed for the duration of the absence of another employee on maternity leave is for a 'substantial' reason for the purposes of any complaint

of unfair dismissal by that employee when the employee on maternity leave returns. It is of course now largely a dead letter as the period of statutory maternity leave will rarely exceed the fifty-two weeks for which a temporary replacement would have to work in order to qualify to make a complaint of unfair dismissal.

28 'Maternity Leave — The IR—RR Survey' Parts 1 and 2 *Industrial Relations Review and Report* Nos. 217 and 218, February 1980, pp. 7 and 2 respectively.

29 W. W. Daniel *Maternity Rights: The Experience of Women* PSI, 1980.

30 The changes were incorporated in the Industrial Tribunals (Rules of Procedure) Regulations, S.I. 1980, No. 884.

31 See House of Commons Debates Vol. 989, col. 1467, 29 July 1980.

32 Ibid. col. 1452 (J. Grant M.P.).

33 *E. T. Marler Ltd.* v. *Robertson* [1974] I.C.R. 72, NIRC, approved by the EAT in *Carr* v. *Allen-Bradley Electronics Ltd.* [1980] I.C.R. 603.

34 Employment Appeal Tribunal Rules, S.I. 1980 No. 2035, rule 27(1). These rules replaced the original 1976 rules. Apart from additions to take account of the EAT's new jurisdiction under EA ss.4 and 5, the new rules make small changes in the procedure for instituting appeals and interlocutory applications.

35 House of Commons Debates Vol. 989, col. 1472, 29 July 1980.

CHAPTER 3

1 The basis for recognition of a right to dissociate on this ground is discussed in ch. 4. For a full summary of the law before the EA amendments, see Wedderburn 'Discrimination in the Right to Organise and the Right to be a Non—Unionist' in F. Schmidt (ed.) *Discrimination in Employment* Almquist and Wiksell International (Stockholm), 1978, especially pp. 401—14.

2 Organisations falling within the definition of a trade union in TULRA s.28(1) may apply to be entered in the list of trade unions maintained by the Certification Officer under TULRA s.8. This is a purely administrative process, the principal advantages of which are income and capital gains taxes relief under the Finance Act 1974 s.28 in respect of investment income and capital gains used to pay provident benefits. Only unions entered in the list may apply for a certificate of independence. On the independence criteria, see the

volumes for the years 1976–80 of the *Annual Report of the Certification Officer* HMSO. The leading cases on the meaning of independence are *Blue Circle Staff Association* v. *Certification Officer* [1977] I.C.R. 224 and *Squibb UK Staff Association* v. *Certification Officer* [1978] I.C.R. 235.

3 *City of Birmingham District Council* v. *Beyer* [1977] I.R.L.R. 211. Contrast Sex Discrimination Act 1975 s.6(1) and Race Relations Act 1976 s.4(1) which make discrimination in recruitment by employers on grounds of sex, marital status and race unlawful, although the only effective remedy provided is compensation.

4 Cf. the inconsistency referred to above between EPCA s.23(1)(b) as limited in UMA employment by s.23(2A)(a) and (2B) and s.58(1)(b) which is not so limited.

5 *Sulemanji* v. *Toughened Glass* [1979] I.C.R. 799; and see *Taylor* v. *Co-operative Retail Services Ltd.* [1981] I.R.L.R. 1.

6 *Robb* v. *Leon Motor Services Ltd.* [1978] I.C.R. 506; *British Airways Engine Overhaul Ltd.* v. *Francis* [1981] I.R.L.R. 9.

7 [1978] I.C.R. 405. On an appeal concerned with the amount of compensation awarded, the employer did not contest the industrial tribunal's finding that his threat to close the business should he be required to recognise the TGWU (intended to influence employees' responses to a questionnaire from ACAS in the course of its inquiries into a recognition reference under the now repealed procedure in EPA ss.11–16) was action short of dismissal within s.23(1).

8 McCarthy's phrase, House of Lords Debates Vol. 410, cols. 603–04, 12 June 1980. The exposition of the problems consequent on the amendment of EPCA s.23(1)(c) by EA s.15(1) are forcefully and succinctly expressed by Wedderburn (ibid. cols. 585–9, 594 and 606) and McCarthy (cols. 603–05).

9 [1973] I.C.R. 366, 381.

10 *Langston* v. *AUEW* [1974] I.C.R. 180 and (No. 2) 510.

11 In EPCA ss.76A and 76B this covers not only basic award and compensatory award compensation but also additional award compensation for total non-compliance with an order for re-instatement or re-engagement. It does not include an award of compensation for partial non-compliance with a reinstatement or re-engagement order under EPCA s.71(1).

12 *Heaton's Transport* v. *TGWU* [1973] A.C. 15; *Howitt Transport* v. *TGWU* [1973] I.C.R. 1, and *General Aviation Services* v. *TGWU* [1976] I.R.L.R. 224. See too B. A. Hepple 'Union Responsibility for Shop Stewards' (1972) 1 *Industrial Law Journal* 197. See further p. 196.

13 The Under Secretary of State for Employment acknowledged this

possibility: House of Commons Standing Committee A, cols. 1093–1100, 11 March 1980. On the expanded ambit of unlawful means after the 1980 Act, see pp. 216–17.

14 EA ss.10 and 15 are not quite so widely drawn as the comparable provision on joinder in IRA s.119, which was not limited to where pressure was exercised because of an individual's non-membership of a union. Further, organising the industrial action was independently actionable as an unfair industrial practice under IRA s.33(3)(a).

CHAPTER 4

1 W. E. J. McCarthy *The Closed Shop in Britain* Blackwell, 1964, p. 3.

2 For preliminary reports on the LSE closed shop project (commissioned and financed by the DE), see J. Gennard *et al.* 'The Content of British Closed Shop Agreements' (1979) 87 *DE Gazette* 1088, 'The Extent of Closed Shop Arrangements in British Industry' (1980) 88 *DE Gazette* 16, 'Throwing the Book: Trade Union Rules on Admission, Discipline and Expulsion' (1980) 88 *DE Gazette* 591. All references in the text to the findings of the LSE project are based on these articles. See too R. Benedictus 'Closed Shop Exemptions and their Wording' (1979) 8 *Industrial Law Journal* 160.

3 The SSRC's Industrial Relations Research Unit based at Warwick University has been responsible for several research projects and publications of relevance to closed shop issues, see in particular: B. Weekes, M. Mellish, L. Dickens and J. Lloyd *Industrial Relations and the Limits of Law* Blackwell, 1975, ch. 2; B. Weekes 'Law and the Practice of the Closed Shop' (1976) 5 *Industrial Law Journal* 211; M. Hart 'Why Bosses Love the Closed Shop' *New Society* 15 February 1979; W. Brown (ed.) *The Changing Contours of British Industrial Relations* Blackwell, 1981, ch. 4.

4 *Edwards* v. *SOGAT* [1971] Ch. 354, 376. See too *Lee* v. *Showmen's Guild* [1952] 2 Q.B. 329 and *Nagle* v. *Fielden* [1966] Ch. 633.

5 *McInnes* v. *Onslow-Fane* [1978] 1 W.L.R. 1520, 1528.

6 Weekes *Industrial Law Journal* 216–17.

7 *Gayle* v. *John Wilkinson & Sons* [1978] I.C.R. 154 where the EAT accepted advice from Mr. Bill Sirs, one of its lay members, as to the unreality of requiring management to question information given

by shop stewards in the circumstances of that case; *Lakhani* v. *Hoover Ltd.* [1978] I.C.R. 1063, and *Blue Star Ship Management Ltd.* v. *Williams* [1978] I.C.R. 770. Cf. the apparently stricter onus on the employer in *Leyland Vehicles Ltd.* v. *Jones* [1981] I.C.R. 428.

8 *Jeffrey* v. *Laurence Scott Ltd.* [1977] I.R.L.R. 466. If he cannot rely on EPCA s.58(3), the fairness of the dismissal then falls to be determined under the normal provisions in s.57.

9 *Curry* v. *Harlow District Council* [1979] I.C.R. 769; *Taylor* v. *Co-operative Retail Services Ltd.* [1981] I.R.L.R. 1.

10 *Rawlings* v. *Lionweld Ltd.* [1978] I.R.L.R. 481; *Home Counties Dairies Ltd.* v. *Woods* [1977] I.C.R. 463 and *Beaumont* v. *Libby McNeil Ltd., The Times* 10 October 1978.

11 Lord McCarthy, House of Lords Debates Vol. 410, col. 287, 10 June 1980.

12 The Under Secretary of State, House of Commons Standing Committee A, cols. 788 and 792, 28 February 1980. The interpretation of conscience under the IRA was presumably what the government had in mind. The one exception to the requirement of union membership common to both the agency shop and approved closed shop provisions of the IRA was for workers who objected to union membership on grounds of conscience. In the only decision on the ambit of that exception of any precedent value, the NIRC effectively confined it to religious belief: *Hynds* v. *Spillers-French Baking Ltd.* [1974] I.T.R. 261.

13 Lord Hailsham, House of Lords Debates Vol. 411, cols. 934–35, 7 July 1980; see too House of Commons Debates Vol. 983, col. 556, 23 April 1980.

14 It should be noted that EPCA s.58(3E) prevents avoidance of this exception by restricting the relevant class of employees by reference to union membership or objection to it. Thus an employee who had both been a member of a specified union and left it at a date before the UMA took effect arguably could not be denied the benefit of s.58(3B) on the grounds that the relevant class comprised those who belonged to specified unions at a date before the UMA came into operation.

15 See further R. Simpson and J. Wood *Industrial Relations and the 1971 Act* Pitman, 1973, pp. 120–25.

16 Lord Gowrie, House of Lords Debates Vol. 414, col. 1493, 13 November 1980.

17 W. E. J. McCarthy, 'Closed Minds and Closed Shops' (1980) *Federation News* 145, 146–7 (on the consultative draft Code). Cf. *Handbook on the Employment Act 1980* TUC, 1981, especially paras. 9–12, 65.

18 For our analysis of Section D of the Closed Shop Code on 'Union Treatment of Members and Applicants', see pp. 111–13, 120–2.

19 House of Commons Select Committee on Employment 1979–80, Second Report, 822, paras. 16–20.

20 For an elaboration of this argument see N. Beloff *Freedom Under Foot: The Battle Over the Closed Shop in British Journalism* Temple Smith, 1976. Cf. dicta by Lord Denning that interference with press freedom is unlawful means for the purposes of tort liability (*Associated Newspapers Group* v. *Wade* [1979] I.C.R. 664, 690–91), and by Lord Scarman that it justifies exercise of the residual discretion to grant interlocutory injunctions (*Express Newspapers* v. *MacShane* [1980] I.C.R. 42, 65).

21 *Federation News* p. 147.

22 Cases 7601/76, 7806/77. Opinion of the Commission, para. 160. Three of the seventeen members of the Commission, including the British representative, dissented from the opinion that English law violated Article 11.

23 In a case where the legality of the Greater London Council's closed shop was challenged, it was confirmed that the Convention did not form part of English law: *R* v. *GLC, ex parte Burgess* [1978] I.C.R. 991.

CHAPTER 5

1 On the common law, see N. Citrine *Trade Union Law* Stevens, 3rd edn, 1967, K. W. Wedderburn *The Worker and the Law* Penguin, 2nd edn, 1971, chs. 9 and 10; C. Grunfeld *Modern Trade Union Law* Sweet and Maxwell, 1966, Parts 2 and 3; R. Kidner *Trade Union Law* Stevens, 1979, Part 1; P. Davies and M. Freedland *Labour Law: Text and Materials* Weidenfeld and Nicolson, 1979, ch. 7.

2 Confirmed by TULRA s.2, which also provides that trade unions may make contracts and sue and be sued in their own name, subject to TULRA s.14. Donovan proposed that unions should be granted corporate status (para. 782); under the IRA, only registered organisations of workers became corporations (s.74) but unregistered organisations could be sued in their own name (s.154).

3 *Faramus* v. *Film Artistes' Association* [1964] A.C. 925, 942. See too *Martin* v. *Scottish TGWU* [1952] 1 All E.R. 691.

4 For the leading cases on this point, see ch. 4, n. 4.

5 TULRA ss.10–12 and Schedule 2, provisions which were in fact

amended with regard to superannuation funds by EA Schedule 1, paras. 2 and 3.

6 J. Gennard *et al.* 'Throwing the Book: Trade Union Rules on Admission, Discipline, and Expulsion' (1980) 88 *DE Gazette* 591. References to the LSE research (on which see further ch. 4 n. 2) in this chapter are mainly to this article.

7 See *Lawlor* v. *UPW* [1965] 1 All E.R. 353; cf. *White* v. *Kuzych* [1951] A.C. 585.

8 Paras. 610–15. See paras. 650–51 for Donovan's proposals on admission and discipline, and paras. 658–59 on the independent review body. The Labour government endorsed the Donovan policy in paras. 115–17 of *In Place of Strife*.

9 For a full elaboration of this argument, see B. Weekes, M. Mellish, L. Dickens and J. Lloyd *Industrial Relations and the Limits of Law* Blackwell, 1975, ch. 3.

10 There were thirty-three applications of which sixteen were withdrawn and seven, including four concerning closed shop employment, succeeded: Under Secretary of State for Employment, House of Commons Standing Committee A, col. 474, 19 February 1980. On the drafting deficiencies of TULRA s.5, see K. W. Wedderburn 'The Trade Union and Labour Relations Act 1974' (1974) 37 *Modern Law Review* 525, 533–34.

11 *TUC Report 1980* p. 344.

12 It should be noted both that the right is confined to 'employees' and would be employees (not self-employed persons), and that by virtue of the definition of UMA, on which see ch. 4, a specified union must be an independent trade union so that the right can only be exercised against independent trade unions.

13 See *TUC Disputes Principles and Procedures* 1979. According to their 'Preface', the 'Principles' are not intended to be a legally enforceable contract. However under 'Regulations Governing Procedure' a TUC Disputes Committee shall be guided by the Principles: Regulation 'P'. The TUC Rules (which are a legally enforceable contract) refer to the Regulations, and require affiliated organisations to comply with the awards of TUC Disputes Committees (Rule 12(e) and (h)). In October 1977 EMA, an affiliated organisation, issued a writ against the TUC directly challenging the legal validity of a TUC Disputes Committee decision, but the action was not proceeded with: see facts of *EMA* v. *ACAS* [1980] I.C.R. 215. Whether this action was well founded or not, it is clear that Bridlington decisions are challengeable in the courts at least indirectly in actions brought by individuals against affiliated organisations: *Rothwell* v. *APEX* [1976] I.C.R. 211 (p. 102).

See C. Ball 'The Resolution of Inter-Union Conflict: The TUC's Reaction to Legal Intervention' (1980) 9 *Industrial Law Journal* 13.

14 See e.g. Collins and NUFSO (IRC) *TUC Report 1979* p. 364.

15 'The Independent Review Committee: The Success of Voluntarism?' *Industrial Relations Review and Report* No. 208, September 1979, p. 2.

16 Mayhew-Smith and ACTT (IRC) *TUC Report 1979* p. 385.

17 Ward and TGWU (IRC) *TUC Report 1980* p. 347.

18 House of Lords Debates Vol. 411, col. 898, 7 July 1980 (Lord Gowrie); see too House of Lords Debates Vol. 409, col. 1373, 3 June 1980.

CHAPTER 6

1 *Secretary of State for Employment* v. *ASLEF* [1972] I.C.R. 7 and 19. See further R. Simpson and J. Wood *Industrial Relations and the 1971 Act* Pitman, 1973, pp. 195–215.

2 However TULRA s.6 which was inserted against the wishes of the minority Labour government in 1974 and repealed in 1976 did require union rules to provide for the election of the governing body and officials other than officers and for the conduct of elections. Some of the information on the evolution of Conservative Party policy on trade union ballots was kindly provided by J. Hutton of the Oxford Management Centre.

3 House of Commons Debates Vol. 896, cols. 1865–6, 30 July 1975 (Secretary of State for Employment).

4 House of Commons Debates Vol. 894, cols. 37–8, 23 June 1975.

5 The Funds for Trade Union Ballots Regulations, S.I. 1980 No. 1252.

6 Whether or not an official is an employee of the union may be a difficult question. See e.g. *AEU* v. *Ministry of Pensions* [1963] 1 W.L.R. 441 ('sick steward' held to be an employee for purposes of social security).

7 *Funds for Union Ballots* Certification Office, 1980.

8 See House of Commons Standing Committee A, col. 209, 5 February 1980.

9 Ibid. col. 208, and House of Lords Debates Vol. 409, col. 1295, 3 June 1980.

10 See House of Commons Standing Committee A, col. 105, 29 January 1980. This addition was requested by the CBI. Under the

first scheme, such a question could only be covered if other questions in the same ballot related to a purpose within the scheme e.g. whether or not to take industrial action over the offer. For the assurance referred to in the text see House of Lords Debates Vol. 409, col. 1279, 3 June 1980.

11   It appears that a ballot for the purposes of the 1913 Act is not within EA s.1, although it could arguably be included as a ballot on amending the rules within s.1(3)(d) and reg. 4(d) of the first scheme. Cf. Wedderburn's view that the 1913 Act was left out because it would be strange for a ballot on whether a union should spend funds for political purposes to be publicly subsidised: House of Lords Debates Vol. 409, col. 1291, 3 June 1980.

12   House of Commons Standing Committee A, col. 209, 5 February 1980 (our italics).

13   The leading authority is *NUGSAT* v. *Albury Bros. Ltd.* [1979] I.C.R. 84. See generally P. Davies and M. Freedland *Labour Law: Text and Materials* Weidenfeld and Nicolson, 1979, pp. 168–72.

14   House of Lords Debates Vol. 409, col. 1302, 3 June 1980.

15   Ibid. col. 1331 (Lord Gowrie).

CHAPTER 7

1   R. Lewis 'The Legal Enforceability of Collective Agreements' (1970) 8 *British Journal of Industrial Relations* 313. Another difficulty would be the interpretation of 'status quo' clauses which often accompany peace obligations: S. Anderman 'The "Status Quo" Issue and Industrial Disputes Procedures: Some Implications for Labour Law' (1975) 4 *Industrial Law Journal* 131. Such problems would be relevant to the withdrawal of TULRA immunities from action in breach of procedure agreements as envisaged by the Green Paper (paras. 220–1).

2   The Safety Representatives and Safety Committee Regulations, S.I. 1977 No. 500; Health and Safety Commission Code *Safety Representatives and Safety Committees* (1978) plus *Guidance Notes*. See too a further Code *Time Off for the Training of Safety Representatives* (1978).

3   On 13 November 1980: House of Commons Debates Vol. 992, cols. 647–764; House of Lords Debates Vol. 414, cols. 1492–1545.

4   House of Commons Select Committee on Employment 1979–80, Second Report, 822 and Secretary of State's Observations on

this Report, 848. The Committee's scrutiny of the codes was part of its inquiry into the legal immunities of trade unions.

5 House of Commons Select Committee on Employment, 1979—80, Minutes of Evidence, 462 (vi), qq. 325—7. *Annual Report 1980* ACAS, 1981, p. 9.

6 Enoch Powell's phrase: Select Committee Report, para. 22.

7 R. Simpson and J. Wood *Industrial Relations and the 1971 Act* Pitman, 1973, pp. 106—18; B. Weekes, M. Mellish, L. Dickens and J. Lloyd *Industrial Relations and the Limits of Law* Blackwell, 1975, chs. 5 and 6; R. Lewis and G. Latta 'Bargaining Units and Bargaining Agents' (1972) 10 *British Journal of Industrial Relations* 84; M. Hart 'Union Recognition in America — The Legislative Snare' (1978) 7 *Industrial Law Journal* 201.

8 On the significance of 'associated' employer in this context see p. 18 and on its legal definition, p. 27.

9 B. Doyle 'A Substitute for Collective Bargaining? — The Central Arbitration Committee's Approach to Section 16 of the Employment Protection Act 1975' (1980) 9 *Industrial Law Journal* 154.

10 R. Simpson 'Judicial Control of ACAS' (1979) 8 *Industrial Law Journal* 69; B. James and R. Simpson 'Grunwick v. ACAS' (1978) 41 *Modern Law Review* 573.

11 *Powley* v. *ACAS* [1978] I.C.R. 123, 135. Contrast *National Employers' Life Assurance* v. *ACAS* [1979] I.C.R. 620.

12 *Grunwick Processing Laboratories Ltd.* v. *ACAS* [1978] I.C.R. 231, 268.

13 For different views on the Grunwick dispute: J. Rogaly *Grunwick* Penguin, 1977; G. Ward *Fort Grunwick* Temple Smith, 1977; J. Dromey and G. Taylor *Grunwick: The Workers' Story* Lawrence and Wishart, 1978. Report of a Court in Inquiry under Lord Justice Scarman into a dispute between Grunwick Ltd. and APEX, Cmnd. 6922, HMSO, 1977. The Grunwick affair is treated as a case study in P. Elias, B. Napier and P. Wallington *Labour Law: Cases and Materials* Butterworth, 1980, pp. 29—59.

14 *Grunwick Ltd.* v. *ACAS* [1978] I.C.R. 231, 262.

15 See ch. 5, n. 13.

16 *UKAPE* v. *ACAS* [1980] I.C.R. 201 and *EMA* v. *ACAS* [1980] I.C.R. 215. See Simpson (1980) 9 *Industrial Law Journal* 125. Cf. M. Elliott 'ACAS and Judicial Review' (1980) 43 *Modern Law Review* 580.

17 [1980] I.C.R. 201, 210.

18 EPA s.126(1) as amended by EA Schedule 1, para. 6. EPA s.126(1) defines 'collective bargaining' as 'negotiations relating to or connected with one or more of the matters specified in' TULRA s.29(1)

– the definition of 'trade dispute' which we discuss in ch. 9.

19 See ch. 6, n. 13.

20 *Annual Report 1980* ACAS, 1981 p. 32. Part II of this Report reviews ACAS's involvement in union recognition and chronicles the many difficulties it experienced under EPA ss.11–16.

21 See L. Dickens 'ACAS and the Union Recognition Procedure' (1978) 8 *Industrial Law Journal* 150; B. Weekes 'ACAS – An Alternative to Law?' (1979) 8 *Industrial Law Journal* 147.

22 Confirmed by *R. v. CAC, Ex. parte Deltaflow Ltd.* [1978] I.C.R. 534. This basic limitation was explained in P. Wood 'The Central Arbitration Committee's Approach to Schedule 11 to the Employment Protection Act 1975 and the Fair Wages Resolution' (1978) 7 *Industrial Law Journal* 65. Contrast B. Bercusson 'The New Fair Wages Policy: Schedule 11 to the Employment Protection Act' (1976) 5 *Industrial Law Journal* 129 and *Fair Wages Resolutions* Mansell, 1978, Part IV.

23 *R. v. CAC, Ex parte North West Regional Health Authority* [1978] I.C.R. 1228; but Schedule 11 was held to be available to part-time teachers in further education: *R. v. CAC, Ex parte Gloucestershire County Council* [1981] I.C.R. 95.

24 *R. v. CAC, Ex parte TI Tubes Ltd.* [1978] I.R.L.R. 183, 184.

25 House of Commons Standing Committee A, col. 1672, 27 March 1980; House of Lords Debates Vol. 410, col. 802, 13 June 1980.

26 House of Lords Debates Vol. 410, col. 807, 13 June 1980.

27 L. Dickens, M. Hart, M. Jones and B. Weekes *A Response to the Government's Working Paper on Amendments to Employment Protection Legislation* Discussion Paper, SSRC Industrial Relations Research Unit, University of Warwick, 1979, pp. 50–52; M. Jones 'CAC and Schedule 11: The Experience of Two Years' (1980) 9 *Industrial Law Journal* 28; *Employment Bill Briefing No. 6* Low Pay Unit, 1980.

28 *Annual Report 1979* CAC, 1980 p. 23.

29 Ibid.

30 *Annual Report 1978* CAC, 1979, p. 18.

CHAPTER 8

1 See ch. 7 n. 13.

2 G. Howell *Conflicts of Capital and Labour* Macmillan, 2nd edn, 1890, pp. 309–10.

3 House of Commons Select Committee on Employment 1979–

1980, Minutes of Evidence, 462 (ii), 27 February 1980, p. 39.

4 Ibid.

5 *Report of the Committee of Inquiry on Industrial Democracy* HMSO, Cmnd. 6706, 1977 ('Bullock Report'), pp. 4–7.

6 *Trade Unions in a Changing World: The Challenge for Management* CBI, 1980.

7 *Associated Newspapers Group Ltd.* v. *Wade* [1979] I.C.R. 664, 695. For a similar line of reasoning in an undefended secondary picketing case, see *United Biscuits* v. *Fall* [1979] I.R.L.R. 110.

8 *Hunt* v. *Broome* [1974] I.C.R. 84, 89.

9 Ibid. p. 90, Cf. Lord Salmon at p. 96.

10 House of Commons Select Committee on Employment loc. cit., p. 45.

11 Ibid. pp. 36–7.

12 Public Order Act 1936 s.5 as substituted by the Race Relations Act 1976 s.79(6).

13 *R* v. *Jones* [1974] I.C.R. 310, 318.

14 *R* v. *Jones* [1974] I.C.R. 310: *R* v. *Tomlinson* [1974] I.R.L.R. 347; and see J. Arnison *The Shrewsbury Three* Lawrence and Wishart, 1974.

15 House of Commons Debates Vol. 979, col. 239, 19 February 1980.

16 The quotations come from, respectively: House of Commons Standing Committee A, col. 1306, 18 March 1980; ibid col. 1326; ibid col. 1357.

17 E. Batstone, I. Boraston and S. Frenkel *Shop Stewards in Action* Blackwell, 1977.

18 House of Commons Debates Vol. 976, cols. 67, 75–6, 17 December 1979.

19 [1974] I.C.R. 84, 96; cf. Lord Reid at p. 92.

20 House of Commons Debates Vol. 979, col. 255 19 February 1980, and Standing Committee A, col. 1348 18 March 1980.

21 House of Commons Select Committee on Employment 1979–80, Second Report, 822, para. 11.

22 W. E. J. McCarthy, 'The Trouble with the Picketing Code' *New Society* 4 September 1980, p. 452.

23 House of Commons Debates Vol. 976, col. 170, 17 December 1979.

24 *Rookes* v. *Barnard* [1964] A.C. 1129, 1211.

25 House of Commons Standing Committee A, col. 1490, 25 March 1980.

26 *Wilkes Ltd.* v. *Bunn, Financial Times* 27 March 1981.

27 See *TUC Report 1978*, pp. 483–6; M. Rutherford 'Mrs. Thatcher's Overmighty Baron' *Financial Times* 22 February 1980; cf. House

of Commons Select Committee on Employment 1979–80, Minutes of Evidence, 462 (ii), 27 February 1980, p. 35, q. 6.

28 S. Anderman and P. Davies 'Injunction Procedure in Labour Disputes – II' (1974) 3 *Industrial Law Journal* 30, 33; see too K. W. Wedderburn 'Contempt of the NIRC' (1974) 37 *Modern Law Review* 187.

29 *Duport Steels Ltd.* v. *Sirs* [1980] I.C.R. 161, 184–5.

CHAPTER 9

1 *NWL Ltd.* v. *Woods* [1979] I.C.R. 867, 886. Noted by R. Simpson (1980) 43 *Modern Law Review* 327.

2 For a more detailed analysis of the golden formula as interpreted up to 1976 see R. Simpson 'Trade Dispute and Industrial Dispute in British Labour Law' (1977) 40 *Modern Law Review* 16.

3 See Wedderburn 'Labour Injunctions and Trade Disputes' (1978) 41 *Modern Law Review* 80, 84.

4 *Hadmor Productions Ltd.* v. *Hamilton* [1981] I.R.L.R. 210, 216.

5 House of Lords Debates Vol. 410, col. 695, 12 June 1980.

6 *Conway* v. *Wade* [1909] A.C. 506 affirmed on this point by Lord Scarman in *Express Newspapers Ltd.* v. *MacShane* [1980] I.C.R. 42, 64.

7 For a full exposition of this decision and its importance see Wedderburn 'Gilt Back on the Formula' (1980) 43 *Modern Law Review* 319.

8 House of Commons Debates Vol. 982, col. 1499, 17 April 1980.

9 House of Lords Debates Vol. 409, col. 901, 20 May 1980.

10 House of Lords Debates Vol. 411, col. 1137, 8 July 1980.

11 See K. W. Wedderburn 'The Trade Union and Labour Relations Act 1974' (1974) 37 *Modern Law Review* 525, 537–8.

12 For a discussion of the full significance of the decision for the integrity of TULRA s.14(1) see R. Simpson 'Gouriet: Labour Law Aspects' (1978) 41 *Modern Law Review* 63, 64–5.

13 For a readable and still relevant account see K. W. Wedderburn, *The Worker and the Law* 2nd edn, 1971, chs. 7 and 8. For the fullest account see *Clerk and Lindsell on Torts* 15th edn, 1982, ch. 15 (forthcoming).

14 House of Commons Debates Vol. 982, cols. 1485–90, 17 April 1980.

15 See Wedderburn 'Secondary Action and Gateways to Legality: A Note' (1981) 10 *Industrial Law Journal* 113.

16 House of Lords Debates Vol. 410, col. 736, 12 June 1980.

17 House of Lords Debates Vol. 411, cols. 1097–8, 8 July 1980.

18 Lord Wedderburn ibid. cols. 1143–4.

19 *Report of Inquiry into certain Trade Union Recruitment Activities* Cmnd. 7706, HMSO, 1979.

20 House of Commons Standing Committee A, cols. 1530 and 1534–5, 25 March 1980.

21 House of Lords Debates Vol. 411, col. 1148, 8 July 1980.

22 House of Commons Standing Committee A, col. 1571, 25 March 1980.

23 *Hadmor Productions Ltd.* v. *Hamilton* [1981] I.R.L.R. 210, 215.

24 See House of Commons Standing Committee A, cols. 513–9, 19 February 1980; House of Lords Debates Vol. 410, cols. 347–52, 10 June and cols. 764–8, 13 June 1980; Vol. 411 cols. 1152–9, 8 July 1980.

25 See P. Davies and S. Anderman 'Injunction Procedure in Labour Disputes – I' (1973) 2 *Industrial Law Journal* 213, 222–3 ff.

26 *Duport Steels Ltd.* v. *Sirs* [1980] I.C.R. 161, 193.

27 House of Lords Debates Vol. 410, cols. 780–2, 13 June 1980.

28 C. Whelan 'Military Intervention in Industrial Disputes' (1979) 8 *Industrial Law Journal* 222; G. Morris 'The Police and Industrial Emergencies' (1980) 9 *Industrial Law Journal* 1.

29 See Simpson and Wood *Industrial Relations and the 1971 Act* Pitman, 1973, pp. 195–215.

30 For the opinion of the Attorney-General on the application of these offences, see House of Commons Standing Committee B, cols. 581–3, 3 March 1981.

CHAPTER 10

1 House of Commons Standing Committee A, col. 1389, 20 March 1980 (E. Varley MP).

2 *Trade Unions in a Changing World: The Challenge for Management* CBI, 1980, p. 22.

3 J. Donaldson 'Lessons from the Industrial Court' (1975) 91 *Law Quarterly Review* 181, 191–192. (Quoted in J. A. G. Griffith *The Politics of the Judiciary* Fontana, 1977, p. 76.)

4 See J. A. G. Griffith op. cit. especially chapters 2, 3 and 9; Wedderburn 'Industrial Relations and the Courts' (1980) 9 *Industrial Law Journal* 65; R. Miliband *The State in Capitalist Society* Weidenfeld and Nicolson, 1969, pp. 138–148. For a fascinating analysis of judicial ideology in a different country and time see

'The Social Ideal of the Reich Labour Court' in O. Kahn-Freund *Labour Law and Politics in the Weimar Republic* (edited and introduced by R. Lewis and J. Clark) Blackwell, 1981.

5   House of Lords Debates Vol. 419, cols. 271–292, 1 April 1981 (Lord Gowrie); House of Commons Select Committee on Employment 1980–1981, Minutes of Evidence, 282(i), 8 April 1981 (Lord Chancellor).

6   House of Commons Debates Vol. 26, col. 1022, 30 May 1911.

7   See R. Hyman 'Green Means Danger? Trade Union Immunities and the Tory Attack' in *Politics and Power 3* Routledge and Kegan Paul, 1981. For Wedderburn's critique of the Green Paper see House of Commons Select Committee on Employment 1980–1981, Minutes of Evidence, 282(ii), 6 May 1981.

Table of Statutes

1847   Harbours Docks and Piers Clauses Act: *215*
1863   Telegraph Act s.45: *222*
1871   Trade Union Act: *8*
1875   Conspiracy and Protection of Property Act: *3*
         s.3: *164, 184*
         s.5: *174, 222, 227*
         s.7: *157–8, 160, 163, 164, 171–2*
1886   Riot Damages Act: *162*
1906   Trade Disputes Act: *4, 176, 184–5*
         s.1: *198*
         s.2: *158, 172*
         s.3: *201, 213*
         s.4: *184, 195*
         s.5(3): *184, 186, 190–1*
1909   Trade Boards Act: *8*
1913   Trade Union Act: *100, 124, 131, 244*
1915   Munitions of War Act: *1*
1920   Emergency Powers Act: *1, 221*
1927   Trade Disputes and Trade Unions Act: *1*
1936   Public Order Act s.5: *162*
1938   Road Haulage Wages Act: *147, 151–2, 223*
1949   Civil Aviation Act: *151*
1953   Post Office Act s.58: *222*
1959   Highways Act s.121: *160, 161, 172*
1959   Terms and Conditions of Employment Act s.8: *147, 150*
1960   Films Act: *151*
1960   Road Traffic Act: *151*
1964   Emergency Powers Act: *221*
1964   Police Act s.51: *162*
1964   Trade Union (Amalgamations etc.) Act: *124, 128, 131*

1965 Redundancy Payments Act: *12*
1965 Trade Disputes Act: *5, 184, 199, 213*
1966 Prices and Incomes Act: *14*
1970 Equal Pay Act: *12, 15, 45*
1970 Merchant Shipping Act: *221–2*
1971 Industrial Relations Act: *1, 12, 17–18, 19–22, 105, 121, 180, 184, 224, 225, 231*
    s.3: *138*
    s.5: *61, 63, 66, 71–2, 80*
    ss.6–18: *76, 80–1, 90–1*
    s.24(4): *82*
      (6): *30*
    s.27(1)(a): *33*
    s.33(3)(a): *72, 239*
    ss.34–36: *136, 137*
    ss.44–55: *141*
    s.65: *105, 109, 113, 125–6*
    s.74: *241*
    s.117: *197*
    s.119: *239*
    s.134: *158, 161, 172*
    ss.138–145: *221*
    ss.141–145: *125, 134*
    s.147: *183*
    s.154: *241*
    s.167(1): *33, 190*
    Schedule 4: *105, 106, 126*
1973 Independent Broadcasting Authority Act: *151*
1974 Finance Act s.28: *237*
1974 Health and Safety at Work etc. Act: *12, 15, 16*
1974– Trade Union and Labour Relations Acts: *5–6, 12, 15, 185*
1976 s.1A: *96*
    s.2: *8, 99, 241*
    s.5: *105–6, 109*
    s.6: *105–6, 243*
    s.7: *105–6*
    s.8: *237*
    ss.10–12: *100*
    ss.13–17: *134–5, 145, 225, 244*
    s.13: *73, 159, 171, 175–8, 196, 197, 210, 215, 216, 219*

(1): *176–7, 199, 201, 202–9, 210–12, 213, 214*
(2): *177, 213*
(3): *177–8, 184, 202, 209, 212–17*
(4): *177–8, 198*
s.14: *73, 178, 196, 219, 225, 241*
s.15: *152–162, 165–172, 174, 175–7, 207–8, 219*
s.17: *218–20*
s.18: *9, 136–7*
s.28(1): *99, 237*
s.29: *185–92, 198, 203, 245–6*
s.30: *62, 82, 83–5, 133, 169, 170, 207*
Schedule 1 para. 6(5): *82*
Schedule 2: *100*
1975   Employment Protection Act: *12, 15, 16*
s.1(2): *17, 143, 144*
s.2: *146*
s.3: *147*
ss.4–6: *17*
s.6: *138, 139*
ss.11–16: *15, 16, 17–18, 130, 136, 140–7, 149, 223*
ss.17–21: *15, 16, 17–18*
ss.99–107: *14, 15, 16, 43–5, 132–3, 169*
s.126(1): *145, 245*
Schedule 1 para. 11(1): *139*
Schedule 11: *15, 16, 136, 147–51, 152, 223*
1975   Sex Discrimination Act: *12, 46, 48, 100, 238*
1975   Social Security Pensions Act s.31(5): *15*
1976   Race Relations Act: *12, 100, 162. 238*
1977   Criminal Law Act: *3, 164, 165, 184*
1977   Torts (Interference with Goods) Act: *165*
1978   Employment Protection (Consolidation) Act: *12*
s.1: *32*
ss.12–18: *14, 41–3*
ss.19–22: *26, 27*
s.23(1)(a): *63*
(b): *63, 69, 93, 238*
(c): *13–14, 66–9, 70, 71, 93, 211, 216*
(2): *63*
(2A): *64, 93, 238*
(2B): *64, 93, 238*

s.24(3): *65*
s.25(2): *70, 73*
s.26: *65, 70, 73*
s.26A: *69–70, 73, 93–4*
s.27: *13, 62, 145*
s.28: *62, 135*
s.31: *236*
s.31A: *46–7*
s.33: *50–1*
s.45: *51, 52–3*
s.47: *51–3*
s.53: *32*
s.55: *33–4*
s.56: *53–4*
s.56A: *53–4*
s.57: *240*
  (1)(b): *67*
  (3): *30–3, 54, 67*
s.58: *13*
  (1)(a): *62*
   (b): *62, 66, 88, 93, 238*
   (c): *66, 67*
  (2): *63*
  (3): *83, 85, 86–7, 89, 92*
  (3A): *86, 87–8*
  (3B): *86, 88–9, 240*
  (3C): *86, 89–91*
  (3E): *90, 240*
s.58A: *64, 89–91*
s.59: *39*
s.60: *48–9*
s.61(1): *54*
s.62: *13, 73, 183*
s.63: *73*
s.64(3): *26, 27, 62–3*
s.64A: *27–9, 48*
s.65: *14*
s.71(1): *238*
s.73(7A): *36–7*
  (7B): *37–8*

(8): *38–9*
s.74: *73, 119*
ss.76A–76C: *39, 70, 72, 92*
s.76A: *70, 73*
s.76B: *71–2, 211*
s.76C: *71–2, 211*
s.77: *65*
s.83: *34*
s.86: *52, 53*
s.91(2): *30–1*
s.96(2)(3): *14*
s.132(2)(3): *114*
s.136(3): *118*
s.142: *34*
s.149: *26*
s.153(1): *52, 62*
s.153(4): *27–8*
Schedule 2: *54*
1980 Employment Act
s.1: *123, 127–32, 135, 216, 244*
s.2: *123, 127, 129, 132–3, 135, 216, 217*
s.3: *136, 139–40, 172, 216*
s.4: *81–2, 99, 103, 104, 108–22, 174, 216, 217, 237*
s.5: *81–2, 99, 108–22, 133, 174, 216, 237*
s.6: *30–3, 54, 67*
s.7: *64, 86–91, 216*
s.8(1): *27–9, 48*
    (2): *34*
s.9: *36–9*
s.10: *39, 70, 73, 74, 92, 119, 133, 196, 211, 216, 239*
s.11: *51–2*
s.12: *52–4*
s.13: *46–7*
s.14: *41–3*
s.15(1): *13–4, 66, 93, 211, 216*
    (2): *64, 66, 93*
    (3): *65*
    (4): *69–70, 73, 93–4, 119, 133, 196, 216, 239*
s.16: *153, 171, 172, 179, 180, 225*
    (1): *159, 165–72, 174, 175–7, 207–8, 219*

(2): *160, 171, 175–8, 208*
s.17: *6, 159, 178, 185, 189, 190–1, 192, 194–5, 202–9, 212, 225*
   (1): *202, 204, 212*
   (2): *153, 190, 202, 203, 204, 207, 208*
   (3): *202, 204–6, 208*
   (4): *168, 202, 206–7*
   (5): *202, 207–8*
   (6): *205*
   (7): *203, 207*
   (8): *184, 202, 212–17*
s.18: *71, 86, 178, 209–12, 225*
s.19(a): *96*
   (b): *140*
   (c): *147, 151*
Schedule 1 paras. 2 and 3: *241–2*
         para. 4: *139*
         para. 6: *145*
         para. 17: *114*
         para. 23: *54*
Schedule 2: *145*
1980 Social Security Act: *40–1, 50*
1980 Social Security (No. 2) Act: *40–1*
1981 Finance Act: *40*

Statutory Instruments

1977 Safety Representatives and Safety Committees Regulations S.I. 1977 No. 500: *16, 244*
1979 Employment Protection (Handling of Redundancies) Variation Order S.I. 1979 No. 958: *43–5*
1979 Unfair Dismissal (Variation of Qualifying Period) Order S.I. 1979 No. 959: *25–7, 48*
1980 Industrial Tribunals (Rules of Procedure) Regulations S.I. 1980 No. 884: *57–9*
1980 Funds for Trade Union Ballots Regulations S.I. 1980 No. 1252: *128–31*
1980 Employment Appeal Tribunal Rules S.I. 1980 No. 2035: *59*

Table of Cases

ABBREVIATIONS

All E.R.	All England Reports
A.C.	Appeal Cases
CA	Court of Appeal
Ch.	Chancery
HL	House of Lords
I.C.R.	Industrial Cases Reports
I.R.L.R.	Industrial Relations Law Reports
I.T.R.	Industrial Tribunal Reports
Q.B.	Queens Bench
W.L.R.	Weekly Law Reports

AEU v. *Minister of Pensions* [1963] 1 W.L.R. 441; [1963] 1 All E.R. 864 *243*

Allen v. *Flood* [1898] A.C. 1 (HL) *4, 214*

American Cyanamid Co. v. *Ethicon Ltd.* [1975] A.C. 396 (HL) *218–19*

Associated Newspapers Group Ltd. v. *Wade* [1979] I.C.R. 664; [1979] I.R.L.R. 201 (CA) *120, 159, 193, 195, 215–16, 241*

BBC v. *Hearn* [1977] I.C.R. 685; [1977] I.R.L.R. 269 (CA) *186, 188, 189*

Beaumont v. *Libby McNeil Ltd., The Times* 10 October 1978 (EAT) *86*

Beaverbrook Newspapers Ltd. v. *Keys* [1978] I.C.R. 582; [1978] I.R.L.R. 34 (CA) *192, 195*

Blue Circle Staff Association v. *CO* [1977] I.C.R. 224; [1977] I.R.L.R. 20 (EAT) *238*

Blue Star Ship Management Ltd. v. *Williams* [1978] I.C.R. 770; [1979] I.R.L.R. 16 (EAT) *85*

257

Bonsor v. *Musicians Union* [1956] A.C. 104 (HL) *101, 113*

Brassington v. *Cauldron Wholesale Ltd.* [1978] I.C.R. 405; [1977] I.R.L.R. 479 (EAT) *67*

British Airways Engine Overhaul Ltd. v. *Francis* [1981] I.C.R. 278; [1981] I.R.L.R. 9 (EAT) *67*

Byrne v. *Foulkes* 1961 unreported *123*

Camellia Tanker Ltd. SA v. *ITF* [1976] I.C.R. 274; [1976] I.R.L.R. 183 (CA) *215*

Carr v. *Allen-Bradley Electronics Ltd.* [1980] I.C.R. 603 (EAT) *58, 59*

CEGB v. *Coleman* [1973] I.C.R. 230; [1973] I.R.L.R. 117 (NIRC) *68*

Chant v. *Aquaboats Ltd.* [1978] I.C.R. 643 (EAT) *64*

Charnock v. *Court* [1899] 2 Ch. 35 *158*

Churchman v. *Joint Shop Stewards Committee of the Workers of the Port of London* [1972] I.C.R. 222 (CA) *179*

City of Birmingham District Council v. *Beyer* [1977] I.R.L.R. 210; [1977] I.T.R. 409 *65–6, 122*

Con-Mech (Engineers) Ltd. v. *AUEW (Engineering Section)* [1973] I.C.R. 620; (No. 2) [1974] I.C.R. 332 (NIRC) *21*

Conway v. *Wade* [1909] A.C. 506 (HL) *187, 192, 194*

Coral Squash Clubs Ltd. v. *Matthews* [1979] I.C.R. 607; [1979] I.R.L.R. 390 (EAT) *57*

Cory Lighterage Ltd. v. *TGWU* [1973] I.C.R. 197 and 339 (CA) *190*

Crofter Hand-Woven Harris Tweed Co. v. *Veitch* [1942] A.C. 435 (HL) *9, 78, 198*

Croydon v. *Greenham (Plant Hire) Ltd.* [1978] I.C.R. 415 (EAT) *59*

Curry v. *Harlow District Council* [1979] I.C.R. 769; [1979] I.R.L.R. 269 (EAT) *85*

Daily Mirror Newspapers Ltd. v. *Gardner* [1968] 2 Q.B. 768 (CA) *201, 214, 216*

Devis & Sons Ltd. v. *Atkins* [1977] A.C. 931; [1977] I.C.R. 662; [1977] I.R.L.R. 314 (HL) *37–8*

Dixon v. *West Ella Developments Ltd.* [1978] I.C.R. 856; [1978] I.R.L.R. 151 (EAT) *63–4*

Drew v. *St. Edmundsbury Borough Council* [1980] I.C.R. 513 (EAT) *64*

Duport Steels Ltd. v. *Sirs* [1980] I.C.R. 161; [1980] I.R.L.R. 112 (HL) *5–6, 159, 180, 193–4, 195, 219–20*

Dutton v. *Hawker Siddeley Aviation Ltd.* [1978] I.C.R. 1057; [1978]
I.R.L.R. 390 (EAT) *236*
EMA v. *ACAS* [1980] I.C.R. 215; [1980] I.R.L.R. 164 (HL); [1979]
I.C.R. 637; [1979] I.R.L.R. 246 (CA) *142–3, 144, 145, 242*
Edwards v. *SOGAT* [1971] Ch. 354 (CA) *78–9, 102–3, 113*
Enessy Co. S.A. v. *Minoprio* [1978] I.R.L.R. 489 (EAT) *32*
Esterman v. *NALGO* [1974] I.C.R. 625 *101, 120*
Express Newspapers Ltd. v. *Keys* [1980] I.R.L.R. 247 *183–4, 188–9*
Express Newspapers Ltd. v. *MacShane** [1980] A.C. 672; [1980]
I.C.R. 42; [1980] I.R.L.R. 35 (HL); [1979] I.C.R. 210; [1979]
I.R.L.R. 79 (CA) *5–6, 159, 192, 193, 194, 195, 202, 206, 219–20,
241*

Faramus v. *Film Artistes' Association* [1964] A.C. 925 (HL) *78–9,
99–100*
Ford Motor Co. Ltd. v. *AEF* [1969] 2 Q.B. 303 *9, 136, 137*

General Aviation Services (U.K.) Ltd. v. *TGWU* [1976] I.R.L.R. 214
(HL) *72, 197*
Gardiner v. *Merton London Borough Council* [1981] I.C.R. 186;
[1980] I.R.L.R. 472 (CA) *28*
Gayle v. *John Wilkinson & Sons (Saltley)* [1978] I.C.R. 154; [1977]
I.R.L.R. 208 *85*
Gouriet v. *UPW* [1978] A.C. 435 (HL) *186, 196, 218, 222*
Grunwick Processing Laboratories Ltd. v. *ACAS* [1978] A.C. 655;
[1978] I.C.R. 231; [1978] I.R.L.R. 38 (HL) *142, 143–4, 146*

Hadmor Productions Ltd. v. *Hamilton* [1981] I.R.L.R. 210 (CA)
187–8, 195, 202–3, 214–15
Heaton's Transport (St. Helens) Ltd. v. *TGWU* [1973] A.C. 15; [1972]
I.C.R. 308; [1972] I.R.L.R. 25 (HL) *20, 72, 169*
Home Counties Dairies Ltd. v. *Woods* [1977] I.C.R. 463; [1976]
I.R.L.R. 380 (EAT) *82, 86*
Howitt Transport Ltd. v. *TGWU* [1973] I.C.R.1; [1972] I.R.L.R. 93
and [1973] I.R.L.R. 25 (NIRC) *72*
Hubbard v. *Pitt* [1975] I.C.R. 77 and 308 (CA) *159, 160*
Hunt v. *Broome* [1974] A.C. 587; [1974] I.C.R. 84; [1974] I.R.L.R.
26 (HL) *161, 163, 172*
Huntley v. *Thornton* [1957] 1 W.L.R. 321; [1957] 1 All E.R. 234 *187*

*Incorrectly spelt McShane in most reports

Hynds v. *Spillers-French Baking Ltd.* [1974] I.T.R. 261 (NIRC) *240*

Jeffrey v. *Laurence Scott & Electromotors Ltd.* [1977] I.R.L.R. 466 (EAT) *85*

Kapur v. *Shields* [1976] I.C.R. 26 *33*

Lakhani v. *Hoover Ltd.* [1978] I.C.R. 1063 (EAT) *85*
Lawlor v. *UPW* [1965] Ch. 712 *101*
Lee v. *Showmen's Guild* [1952] 2 Q.B. 329 (CA) *239*
Leyland Vehicles Ltd. v. *Jones* [1981] I.C.R. 428; [1981] I.R.L.R. 269 (EAT) *85*
Lyons v. *Wilkins* [1896] 1 Ch. 811 and [1899] 1 Ch. 255 (CA) *158, 160*

Marler Ltd. v. *Robertson* [1974] I.C.R. 72 (NIRC) *58*
Marley Tile Co. Ltd. v. *Shaw* [1980] I.C.R. 72; [1980] I.R.L.R. 25 (CA) *63*
Martin v. *Scottish TGWU* [1952] 1 All E.R. 691 (HL) *241*
McInnes v. *Onslow-Fane* [1978] 1 W.L.R. 1520; [1978] 3 All E.R. 211 *79*
Meade v. *Haringey London Borough Council* [1979] I.C.R. 494 (CA) *216*
Merseyside and North Wales Electricity Board v. *Taylor* [1975] I.C.R. 185; [1975] I.R.L.R. 60 *30*
Midland Cold Storage Ltd. v. *Turner* [1972] I.C.R. 230 (NIRC) *179*
Morgan v. *Fry* [1968] 2 Q.B. 710 (CA) *183*

NWL Ltd. v. *Woods* [1979] I.C.R. 867; [1979] I.R.L.R. 478 (HL) *5, 185, 186–7, 188, 189, 191, 194, 195, 206, 219–20*
Nagle v. *Fielden* [1966] 2 Q.B. 633 (CA) *239*
National Coal Board v. *Galley* [1958] 1 W.L.R. 16; [1958] 1 All E.R. 91 (CA) *183*
National Employers Life Assurance Co. Ltd. v. *ACAS* [1979] I.C.R. 620; [1979] I.R.L.R. 282 *245*
National Union of Gold Silver and Allied Trades v. *Albury Bros. Ltd.* [1979] I.C.R. 84; [1978] I.R.L.R. 504 (CA) *132–3*
Neefjes v. *Crystal Products Ltd.* [1974] I.R.L.R. 63; [1973] I.T.R. 616 (CA) *58*

Nelson v. *BBC (No. 2)* [1980] I.C.R. 110; [1979] I.R.L.R. 346 (CA)
36

Nu-Swift International Ltd. v. *Mallinson* [1979] I.C.R. 157; [1978] I.R.L.R. 537 (EAT) *51*

Piddington v. *Bates* [1961] 1 W.L.R. 162; [1960] 3 All E.R. 660 *160, 161*

Post Office v. *Mughal* [1977] I.C.R. 763; [1977] I.R.L.R. 178 (EAT) *26*

Post Office v. *UPW* [1974] I.C.R. 378; [1974] I.R.L.R. 22 (HL) *63–4, 68*

Powley v. *ACAS* [1978] I.C.R. 123; [1977] I.R.L.R. 190 *142*

Quinn v. *Leathem* [1901] A.C. 495 (HL) *4, 156*

R v. *CAC, Ex parte Gloucestershire County Council* [1981] I.C.R. 95 *246*

R v. *CAC, Ex parte North West Regional Health Authority* [1978] I.R.L.R. 404 *149*

R v. *CAC, Ex parte RHM Foods Ltd.* [1979] I.C.R. 657; [1979] I.R.L.R. 279 *151*

R v. *CAC, Ex parte TI Tubes Ltd.* [1978] I.R.L.R. 183 *149*

R v. *Greater London Council, Ex parte Burgess* [1978] I.C.R. 991; [1978] I.R.L.R. 261 *241*

R v. *Jones* [1974] I.C.R. 310; [1974] I.R.L.R. 117 (CA) *154, 163, 164*

Rawlings v. *Lionweld Ltd.* [1978] I.R.L.R. 481 (EAT) *85–6*

Reynolds v. *Shipping Federation Ltd.* [1924] 1 Ch. 28 *78*

Robb v. *Leon Motor Services Ltd.* [1978] I.C.R. 506; [1978] I.R.L.R. 26 (EAT) *67*

Rookes v. *Barnard* [1964] A.C. 1129 (HL) *5, 177, 183, 198, 199, 213*

Rothwell v. *APEX* [1976] I.C.R. 211; [1975] I.R.L.R. 375 *102, 114, 242*

Royal Naval School v. *Hughes* [1979] I.R.L.R. 383 (EAT) *32*

Ryan v. *Shipboard Maintenance Ltd.* [1980] I.C.R. 88; [1980] I.R.L.R. 16 (EAT) *35*

Saggers v. *British Railways Board* [1977] I.C.R. 809; [1977] I.R.L.R. 266; (No. 2) [1978] I.C.R. 1111 [1978] I.R.L.R. 435 (EAT) *83*

Sarvent v. *CEGB* [1976] I.R.L.R. 66 *82–3*

Seaboard World Airlines Inc. v. *TGWU* [1973] I.C.R. 458; [1973] I.R.L.R. 300 (NIRC) *182*

Secretary of State for Employment v. *ASLEF* [1972] I.C.R. 7; (No. 2) [1972] I.C.R. 19 (CA) *21, 125, 182*

Simmons v. *Hoover Ltd.* [1977] I.C.R. 61; [1976] I.R.L.R. 266 (EAT) *182–3*

Spillers-French (Holdings) Ltd. v. *USDAW* [1980] I.C.R. 31; [1979] I.R.L.R. 339 (EAT) *44*

Spring v. *NASD* [1956] 1 W.L.R. 585; [1956] 2 All E.R. 221 *102, 114*

Squibb UK Staff Association v. *CO* [1979] I.C.R. 235; [1979] I.R.L.R. 75 (CA) *238*

Star Sea Transport Corporation v. *Slater* [1979] 1 Lloyd's Reports 26; [1978] I.R.L.R. 507 (CA) *187, 189, 195*

Stratford & Son Ltd. v. *Lindley* [1965] A.C. 269 (HL) *5, 187, 190–1, 201, 214*

Sulemanji v. *Toughened Glass Ltd.* [1979] I.C.R. 799 (EAT) *67*

Taff Vale Railway Co. v. *Amalgamated Society of Railway Servants* [1901] A.C. 426 (HL) *4, 20*

Taylor v. *Co-operative Retail Services Ltd.* [1981] I.C.R. 172; [1981] I.R.L.R. 1 (EAT) *67, 84–5*

Temperton v. *Russell* [1893] 1 Q.B. 715 (CA) *156*

Terry v. *East Sussex County Council* [1976] I.C.R. 536 (EAT) *34*

Thomson & Co. v. *Deakin* [1952] Ch. 646 (CA) *200–1*

Torquay Hotel Co. Ltd. v. *Cousins* [1969] 2 Ch. 106 (CA) *5, 201, 210, 214*

Turley v. *Allders Department Stores Ltd.* [1980] I.C.R. 66; [1980] I.R.L.R. 4 (EAT) *48*

Tynan v. *Balmer* [1967] 1 Q.B. 91 *160–1*

UKAPE v. *ACAS* [1980] I.C.R. 201; [1980] I.R.L.R. 124 (HL) [1979] I.C.R. 303; [1979] I.R.L.R. 68 (CA) *142–3, 144, 145*

United Biscuits (U.K.) Ltd. v. *Fall* [1979] I.R.L.R. 110 *193, 247*

Universe Tankships Inc. of Monrovia v. *ITF* [1981] I.C.R. 129; [1980] I.R.L.R. 363 (CA) *187*

Ward Lock & Co. Ltd. v. *Operative Printers' Assistants' Society* (1906) 22 Times Law Reports 327 *158*

Watling & Co. Ltd. v. *Richardson* [1978] I.C.R. 1049; [1978] I.R.L.R. 255 (EAT) *31*

Weddel & Co. Ltd. v. *Tepper* [1980] I.C.R. 286; [1980] I.R.L.R. 96 (CA) *31*

White v. *Kuzych* [1951] A.C. 585 *101*
Wilkes Ltd. v. *Bunn* 1981 unreported *179*
Wiltshire County Council v. *Guy* [1980] I.C.R. 455; [1980] I.R.L.R.
198 (CA) *35*

Young and Woods Ltd. v. *West* [1980] I.R.L.R. 201 (CA) *28*

Index

Action short of dismissal, 67–9, 93–4,
  131, 216, 224
  see also Right to dissociate
Advisory, Conciliation and Arbitration
    Service (ACAS)
  autonomy, 223
  closed shop, 91
  Codes of Practice, 17, 32, 62,
    138–40
  composition, 15
  functions, 17
  union recognition, 141–7
Ante-natal care, time off for, 46–7
  see also Maternity
Arbitration, see CAC
Armed forces, 221
Associated employer, 18, 27–8, 168,
  206–7

Ballots, see Trade Union Ballots
Bill of Rights, 227
Bridlington Principles, see TUC
Bullock Report, 16, 17

Central Arbitration Committee (CAC)
  awards, 16, 148–51
  fair wages legislation, 151
  judicial review, 149
  union recognition, 144
Certification Officer
  certificate of independence, 62,
    118
  political fund, 124
  trade union ballots, 127–31
Closed shop, 22, 75–98
  action short of dismissal, 93
  'agency', 76, 80, 82, 90
  'approved', 76, 80, 82
  Bridlington Principles, see TUC
  charity contributions, 82

Closed shop, continued
  Code of Practice, 71, 79, 86, 87,
    90–1, 94–7, 103, 109, 111, 114,
    116,122, 140, 216, 223–4
  collective bargaining, 77, 80
  common law, 103
  definition, 75
  Donovan Commission, 77, 79–80,
    104
  European Commission of Human
    Rights, 97
  existing employees, 88–9
  'fair list' of businesses, 211
  formal, 76
  'free rider', 77
  genuine objection, 79, 82, 86–88
  Green Paper, Trade Union
    Immunities, 71, 73, 78, 91, 98
  IRA, 21, 80–1, 91, 240 n.12
  judicial attitudes to, 78–9
  management interest in, 76–7, 81
  religious belief, 62, 82–3, 86
  secret ballots, 86, 89–91, 93
  unfair dismissal, 13, 39, 81–6,
    92–3, 216, 224
  union membership agreements,
    64–9, 81–94, 108–13
  white collar unionism, 76
  Working Paper on, 89, 107
  see also Right to dissociate, Trade
    union membership, UMA
Codes of Practice, 138–40
  see also ACAS, Closed shop,
    Picketing
Collective agreements, 136–8
  contract of employment, 9, 137
  'contracting-out' agreements, 14,
    233 n.17
  Donovan Commission, 8, 10, 18,
    137–8

Collective agreements, *continued*
  enforceability, 8–9, 15, 20, 136–7
  Green Paper, *Trade Union Immunities*, 136–7
  'no strike' clause, 137, 222
Collective bargaining, 9, 10, 136–52
  bargaining units, 20, 141, 144
  bargaining agents, 20, 141
  single employer bargaining, 148–9
  Whitley, 149
  see also Collective agreements, Contract of employment, Recognition, Trade unions, Wages councils
Commission on Industrial Relations (CIR), 17, 141
Contempt of court, 179–80
Conciliation, 8, 15
  see also ACAS
Confederation of British Industry (CBI) policies
  ballots, 127, 132
  Closed Shop Code, 95
  employer solidarity, 157
  service qualification, 29
  strike, positive right, 226
Conspiracy
  civil, 4, 9, 175, 177, 197–9
  criminal, 4, 164, 184
  see also Torts
Contract of employment
  arbitration awards, incorporation of, 16, 148
  collective agreements, incorporation of, 9, 137
  definition of, 28
  fixed term, 33, 36
  freedom of contract, 7
  industrial action, 182–4
  suspension, 227–8
  'task' contract, 35
  termination, 33
  'yellow dog', 61, 200
'Cooling-off' period, 21, 221

Damages, 4, 183, 196–7, 217
Department of Employment, 41–5
Disclosure of information, 15, 16, 18, 20, 145
Discrimination, 12, 46, 100, 238 n.2
Dissociate, *see* Right to dissociate
Donovan Commission (Royal Commission on Trade Unions and

Donovan Commission, *continued*
  Employers' Associations)
  closed shop, 77, 79–80, 104
  collective agreements, 8, 10, 18, 137
  collective bargaining, reform of, 10–11, 136, 138, 140–1
  immunities, 196, 201
  shop stewards, 170
  strike notices, 182
  trade union ballots, 124–5
  unfair dismissal, 29
  union admission and expulsion, 104
  union recognition, 17, 140–1
  'yellow-dog' contract, 61

Earnings related supplement, 40
Economic torts, *see* Torts
EEC Directive on Collective Redundancies, 18, 45
Emergency powers, 220–1
Employment Appeal Tribunal (EAT), 108, 118–19
Employers, *see* Associated Employers, CBI, Green Paper, *Trade Union Immunities*, Small firms, Trade union ballots, Unfair dismissal
Equal Opportunities Commission (EOC), 29, 146
Equal pay, 5, 11, 13, 15, 45
Essential supplies and services, 174, 220–22
European Commission of Human Rights, 97

Fair Deal at Work (1968), 20, 125
'Fair' list of businesses, 211
Fair Wages Resolution, 60, 136, 147, 149–52
Fair wages legislation, 151
Flags of convenience, 187, 192, 194
Freedom of press, *see* Press

Green Paper, *Trade Union Immunities* (1981), 22, 181, 225
  closed shop, 78, 91, 98, 225
  collective agreements, 22, 136, 137, 225
  employers, role of, 230
  essential industries, 221–2
  fair list of businesses, 211
  picketing, 153, 171, 174

Green Paper, *continued*
  positive right to strike, 226−9
  secondary action, 203, 205, 209
  strike ballot, 134, 225
  tort, liabilities in, 191, 196, 202
Grunwick dispute, 142−3, 146, 168
Guarantee payments, 41−3

House of Commons Select Committee
  on Employment, 95, 139, 155,
  169, 173

In Place of Strife (1969), 15, 125, 134
Incomes policies, 11, 14, 18
Independent Review Committee (IRC),
  see TUC
Inducing breach of and interference
  with contract, 4, 5, 153, 176−8,
  199−213
Industrial tribunals, 56−9
  collective rights, 14, 133
  costs, 58−9
  development of, 11−12
  Donovan Commission, 13
  interim relief, 65
  neutrality, 98, 121
  pre-hearing assessment, 58
  procedure, 32, 56−9
  protective awards, 43−4
  trade union recognition, 145
  workload, 26
  see also Compensation, Right to
    dissociate, Trade unions, Trade
    union ballots, UMA, Unfair
    dismissal
Injunction, labour, 2, 5, 158, 178−80,
  184, 194, 196, 214, 217−20
Interference with business by unlawful
  means, 121, 153, 201−3,
  212−17, 225
International Labour Organisation
  (ILO), 61
Intimidation
  civil, 5, 163, 177, 199
  criminal, 158, 163−4
Institute of Personnel Management
  (IPM), 25, 29, 223

Joinder provisions, 69−74, 92, 93,
  119, 224
Judges
  closed shop, attitudes to, 78−9
  industrial conflict, 2−7, 159, 193,
  195

Judges, *continued*
  political role, 228−9
  trade union recognition, 141−7
  trade union rule book, 100−04

Labour injunction, *see* Injunction
Leggatt Report, 209−11
Low paid, 42−3, 136, 149−50

Manpower Services Commission
  (MSC), 45
Maternity
  allowance, 49
  grant, 50
  pay, 12, 13, 49
  rights, 23, 45−56
  see also Ante-natal care, Right to
    return to work
Merchant seamen, 221, 222
Minimum wage, 9, 151

National emergency, *see* 'Cooling-off'
  period, Emergency powers
National Industrial Relations Court
  (NIRC), 20−2, 68, 141, 179, 182,
  228
National Insurance Commissioner, 167

Pensions, 15
Picketing, 153−80
  affray, 163−4
  associated employer, 168
  Code of Practice, 120−1, 153, 162,
    165, 167, 169, 172−5, 179, 216,
    220
  criminal law, 140, 158, 160−5,
    171−2, 173−4, 225
  Donovan Commission, 156, 170
  essential supplies, 174
  flying pickets, 163
  immunities, 158−9, 171−2, 175−8
  implied presence, 175
  intimidation, 158, 163−4
  injunction, 158, 178−80
  mass picketing, 161, 163, 173
  numbers, 161, 173, 176
  nuisance, 158, 160, 175
  'own place of work', 166−8, 172
  peaceful, 154−5, 158−62, 165
  picket organisers, 173−5, 177−9,
    225

Picketing, *continued*
    primary and secondary, distinction,
      153, 157, 167–8, 177, 180
    private detectives, 179
    public order, 172
    secondary, lawful, 207–08
    trade union officials, 159, 168–70
    trespass, 165, 175
    TUC, 156–7, 173
    unlawful assembly, 164
    violence, 154, 164
    watching or besetting, 160, 171–2
    wilful obstruction of the highway,
      160–5, 171–2
    Working Paper (1979), 153, 173
Police, 154–7, 160–5, 171, 173–4,
    179, 221, 225
Posts and telecommunications, 222
Positive right to strike, *see* Strikes
Press, freedom of, 96–7, 215, 219

Recognition of trade unions, 16, 17,
    140–7
    inter union disputes, 15, 141, 146,
      190–1
    see also ACAS, Judges,
      Redundancy
Redundancy
    consultation, 15, 16, 18, 43–5
    EEC Directive on Collective
      Redundancies, 18, 45
    recognised trade unions, 133, 145
    redundancy pay, 11–13, 34, 36
Re-engagement, 36, 65
    see also Unfair dismissal
Registrar of Friendly Societies, 8
Registrar of Trade Unions, 20, 22
Registration of trade unions, 8, 20–2,
    80–1
Reinstatement, 36, 65
    see also Unfair dismissal
Restraint of trade, 8, 107
Right to dissociate, 29, 61–72, 93
    see also Action short of dismissal,
      Closed shop, Joinder provisions,
      Trade unions, Unfair dismissal
Right to return to work, 50–4
    see also Maternity
Right to work, 78–9, 100, 107
Road Haulage Wages Council, 152
Royal Commission on Trade Unions
      and Employers' Associations, *see*
      Donovan Commission

Safety at work
    consult, duty to, 15, 16, 145
    Health and Safety Executive, 16
    industrial injury benefits, 40
    legal regulation of, 8
Secondary action
    associated employer, 206–7
    blacking, 210
    customers and suppliers, 204–5
    immunity, 22, 190, 194–5, 202–9,
      225
    primary action, distinction from,
      203–4, 209, 213, 225
    Working Paper on (1980), 172, 194,
      214
    see also Inducing breach of and
      interference with contract,
      Industrial action, Interference
      with business by unlawful means,
      Intimidation, Picketing
Secret ballots
    closed shop, 86, 89–91, 93
    industrial action, control of, 121
    see also Trade union ballots
Shop stewards, 1, 20–1, 68, 128, 137,
    169–70, 181, 199, 230
Sickness benefit, 40
Small firms, 27–30, 44, 53, 55–6, 153
Social Contract, 12, 16, 18
Social security, 40–1, 227
Steel dispute (1980), 154–5, 164, 193,
    219–20
Strikes
    ballots, 15, 124, 131, 133, 134–5
    benefit entitlement, 40, 167
    contract, breach of, 200
    dismissal, 183
    notices, 182
    official, unofficial, 2, 196, 226–7
    positive right to, 68, 181–221,
      226–9
    threats, 199
    to compel union membership,
      209–12
    unconstitutional, 15, 19
    unfair dismissal, 13–14, 183
    see also Green Paper, *Trade Union
      Immunities*, Injunctions,
      Picketing, Secondary action,
      Torts, Trade dispute

Torts
    electoral malpractices, 123

Torts, *continued*
immunities from liability in, 4–7, 9, 15, 184–222
nuisance, 175
trade unions' liability, 195–7
see also Conspiracy, Inducing breach of and interference with contract, Injunctions, Interference with business by unlawful means, Intimidation, Trade dispute
Trade dispute
definition, 185–9, 203, 210
extraneous motive, 187–9, 194
Green Paper, Trade Union Immunities, 186, 189, 191
'in contemplation or furtherance of', 4, 5, 6, 184–6, 192–5, 201, 206
persons concerned with, 189–92
worker-worker, 190–5, 203
Trade unions
autonomy, 129–31
ballots, *see* Trade union ballots
independent unions, 62, 99
inter-union relations, 64, 69, 102, 114, 122, 190, 224
internal appeals, 114
internal democracy, 124–7
IRA, 3–7, 105–6
right to participate in activities, 11, 13, 62, 63, 65–6, 69
right to organise, 3, 61, 197, 212
right to time off for union duties, 11, 13, 47
rules, 99–122, 128, 131
voluntary unincorporated associations, 8, 99
see also Action short of dismissal, Closed shop, Right to dissociate, Trade union ballots, Trade union membership, TUC
Trade union ballots, 123–35
applications for, 129
canvassing, 129–30
CBI, 127, 132
elections, 124–5
employer, premises on, 123, 132, 217
finance, state, 127–31, 224
mergers, 124, 128
political funds. 124
postal, 123, 126–31

Trade union ballots, *continued*
strike ballots, *see* Strike, ballots
TUC, 127
union membership agreements, 131
wage offers, 131
Working Paper on, 126
workplace ballots, 123, 224
see also Certification Officer, Secret ballots
Trades Union Congress (TUC), 18, 20, 29, 80, 95
ballots, 127, 135
Bridlington Principles, 77, 102, 114, 116, 242 n. 13
Certification Officer, 62
Guides (1979), 18, 156, 169
Independent Review Committee (IRC), 106–7, 114–17
union admission and expulsion, 104–5
union recognition, 143, 145
Trade union membership, 99–122
admission, 99, 103–7
common law rights, 99–103, 112
disciplinary sanctions, 100–5
EAT, 118–19
industrial action, refusal to participate in, 120–2
lapsing provision, 113
terminate, right to, 106
unreasonable exclusion and expulsion, 104–13, 117–22
see also Closed shop, IRC, Trade unions, TUC, UMA

Unemployment, 25, 40, 43, 167
Union Membership Agreements (UMA), 81–94
ballots, 64, 89–91, 131
definition, 82–4
'practice' of, 84, 110
see also Closed shop, Right to dissociate, Trade union membership
Unfair dismissal, 12, 23–39
associated employer, 27
closed shop, 13, 81–86, 92–3, 216, 224
compensation, 36–39
fairness, definition of 30–1
'fixed term contract', 34–5
inadmissible reason, 26–8, 62

Unfair dismissal, *continued*
  joinder provisions, 69–74, 92–3
  pregnancy, 46
  proof, burden of, 30–3
  service qualification, 25–9
  size and administrative sources, 31–3
  strikes, 13–14, 183
  'task' contract, 35
  'waiver' of right, 34–5
  see also Re-engagement, Reinstatement, Right to dissociate, Small firms

Unfair industrial practices, 72, 180
Union only clauses, 71, 211–12

Vicarious liability, 22, 72–3, 137, 195–7
Voluntarism, 7–10, 15–16

Wages councils, 8, 148, 152
Women, 45–56
  health and welfare, 8
  see also Discrimination, Maternity
Work to rule, 181, 182